Subsumption in Kant, Hegel and Marx

# Historical Materialism Book Series

The Historical Materialism Book Series is a major publishing initiative of the radical left. The capitalist crisis of the twenty-first century has been met by a resurgence of interest in critical Marxist theory. At the same time, the publishing institutions committed to Marxism have contracted markedly since the high point of the 1970s. The Historical Materialism Book Series is dedicated to addressing this situation by making available important works of Marxist theory. The aim of the series is to publish important theoretical contributions as the basis for vigorous intellectual debate and exchange on the left.

The peer-reviewed series publishes original monographs, translated texts, and reprints of classics across the bounds of academic disciplinary agendas and across the divisions of the left. The series is particularly concerned to encourage the internationalization of Marxist debate and aims to translate significant studies from beyond the English-speaking world.

*For a full list of titles in the Historical Materialism Book Series available in paperback from Haymarket Books, visit:* www.haymarketbooks.org/series_collections/1-historical-materialism.

# Subsumption in Kant, Hegel and Marx

*From the Critique of Reason to the Critique of Society*

Andrés Saenz de Sicilia

Haymarket Books
Chicago, IL

First published in 2024 by Brill Academic Publishers, The Netherlands
© 2024 Koninklijke Brill NV, Leiden, The Netherlands

Published in paperback in 2025 by
Haymarket Books
P.O. Box 180165
Chicago, IL 60618
773-583-7884
www.haymarketbooks.org

ISBN: 979-8-88890-558-6

Distributed to the trade in the US through Consortium Book Sales and Distribution (www.cbsd.com) and internationally through Ingram Publisher Services International (www.ingramcontent.com).

This book was published with the generous support of Lannan Foundation, Wallace Action Fund, and the Marguerite Casey Foundation.

Special discounts are available for bulk purchases by organizations and institutions. Please call 773-583-7884 or email info@haymarketbooks.org for more information.

Cover art and design by David Mabb. Cover art is developed from *Painting 45, Long Live the New! Kazimir Malevich drawing painted on 'Arbutus' wallpaper by Kathleen Kersey for Morris & Co*, paint and wallpaper on canvas (2016).

Printed in the United States.

Library of Congress Cataloging-in-Publication data is available.

# Contents

Acknowledgments   VII

Introduction   1
  1    Chapter Outline   7

1  **The Invention of a 'Critical' Concept of Subsumption**   11
  1    Kant: Subsumption and Synthesis   11
      1.1  *Subsumption's Role within 'Pure' Cognition*   13
      1.2  *Subsumption and Empirical Concepts*   21
      1.3  *'Reflective' Judgment and the Faculty of Judging*   25
      1.4  *Subsumption and Aesthetic Judgments*   30
      1.5  *Conclusion*   36
  2    Hegel's Critique of Subsumption   38
      2.1  *A New Derivation*   44
      2.2  *From Pure Concepts to Dialectical Categories*   48
      2.3  *Subsumption's Place in the Exposition*   51
      2.4  *Conclusion*   57

2  **Materialism, Social Form and Reproduction**   61
  1    Critical Beginnings   63
  2    The Actuality of Practice   72
  3    Theory of Practice and the Practice of Theory   80
  4    From Practice to Natural-History   85
      4.1  *Material Subject: 'Trans-individuality' and Social Constitution*   85
      4.2  *Practical Object: The 'Mediating Instrumental Field'*   88
      4.3  *Natural-Historical Being: Practice as Production*   91
  5    Against Nature   96
  6    Reproduction-Development   103
  7    Conclusion   110

3  **Capitalist Subsumption: Abstraction in Action**   112
  1    The Conditions of Subsumption: So-Called Original Accumulation   116
  2    Exchange: Subsumption under Value   121
  3    Subsumption in Production   135
  4    Formal Subsumption under Capital   140

|   |   |   |
|---|---|---|
|   | 5 | Hybrid Forms   146 |
|   | 6 | Real Subsumption: The Objective Positing of Capitalist Command   150 |

      6.1  *Cooperation*   152
      6.2  *Division of Labour and Manufacture*   155
      6.3  *Machinery and Large-Scale Industry*   160
  7  Conclusion   165

**4  The Dynamic of Subsumption on a Social Scale**   170
  1  Historicity and Closure   175
      1.1  *Negri: 'Total Subsumption'*   176
      1.2  *Adorno: Subsumption as 'Total Administration'*   184
  2  Rejecting Periodisation   194
  3  Systematic and Reproductive Totality   197
  4  Mediating Reproduction and Development   204
  5  Subjectivation and Living Labour   212
  6  The Generative Dynamic   219
  7  Conclusion   226

**Conclusion**   232

**Bibliography**   243
**Index**   255

# Acknowledgments

The research which forms the basis of this book was undertaken at the Centre for Research in Modern European Philosophy at Kingston University and the National Autonomous University of Mexico between 2012–16. Without the financial support I received from both Kingston University and the Secretaría de Relaciones Exteriores in Mexico during this time, the project would not have been possible.

I am grateful for the intellectual support and guidance I received whilst carrying out this research, notably from Peter Osborne, who saw the project develop from an initial idea to a full draft as well as Etienne Balibar, Alberto Toscano, Peter Hallward, Howard Caygill, Stephen Howard, Iain Campbell, George Tomlinson and Adam Green, who all offered generous and constructive feedback on earlier versions of this material. I also benefited from invaluable conversations, exchanges, debate and intellectual friendship with Sandro Brito Rojas, Maria Chehonadskih, Ed Luker, Kerem Nisancioglu, Stefano Pippa, Lucie Mercier, Hammam Aldouri, Svenja Bromberg, Eric Alliez, Catherine Malabou, Patrick Murray, Elena Louisa Lange, Gilbert Skillman, Stewart Martin, Massimiliano Tomba, Chris Arthur, Rob Lucas, Anthony Iles, Carlos Oliva Mendoza, Diana Fuentes, Jorge Veraza, Andrés Barreda, Enrique Dussel and John Kraniauskas. Sebastian Budgen and colleagues at Historical Materialism supported the idea for this book from an early stage and Danny Hayward provided invaluable assistance along the way. Above all I am indebted to Jane and Enrique, to whom this book is dedicated.

# Introduction

This book focuses on the concept of 'subsumption' as the site of a central problematic in the encounter between modern philosophy and critical social theory. It traces the development of the concept and shifting context of its application in the work of Kant, Hegel and above all Marx, thus following the transformation of the philosophical critique of reason into a radical critique of society. This book does not propose a new interpretation of the concept of subsumption *per se* nor offer a detailed historical reconstruction of its transmission and modification (although interpretive and critical-historical issues are central to the arguments made throughout); rather, it attempts to construct a framework within which to explore the social implications of conceptual relations and conceptual implications of social relations by establishing the continuities and discontinuities, consistencies and contradictions in the use of subsumption, both within and across the theories in question. It is, perhaps, the proposed consistencies that are most significant in the chapters that follow, insofar as they enable the construction of a unique problem of subsumption, inaugurated by Kant and which reaches its apex (if not completion) in Marx's critique of political economy. This project departs from the contention that there exists a necessary inner connection between the transcendental, dialectical and socio-economic contexts in which subsumption is employed, a problematic conceptual core which informs (whether explicitly or implicitly) the sense of every relation that can be described as subsumptive. More, then, than establishing a genealogically interrelated succession of scenarios in which the concept has been used, or explicating the solely analogical function taken on by the concept when deployed outside of an immediate logical context, this book demonstrates that there is a shared conceptual basis from which it is possible to approach ideas such as Kant's claim that 'we can only understand and communicate to others what we ourselves can produce' and Marx's assertion that 'capital does indeed exist from the outset as One or Unity as opposed to the workers as many'.[1] The key to the comprehension of such diverse statements lies in a 'critical' conception of subsumption that refers to the productive and oppressive dimensions of conceptually organised 'systems-in-process' and a dynamic articulation of concepts such as abstraction, composition, form and totality.

Developing an account of this 'critical' concept of subsumption requires a far more expansive and deeper engagement with its conditions, structure and

---

1  Kant 1999a, p. 482; Marx 1993, p. 590.

effects than is normally afforded to it. Adequately grasping these is hindered by the fact that the scope of what subsumption denotes appears at first sight to be both too vast conceptually and too narrow textually. Conceptually, subsumption immediately connects to a vast complex of problems and ideas within philosophy (almost all logic, epistemology and ontology invokes an idea of subsumption taken in its broadest sense, as a mode of classification, inclusion or identification, even where the term itself is not invoked directly) as well as to other disciplines (legal theory, art history, informatics, etc.). Yet textually, none of the authors in question, nor by and large the traditions they have inspired, recognise subsumption as a concept central to their theories or as a distinct philosophical 'problem' worthy of sustained engagement (as they do for example with proximate concepts such as abstraction, contradiction or alienation). This difficulty perhaps explains why no in-depth study dedicated to subsumption has previously been undertaken and why, where it is discussed, there is a sharp disjunction between the term's employment as a strictly philosophical concept and its employment as a technical Marxist concept. The connection between these two aspects, a small number of exceptions notwithstanding, has by and large been treated as a superficial one, of primarily philological interest and incidental to the systemic significance and functioning of Kant, Hegel and Marx's thought.

At the same time, much contemporary philosophy and critical theory has actively problematised the political dimension of logical/ontological relations (*as* political relations) in tandem with a concern over the status of 'the particular' (or with greater logical coherence: 'the singular'), generating a panoply of relational categories which have come to acquire normative status: affinity, constellation, rhizome, multitude, difference and exclusion/exception. A general notion of subsumption often figures here, connected or synonymous with abstraction, as a 'bad' relation or operation against which critique is directed: unilateral, reductive and repressive in its integrative function.[2] However, without penetrating the complexity and productivity of subsumptive relations and their constitutive processes, such moralisms of the abstract/concrete struggle to account for how their political demands and calls might be theoretically articulated with the material conditions and possibilities implicated in their realisation. Alternatively, departing from a more specific but liberally interpreted reading of subsumption in Marx's work, the concept has been employed by authors as diverse as Antonio Negri and Theodor W. Adorno as a periodising marker to register the degree to which qualitative particularity

---

2  See Osborne 2004, p. 21.

has been effaced by the identitarian organisational forces of capital in its progressive colonisation of the human life-world. Again though, whilst grasping certain core aspects of capitalist subsumption, these readings tend to simplify and exaggerate its inner dynamic and effects, undermining the force of subsumption as a critical category through which to comprehend real conditions and conflicts.

By emphasising the consistency and coherence of the problem of subsumption in its 'critical' form, this book aims to overcome at least some of the aporias these philosophical approaches to an oppressive social reality face, drawing out the deeper theoretical issues and structures at stake in the concept. However, the objective of such an approach is not simply to lump together the distinct approaches offered by Kant, Hegel and Marx under a monolithic and all-encompassing notion of subsumption. Instead, drawing out these structural continuities also allows for a stronger conception of where the key theoretical breaks lie between them. In this sense, this book reckons with new dimensions of subsumption that emerge from two fundamental modifications in the scope and context of its theoretical meaning, as well as the political implications that flow from them.

The first of these breaks occurs between the 'classical' (i.e., pre-Kantian) and 'critical' conceptions of subsumption. In its traditional philosophical form, subsumption names the hierarchical *relation* between a 'universal' and 'particular', where the particular is said to be an *instance of* the universal category or concept, and all particulars gathered under the universal share the same relation of logical identity to it. At the same time, subsumption also refers to the *act* (of judgment) that produces this relation, that of *subsuming* the particular under the universal. Here, it has the legal connotations evoked by Kant of determining the universal rule under which an individual case falls, and in this sense it can be conceived as a *problem* of correct judgment. This notion of a logical act/relation of classification is first presented by Aristotle and his commentators but only formalised in the thirteenth century as the famous 'Dici De Omni' where the phrase 'sumere sub' first appears in a text by William of Sherwood, amongst similar formulations by Aquinas, pseudo-Aquinas, Albertus Magnus, Ockham and Buridan. This is then conjoined into 'subsumptio' in the sixteenth century and reaches Kant via authors such as Wolff, Crusius and Baumgarten.[3]

In distinction to this 'classical' sense, the 'modern' or 'critical' concept of subsumption pertains to relations that are effective or actual beyond a purely

---

3  See Watkins 2009.

conceptual sphere of representation, marking a transition from (formal) logic to diverse *logics*. Thus for Kant, Hegel and Marx alike, subsumption is not an abstract operation that effects a 'mere play of representations' but one with a systemic and 'real' significance, insofar as it productively relates heterogeneous orders and their elements (for example, concepts and intuitions) in order to determine the form of the objective or actual through active processes of adaptation, mediation and unification.[4] What is presupposed in this processual idea of subsumption is a given distribution of elements whose initial configuration and function is resolved or suspended by their subsumptive articulation within a new order of being: that specified by the determining forms under which the particulars are subsumed. It is this formative activity – of the dominant relational series upon the subsumed series – which establishes systemic coherence and objectivity, as, for example, in Kant's *Critique of Pure Reason*, where

> experience rests on the synthetic unity of appearances, i.e., on a synthesis according to concepts of the object of appearances in general, without which it would not even be cognition but rather a rhapsody of perceptions, which would not fit together in any context in accordance with rules of a thoroughly connected (possible) consciousness, thus not into the transcendental and necessary unity of apperception.[5]

A critical theory of subsumption must then not simply grasp the logical relation implied by this conceptual synthesis, thus revealing the mediated character of an apparently unmediated presence, but actively seek to establish what the process of synthesis consists in, what its conditions, structure and effects are. In this sense, the theory of subsumption becomes an essential component of critique in that it establishes the connection between some given presence or objectivity and the subject and context of its production, moving from the judgements that 'subsume a particular under an already constituted category' to 'the occlusive constitution of the field of categories themselves'.[6] What is key to this critical procedure is that the two orders of being which appear from a systemic standpoint as 'particular' and 'universal' have the contradictory dual status of a 'specific heterogeneity' and 'generic homogeneity' respectively, a contradiction that is comprehended with reference to a mediating ground of unity irreducible to either order and containing both (what I will term the

---

4  Kant 1998, A102.
5  Ibid., A156/B195.
6  Butler 2001.

*compositional totality* in which they subsist). Kant initiates this critical reorientation, but both the 'field of categories' he establishes and their 'ground of unity' are destabilised by subsequent thinkers, most importantly Hegel. Nonetheless, even in its basic outline, this critical recoding of subsumption generates the specific problem of how to think the articulation of (i) a 'dominant' system of principles of form, (ii) the multitude of particular or 'minor' elements transformed and unified according to these principles and (iii) the compositional totality that is their shared 'medium of existence'.

The second break occurs between the 'critical-philosophical' and 'critical-social' conceptions of subsumption. Consistent in both is the aforementioned impulse to penetrate through the surface level of appearances and establish the real processes and systematic structure though which they are constituted. However, Marx's challenge to philosophy radically alters the stakes of subsumption by contesting the ideal basis and purely subjective compositional totality within which it was thought to occur by Kant and Hegel. Through his 'new materialism' of historical practice, Marx undermines the finality and truth of those underlying syntheses and mediations traced by critical idealism back to purely ideal relations and instead establishes an alternative account of form-determination based on the practical dimension of 'sensuous' activity. Subsumption is no longer an operation restricted to the mental but is transposed to the domain of social practices and their determining relations. For Marx, the 'metabolic' syntheses effected by these practices are the real basis underlying any formal or conceptual syntheses of elements, as well as the ground of unity in which their significance is always, ultimately, registered. Marx does not entirely jettison the notion of a subjective constitution of objectivity, but in contrast to Kant and Hegel, it cannot for him be decoupled from the living, natural dimension of subjective being implied in his idea of 'social humanity', in light of which 'self-sufficient philosophy [*die selbständige Philosophie*] loses its medium of existence'.[7] This means that the 'field of categories' under which individuals and objects are subsumed are not reducible to categories of thought (although, as I will argue, they may still retain a conceptual dimension) but are more broadly conceived as categories of historical being or social forms of existence that determine and are constituted through the collective practice of social individuals. The immense theoretical revolution contained in Marx's early attack on philosophical conceptions of actuality and form are profound and widely recognised as such, if not normally in terms of a discourse of subsumption. By pursuing the problematic of synthesis, mediation

---

7  Marx and Engels 1998, p. 43, translation modified.

and compositional totality through his radical reorientation, new dimensions and insights into both Marx's theory and the concept of subsumption itself become available to us: in particular, the unique dialectical unity of conceptual relations and socio-natural being implied in Marx's idea of a 'logic of the body politic' and the historically determined co-ordinates of that logic encapsulated in the idea of 'social form'.

As I will show, Marx's key break with Kant and Hegel turns precisely on his construction of subsumption as a fundamentally historical problem. For German idealism, the compositional totality mediating subsumptive relations is marked by a structure of reflexive or speculative closure which delimits the possibilities of the field of form-determining categories according to a self-referential horizon (philosophy's 'medium of existence'). For Marx however, the compositional totality – 'society' – is constituted in the tension between its own immediate horizons (that act as a form of structural limitation) and the open series of possibilities that are both immanently present and active within those horizons, and yet at the same time transcend the latter. The structural closure of the totality of composition that would for Kant and Hegel constitute a final limit is thus for Marx never more than provisional, constituted as it is in an open process of historical development that exceeds reduction to a basic framework of substantial social action, or, in the form in which that idea of action is fully developed, *social reproduction*. It is precisely through such a dialectical thinking of history and nature (as the 'socio-natural') that Marx is able to articulate his own original conception of freedom that places the finality of any form or structure of subsumptive determination in question. At the same time, Marx is also able to refine his analysis of those forms and structures in relation to the (historically) 'specific logic of the specific object', namely bourgeois society, giving rise to his theory of the 'subsumption of labour under capital'. Here, subsumptive relations appear in a historically specific form under certain conditions of social reproduction and with their own unique 'field of categories' which Marx elaborated through his critique of political economy. The problem of subsumption in a capitalist context turns on how these categories ('social forms' or 'real abstractions') are articulated with and affect the wider sphere of subjective and objective elements that they subsume as well as the compositional structure that grounds their social power and actuality (society or 'the body politic'). This is a problem which Marx, given his own apparent hesitation with regard to the theory of subsumption, only partially engaged with in explicit terms, although in a broader sense it also characterises a fundamental aspect of his critical project taken as a whole. Nonetheless, if developed in more detail and with greater conceptual rigour, in a manner adaptable to both the concrete specificities and open possibilities of the social process, a critique of capitalist subsumption can offer a compelling theorisation of the precise mechanisms of capitalist power, their supporting frameworks and developmental dynamics. Such a critique will enable us to specify with greater clarity what exactly is at stake in contemporary forms of domination and the struggles to supersede them: That is, to know what we really mean when we say that something is 'subsumed'.

## 1    Chapter Outline

The first chapter of this book presents an exposition and critical reconstruction of the concept of subsumption in the writings of Kant and Hegel. In analysing the various forms of subsumptive judgement presented by Kant in his first and third critiques it offers an account of the basic problem and modifications of the concept in its critical-philosophical form, i.e., as a concept that still denotes logical inclusion or categorisation (as in its 'classic' form), but equally functions (1) as a productive relation of determination between elements that are *not* formally homogenous, (2) as the mediating condition of an apparently self-sufficient totality and (3) as a process dependent on a pre-existing ground of unity (a *totality of composition* within which both the subsumed and subsuming entity exist). Following this, the chapter moves on to a reading of subsumption in Hegel's work, focusing on how his critique of Kant, specifically of transcendental logic and the transcendental subject, leads to a new form of (speculative) totality and thus a new context for subsumption. Subsumption here no longer functions to mediate heterogeneous faculties in a static structural context (transcendental apperception) but rather appears as a form of mediation specific to different stages in a process of dialectical development, thus breaking with both the fixed transcendental categories and principles that are the 'functions' of subsumption for Kant and the individual consciousness that acts as the compositional totality within which Kantian subsumption occurs. This expands and deepens the 'critical' concept of subsumption, although Hegel will ultimately criticise its logical insufficiency as an unresolved opposition that contradicts its apparent unification of universal and particular. Hegel thus establishes a dynamic, developmental and social-relational theory of subsumption, whilst also highlighting the constraining, abstractive and repressive dimensions of subsumption, all of which set the scene for Marx's appropriation of the concept.

The second chapter of the book presents a reconstruction of Marx's 'new materialism' and its 'logic' of natural-historical being by tracing Marx's transformation of philosophical critique on the basis of his famous assertion that 'all mysteries which lead theory to mystification find their rational solution in human practice and in the comprehension of this practice'.[8] It asks how such practice can be understood as distinct from philosophical, that is, purely intellectual activity, and how it transforms the determinations and implications of subsumption in its critical sense by situating it within a new 'medium of existence' (human practice). The chapter explores both the continuities in Marx's critical adoption of Hegel's dialectical framework (as a critique of appearances and the exposition of constitutive subject-object mediations) and the divergences contained in his development of a materialist account of activity and actuality. This latter aspect passes through stages of increasing conceptual richness and critical effectivity in Marx's texts, grounding itself in the concepts of 'activity', 'praxis', 'labour', 'social production', and finally, in a general theory of 'social reproduction', which I argue, following Bolívar Echeverría, is the most developed formulation of Marx's materialism. Through this concept of socially reproductive activity, the underlying syntheses exposed in the idealist critique of subsumptive relations are reconceived as metabolic interactions between productive subjects and natural objectivity, giving rise to 'socio-natural' or 'trans-naturalised' forms whose objectivity is determined with reference to a practical (rather than intellectual) totality: society. This practical totality, the socio-natural forms that exist within it, and the metabolic syntheses of labour that produce them, are all co-determined by structures of social and practical relationality which are historically variable and in a process of constant contestation. Accounting for this variability necessitates the analytic movement from the general (i.e., transhistorical) theory of social reproduction to its specific and evolving historical configurations. The chapter thus finally explores the double aspect of every social process as at once a process of social reproduction (by which a given configuration of social being is sustained) and at the same time a process of historical development (by which a determinate course of social becoming unfolds).

Chapter 3 moves on to systematically reconstruct Marx's theory of capitalist subsumption from the various discussions of subsumption within his critique of political economy, beginning in the late 1850s. In doing so, it brings together the idea of a productive, constitutive process of conceptual subsumption developed in chapter 1 with Marx's materialism of the social reproduction process as outlined in chapter 2. It aims to show how the reproduction of capitalist societies takes place on the basis of a mediating relation of subsumption under economic abstractions, operative at two distinct but interconnected

---

8  Marx 1978, Suchting 1979, pp. 21–2.

levels: (1) subsumption to the abstract universality of value and 'impersonal' market forces in the process of commodification and exchange and (2) subsumption to direct capitalist command in the production process. These two moments reciprocally form what I identify as the 'distinctive synthesis' of capitalist subsumption, by means of which the formal-economic determinations of circulation are grounded in and progressively come to modify the metabolic syntheses of production. I analyse the multiple forms of subsumption to capital outlined by Marx ('formal', 'hybrid' and 'real') as that which allows abstract economic categories to be articulated with concrete productive practices in diverse ways, and develop their full implications both in terms of the command relations governing production and the objective structure and output of the labour process.

Chapter 4 takes a more problematising tack, departing from the insufficiencies of Marx's account of capitalist subsumption and the theoretical ambiguities arising from them. I argue that further determinations of the concept have to be developed in order to overcome the opposition between Marx's abstract, linear schema of forms of subsumption and their concrete historical actualisation. To this end, I propose a dynamic conception of subsumption that mediates between the two in order to establish the *systematic necessity* but *historical contingency* of capitalist subsumption. I begin by criticising the two interpretive extremes that have dominated the Marxist discourse of subsumption. The first of these is the crude historical schematisation of the transition from formal to real to 'total' subsumption found in the works of Antonio Negri and Theodor W. Adorno. Here, I reject the idea that the dynamic of subsumption constitutes either an extensive template of world-historical development or 'a theory of the internal periodisation of the capitalist mode of production,' as Jason Read has it.[9] I subsequently engage with the 'systematic dialectics' of theorists such as Christopher J. Arthur and Moishe Postone. Whereas the first approach fails to adequately think historical openness and developmental complexity in its conception of the subsumptive dynamic, the second excises the antagonistic character of the subsumptive process, reducing class struggle and the power relations driving social development to functional residues of a self-moving logical subject reminiscent of Hegel's concept. Both extremes threaten to impress closure unto the theory of subsumption, either diachronically (closure to historical contingency, as in the first case) or synchronically (closure to systemic externality, as in the second case), reducing subsumption to either a linear developmental *telos* of modern society or a generic, cellular tendency

---

9   Read 2003, p. 107.

of capital. A dynamic conception of subsumption, by contrast, mediates these systematic and historical aspects in order to establish the reciprocal relationship between 'local' mechanisms of direct command (forms of subsumption through which labour is controlled in the production process) and a 'global' system of domination. I therefore go on to explore what effects, conditions, conflicts and possibilities are generated by the increasing dominance of capitalist reproduction as *the* primary form of global social reproduction, how it interacts with non-capitalist forms of objectivity and subjectivity: absorbing them, altering them, abolishing them or being resisted and altered by them in turn. Finally, I consider how this approach can open the path for further critical engagements, at various levels of concretion, with the ongoing processes of subsumption and resistance across the globe.

CHAPTER 1

# The Invention of a 'Critical' Concept of Subsumption

### 1   Kant: Subsumption and Synthesis

Judgment, in its various forms and occasions, lies at the heart of Kant's critical philosophy. Indeed, read in strictly methodological terms, the Kantian project might be best understood as an attempt to systematically transpose the basic logical forms of judgment structuring discursive reason onto the various spheres of rational activity characterising human life (knowledge, practice, taste, etc.) in order to secure their objective validity. At the centre of this judicial enterprise lies the act of subsumption: the process through which the particular content of the various domains is brought to bear under the universal judgment-forms which Kant prescribes to them. Consequently, understanding the modes of subsumption operative in the various species of judgment, the particular configurations of the faculties at work in each and the circumstances that occasion them, is crucial to grasping the way in which Kant's thought functions as a systematically oriented whole as well as highlighting the multiple points of tension at which this Kantian system threatens to break down or transgress its own limits.

In its most general sense, subsumption is for Kant the process which determines the application of a concept to a representation, or the representing concretely of a particular under a concept. This act is modelled on the minor premise of a syllogistic judgment, in which a given *universal* rule (such as 'all men are mortal') is applied to a *particular* case ('Caius is a man') and from which an inferential judgment can flow, establishing all the implications of the rule within the particular ('Caius *is* mortal'). Indeed, this kind of syllogistic judgment is the model for Kant's entire theory of rational cognition, within which subsumption functions as the mediating act connecting particular representations with the predicates, or 'marks' [*Merkmale*], of universal concepts:

> Reason, considered as the faculty of a certain logical form of cognition, is the faculty of inferring, i.e., of judging mediately (through the subsumption of a condition of a possible judgment under the condition of something given). The given judgment is the universal rule (major

premise, *major*). The subsumption of the condition of another possible judgment under the condition of the rule is the minor premise (*minor*). The actual judgment that expresses the assertion of the rule in the subsumed case is the conclusion (*conclusio*). The rule says something universal under a certain condition. Now in a case that comes before us the condition of the rule obtains. Thus what is valid universally under that condition is also to be regarded as valid in the case before us (which carries this condition with it). We easily see that reason attains to a cognition through actions of the understanding that constitute a series of conditions.[1]

In his pre-critical essay from 1762 on 'The False Subtlety of the Four Syllogistic Figures', Kant works through the compositional structure of this 'series of conditions', as an assemblage of 'marks' constituting a concept. The composite unity of marks in a concept is what gives the rule for determining a (logical) subject as one specific thing rather than another.[2] In its genesis, Kant explains, such a concept is always abstracted 'as a characteristic mark' from other 'subordinate concepts' – i.e., those that are subsumed under it – and thus carries up and totalises the characteristic marks belonging to these subordinate concepts; with this, the conditions are carried up.[3] These 'subordinate' conditions, however, are only *mediately* related to the concept in question, as they do not correspond to its minimal definition; the operation which renders the relation immediate (for consciousness) is the syllogistic inference. Thus for Kant, it is mistaken to think that logic begins with concepts, because prior to them, as their generative requirements, are judgments and syllogisms:

> A distinct concept is only possible by means of a *judgment*, while a *complete* concept is only possible by means of a *syllogism*. A distinct concept demands, namely, that I should clearly recognise something as a characteristic mark of a thing; but this is a judgment. In order to have a distinct concept of a body, I clearly represent to myself impenetrability as a characteristic mark of it. This representation, however, is nothing other than the thought: *a body is impenetrable*. The only thing which needs to be remarked upon in this connection is the fact that this judgment is not the distinct concept itself, but rather the action, by means of which the

---

[1] Kant 1998, A330, emphasis added.
[2] See Pippin 1976, p. 158.
[3] Kant 1992a, § 2.

distinct concept is actualised. For the representation of the thing which comes into being after the operation is distinct.[4]

Concepts are therefore developed and connected with each other, as well as their objects, through elementary *acts* of judgment, and their unity is not apprehended passively but must be *produced*. In prioritising the active, dynamic aspect of thought in this way, Kant establishes the centrality of subsumption as the core operation underlying the logical relationship between universals and particulars, which brings the latter under the former *immediately* in imagination.

The problem of correspondence between concept and object, or rule and case, which has troubled philosophy since the time of the Greeks, is for Kant not therefore primarily about recognition or classification but rather *production* (recognition, as we will see, is only the final moment which consummates the subsumptive process).[5] As Kant declares in a letter from 1794, 'we can only understand and communicate to others what we ourselves can produce'.[6] Thinkability and, more importantly, objectivity, must be produced through acts and series of judgments, at the heart of which lie subsumptive operations.

### 1.1   *Subsumption's Role within 'Pure' Cognition*

This notion of the productivity of subsumptive judgment is fundamental for Kant's account of how objective experience is constituted through 'pure' cognition, that is, cognition of objects grounded in an accord between the faculties of sensibility and the understanding, established logically prior to any particular content which it might give rise to. Here, subsumption is the common thread and key link in Kant's transposition of general or formal logic into a 'transcendental logic' of experience, as, in Carsten Held's words, it is 'both the paradigmatic activity of the mind in forming judgments and the paradigmatic explication of what Kant means when he characterises the activities of the understanding as acts of "determination".'[7] However, the problem of transcendental subsumption is not straightforwardly one of subordination to higher concepts as it is in its purely logical form, but rather depends first and foremost on the adaptation, or 'schematisation', of 'entirely unhomogeneous'

---

4   Kant 1992b, § 6.
5   See Adorno 2001, p. 131.
6   Kant 1999a, p. 482.
7   Held 2000, p. 104.

sources of representations to one another, such that they can be articulated as a single 'series of conditions' structured according to the universal-particular relationship.

For Kant, the objectivity of experience can only be secured by establishing its thoroughgoing interconnectedness and consistent unity as a 'whole of compared and connected representations'. This interconnection cannot, however, be derived from experience, as it would lack the *a priori* necessity required for the truly lawful definition of objectivity to which Kant aspires: '[E]xperience never gives its judgments true or strict but only assumed and comparative universality (through induction)'.[8] Instead, in the *Critique of Pure Reason*'s infamous 'transcendental deduction', Kant attempts to establish the validity of a universal, law-governed structure of experience which would *a priori* condition – although not generate – every possible object of empirical experience. To this end, in the deduction, sensible intuitions are posited as necessarily, rather than contingently, subject to a set of conceptual laws of relation ('concepts of the object of appearances in general') which order and organise them discursively in order to constitute the coherent continuum of conscious experience (the 'series of conditions'). This 'transcendental use' of the understanding is the means by which experience attains its *objective* character and can be categorically distinguished from a mere 'rhapsody of perceptions' or the habitual aggregation of empirical sensations.[9]

In the terms of subsumptive judgment outlined above, in objective cognition, the understanding gives a general rule (concept) for a possible condition (intuition), such that the sensibly given manifold is determined as a particular instance of the universal (an 'object in general'). The basic syllogistic moments are thus transposed and absolutised by Kant as transcendental conditions of experience such that, articulated in this way, representations given by the faculties of sensibility and understanding can be shown to logically occupy the opposing poles of the subsumptive relation – as subject and predicate, particular and universal. However, given the absolute heterogeneity of intuitions and concepts, the relationship cannot simply be one of species to genera (i.e., of that of subordinate marks to a higher concept), but must rather be one of pure form to pure matter such that 'sensibility gives the mere material for thought, but the understanding rules over this material and brings it under rules or concepts'.[10] Kant retains a broadly Aristotelian dualism here, opposing 'a matter

---

8   Kant 1998, B4.
9   Kant 1998, A156.
10  Kant 1992a, §1.

for cognition from the senses' to 'a certain form for ordering it from the inner source of pure intuition and thinking'.[11] Indeed, this hylomorphic conception of the relations between sensible and conceptual *representations* (rather than *substances*, as in the classical Aristotelian theory) is fundamental to Kant's account of cognition; for him, matter and form 'are two concepts which lie at the basis of all other reflection, so very inseparably are they bound up with the use of the understanding'.[12] The matter/form opposition is fused by Kant with the epistemic conception of syllogistic inference, thus modelling the production of the unity of experience on the cognitive structure of judgment acts, whilst the relation and distinction between its unified elements is conceived of in a hylomorphic fashion.

The problem which Kant faces as a result of this original conjunction is one of commensuration: How can the manifold of intuition given by sensibility and the conceptual rules of objectivity given by the understanding be articulated within the syllogistic form, that is, as a series of interconnected 'marks' that can be arrayed in hierarchical relation? For this to occur, the matter (intuition) and form (concept) of cognition must be 'for' each other; there must be homogeneity between the two faculties:

> In all subsumption of an object under a concept the representations of the former must be homogeneous with the latter, i.e., the concept must *contain* that which is represented in the object that is to be subsumed under it, for that is just what is meant by the expression 'an object is contained under a concept'.[13]

Both sensibility (the source of intuitions) and the understanding (the source of concepts), however, are taken by Kant to be fundamental and heterogeneous faculties, neither of which 'is to be preferred to the other' and that furthermore 'cannot exchange their functions'.[14] Therefore, Kant asks:

> How is the subsumption of the latter [intuition] under the former [concept], thus the application of the category to appearances possible, since no one would say that the category, e.g., causality, could also be intuited through the senses and is contained in the appearance?[15]

---

11   Kant 1998, A86/B118, emphasis added.
12   Kant 1998, A 266/B 322.
13   Kant 1998, A137/B176.
14   Kant 1998, A51/B75.
15   Kant 1998, A138/B177.

The subsumption of intuitions under concepts cannot merely be a matter of recognition or resemblance, as this would tautologically presuppose the pre-existence of conceptual marks *in* the sensible manifold, which the understanding would only have to 'recognise' or reflect (thus restricting the problem only to asking *quid facti?*). Hence, for this subsumption to proceed, a conformity between the matter of intuition and the form of its thinkability has to first be established. Consciousness cannot simply incorporate the manifold as a series of subordinate marks (what Kant calls an 'image') into its higher order concepts but must first determine intuitions *as* marks of the same kind, of the same order of representation. Kant therefore seeks a solution which does not presuppose its result as its cause: '[W]e must be able to show how *pure concepts* can be applicable to experiences'.[16]

Kant's well-known solution is to introduce a 'third thing' common to both concepts and intuitions, which acts as a 'mediating representation' between the understanding and sensibility. This third thing, which Kant calls a 'transcendental schema', is a 'function of the power of judgment' that specifies 'the formal condition under which something can be given in intuition' and therefore has both a sensible and intellectual dimension.[17] The schema can do this by establishing a relation between both faculties of representation in virtue of their shared seat in the domain of 'inner sense'. As Kant establishes in the transcendental aesthetic, the pure form of inner sense is *time*, 'that in which [representations] must *all* be ordered, connected and brought into relations'.[18] The common element found in both sources of representation is thus a *time-determination*, so that 'an application of the category to appearances becomes possible by means of the transcendental time-determination which, as the schema of the concept of the understanding, *mediates the subsumption* of the latter under the former.'[19] Through their schematisation, the pure concepts of an object in general are transposed into a series of generic temporal relations or 'compositions' which can be applied as conditions of *formal* organisation to the *matter* of sensibility. Whereas the pure concepts specified abstract functions or rules of unity, their schemata turn these into rules for the temporal synthesis of intuitive representations, that is, rules for the determination of inner sense 'in one concept in accord with the unity of apperception.'[20]

---

16   Ibid., translation modified.
17   Kant 1998, A247/B304.
18   Kant 1998, A99, emphasis added.
19   Kant 1998, A139/B178, emphasis added.
20   Kant 1998, A142/B181. 'By synthesis in the most general sense, however, I understand the

It is worth recalling that the 'pure concepts' of the understanding are presented by Kant as the forms taken by the judgments of the understanding – which he considers to be the fundamental logical 'functions' constituting discursive reason as such – when transcendentally adapted to objects of experience. What Kant addresses here is the need for a further mediation that would account for the interrelation of concepts and objects. This is precisely the work that 'schematism' does: '[I]f this condition of the power of judgment (schema) is missing, then all subsumption disappears; for nothing would be given that could be subsumed under the concept'.[21]

It is accordingly through the schema that Kant claims to have overcome the problematic heterogeneity of sensibility and understanding, setting into motion the productive encounter of the two elements of experience: the 'empty' functions of the concepts that iterate a pure universality and the blind contingency of intuitions characterised by radical singularity. It is by virtue of this interface that the faculties relate to each other systematically, subjecting appearances to general rules of synthesis that make them fit for a thoroughgoing connection in *one* experience. Schematism is thus a requisite condition for subsumption in reason's transcendental use; it is what allows the application of pure concepts to sensible representations, by adapting them to the temporal form of intuition – a process that Kant calls *Hypotyposis* (rendering in terms of sense). Each of the 'pure concepts' is schematised as a universal time determination or 'pure image' of the time series, which can then be represented empirically, exhibited in intuition as a concrete 'composition': In this sense, for example, 'the schema of actuality is existence at a determinate time', while 'the schema of necessity is the existence of an object at all times', etc.[22] In this way, the subsumption of the manifold under the schematised categories circumscribes the general limits of experience *a priori*, binding empirical content together in a law-like manner that enables it to be thought and, crucially for Kant, 'communicated'.[23] In distinction from the contingent contents of exper-

---

       action of putting different representations together with each other and comprehending their manifoldness in one cognition.' A77/B103.

21    Kant 1998, A247/B304.
22    Kant 1998, A145/B184.
23    'The composition itself is not given; on the contrary, we must produce it ourselves: we must *compose* if we are to represent anything *as composed* (even space and time). We are able to communicate with one another because of this composition. The grasping (apprehensio) of the given manifold and its reception in the unity of consciousness (apperceptio) is the same sort of thing as the representation of a composite (that is, it is only possible through composition), if the synthesis of my representation in the grasping of it, and its analysis insofar as it is a concept, yield one and the same representation (recip-

ience derived *a posteriori*, it is not a case of finding out *if* there is, for example, a causal connection between appearances, but only of establishing *what* the causal connection is, as without this connection experience would lack basic consistency.

That schematised concepts specify only the rules for *combining* representations given in intuition consolidates the reciprocal dependence of sensibility and the understanding in cognition, for this relating can only be exhibited *between* such sensible representations. More precisely: Sensible representations are given conceptual determinacy (i.e., objectivity) by their articulation within the time series, but the time series is itself only populated – and thus actualised – by these representations in conceptual relation. In terms of the four sub-groups in the table of categories, this means that:

Quantity    *generates* substantial time (*the time series*)
Quality     fills it (*the content of time*)
Relation    *joins* the perceptions amongst themselves to all time, creating continuity (*the order of time*)
Modality    determines whether and how the object *belongs* to time (*the scope or sum total of time*)

Through the mediation of the schemata, the subsumptive operation consists in a double articulation which posits the time series itself in the very same act that determines the objectivity of phenomena within it. This is nothing more than that which is expressed in Kant's famous dictum that 'the conditions of the possibility of experience in general are at the same time conditions of the possibility of the objects of experience', which is here grasped in terms of the process of the temporalised unfolding of these conditions.[24] What clearly manifests itself here is the way in which the schemata establish a zone of limitation through which experience and its object are reciprocally *realised* by being *restricted* to their common temporal interface. 'The schemata of sensibility first realise the categories, yet they likewise also restrict them, i.e., limit them to conditions that lie outside the understanding (namely, in sensibility)', in order for them to be more than the mere 'play of representations', whilst conversely, perceptions only become objectively cognised through their restriction to a mode of combination derived from outside of sensibility itself (i.e., the categories).[25]

---

      rocally bring forth one another). This agreement is related to something that is valid for everyone, something distinct from the subject, that is, related to an object since it lies exclusively neither in the representation nor in consciousness but nevertheless is valid (communicable) for everyone' (Kant 1999a, p. 482).

24    Kant 1998, A 158/B197.
25    Kant 1998, A146/B186.

The process of synthetic composition enabled by the transcendental schema is therefore that *through which* and *in which* subsumption occurs. 'Subsumption' and 'synthesis' here refer to two parallel descriptions of the *same process* grasped from differing theoretical levels or standpoints. Whereas synthesis denotes the real *productivity* of the process of combination that unifies multiple representations according to a schematised category, subsumption simply denotes the concrete *representing* of those synthesised representations under that category, presupposing the very homogeneity or 'logical identity' between them that synthesis establishes (the particular and the universal must be 'for' each other). So whilst it is clear that synthesis is a condition for transcendental subsumption, it is not clear that subsumption is anything other than synthesis viewed from the perspective of the judgment it enables. Subsumption would, in this case, simply be the systemic (i.e., apperceptive) consciousness of the process of synthesis, only making sense retroactively from the perspective of its completion. In terms of their presentation, the logical order of these moments is as follows: (1) schematisation translates the pure categories into rules for (2) acts of temporal synthesis which, once effected, result in (3) the subsumption of intuitions under the pure concepts, thereby allowing the manifold to be thought objectively. The sequential construction of this operation reflects a crucial difference between the transcendental form of judgment and its purely logical prototype because in the latter case the subsumptive operation is *analytically reversible*, as the forms of judgment permit consciousness to survey its conceptual horizons across multiple poles: inductively and deductively, traversing the vertical plane of conceptual 'marks' related to each other as grounds and consequences. Synthesis according to pure concepts, however, is from the standpoint of consciousness a totally irreversible process of composition that simultaneously determines the inner constitution and outer limit of experience. In the transition made by Kant from general logic to its transcendental equivalent, this irreversibility is the result of adding a condition that lies outside of reason, namely sensible intuitions.[26]

There is a further dimension to the tension between subsumption and synthesis at the level of transcendental subjectivity: Whereas synthesis describes the *process* of composition effected between representations, subsumption designates the punctual *act* of judgment which binds these synthesised representations to apperceptive consciousness, the 'I' through which subjectivity subsists. The dynamic of synthesis and subsumption established above is therefore itself grounded in a second constitutive procedure, which relates determ-

---

26  See also Kant 1998, A331/B388.

ining acts of subsumption to the transcendental consciousness which is their unifying *topos*. Subsumption is always subsumption *by* transcendental subjectivity, which is the ground of unity for the multiple moments of synthesis (we could contrast this with the fact that, for Kant, it is the imagination that synthesises under the guidance of schematised concepts). As we saw in the analysis of the time-series, however, this ground of apperception is only itself brought into being in the act of subsumption through which the time series and its objects are simultaneously determined. These two double-movements, between intuitions and concepts and between the subsumptive act and its subject, are together what constitute apperceptive consciousness as the transcendental space of experience.

The account of subsumption given by Kant in the *Critique of Pure Reason* thus establishes a general theory of cognitive production in which subsumptive acts confer an objective form (i.e., universal intelligibility) onto a matter (the manifold of intuition) which has a merely subjective and arbitrary mode of appearance. The necessity of schematisation demonstrates that subsumption under the categories cannot simply consist in the application of 'internal' cognitive concepts to 'external' objects but must entail the subject's purely internal mediation of its two modes of representing: on the one hand, its sensible form of affection, and on the other, its discursive form of intellect. This is necessary because intuitions 'do not represent the object as it is in itself but only express the manner in which the subject is affected by the object, in accordance with his particular constitution, and so the object is presented only as it *appears* to us, that is, indirectly'.[27] Synthetic judgments thus enable the transition from a subjective and arbitrary order of representation to an objective and universal one. Within this context, subsumption is the operation that raises the singularity of intuition into universally thinkable – and communicable – form. As Cicovacki points out: 'Kant's idea is to show that by means of judging we overcome the privacy and idiosyncrasy of the given and turn them into communicable and intersubjective experience.'[28] In light of this, Kant's claim that philosophical cognition 'considers the particular only in the universal' need not necessarily be read, as Hegel does, as an admission of the reductive character of transcendental cognition.[29] Rather than the subsumptive process abstracting

---

27  Kant 1999a, p. 538.
28  Cicovacki 2001, p. 56.
29  'Subsumption under the species alters what is immediate. We strip away what is sensory, and lift out the universal ... The alteration underway here is called *abstracting*. It seems absurd if what we want is knowledge of external objects, to alter these external objects by our very [abstractive] activity upon them ... The alteration consists in the fact that we

*away* from a set of original concrete determinations, which fix an object here and now before us, and reducing it to an empty abstraction, what is central to Kant's thesis is the idea that to know an object depends on it being internally *composed* according to the universal categories of experience; indeed, knowing it is nothing other than the theoretical affirmation of this conformity. Hence the discourse which reads subsumption as concerned primarily with abstraction occludes the productive act of synthesis subtending in the logical identity between universal and particular; it is not simply a case of abstracting *from* the singularity of sensation but rather of transcendentally inscribing sensation *within* the order of cognitive intelligibility.

### 1.2  Subsumption and Empirical Concepts

Parallel to the theory of transcendental subsumption which dominates in the first *Critique*, Kant also develops a minor (although far more philosophically orthodox) account of subsumption in relation to the use of 'empirical' concepts, i.e., concepts that specify distinct aggregates of 'marks' that can be differentiated in experience as particular kinds of objects – as opposed to the pure concepts of an object *in general*. At stake in this type of subsumption is the thinkability of identity and difference *within* the continuum of experience, which entails the presence to consciousness of the distinctness of an *a*, as opposed to a *b* or a *c*. In other words, the subsumption of 'many' empirical objects under a generic (but not pure) 'one', a '*conceptus communis*'. Such concepts are 'rational abstractions' (to borrow a term from Marx) which consciousness uses to represent empirical regularities, such as, for example, a dog:

> The concept of a dog signifies a rule in accordance with which my imagination can specify the shape of a four-footed animal in general, without being restricted to any single particular shape that experience offers me or any possible image that I can exhibit *in concreto*.[30]

In the case of transcendental subsumption, both the content of pure concepts and the rule for their application are given immediately by the understanding so that, under the legislating power of the understanding and with the mediation of schematism, subsumptive judgment under these concepts is effected 'mechanically'.[31] By contrast, in the case of empirical concepts, neither

---

separate off what is singular or external, and hold the truth of the thing to lie in what is universal rather than in what is singular or external' (Hegel 2008, pp. 12–13).

30  Kant 1998, A141/B180.
31  Kant 2000, v.

the concept's content nor the rule for its application are given to the imagination transcendentally. There is thus no guarantee of the correct subsumption of objects under empirical concepts: The process of 'determining whether something stands under a given [empirical] rule' belongs to the domain of what Kant calls 'the healthy understanding', an art that 'cannot be taught but only practised'.[32] For Kant, this raises the possibility of erroneous judgments about whether something is an *a* or not, which happen when one 'understands the universal *in abstracto* but cannot distinguish whether a case *in concreto* belongs under it'.[33] The principal gesture of transcendental philosophy – the separation of the *a priori* and *a posteriori* domains of judgment – is intended precisely to immunise experience against this uncertainty at its most fundamental level, that of objective form as such, but it nonetheless remains pertinent in the context of empirical judgments, manifesting as the problem of correspondence between *specific* concepts and objects. This is why it makes sense – within transcendental limits – to ask, 'Is it a dog?' but not to ask, 'Does it have a cause?' Whilst the former refers to a merely *possible* correspondence of concept and object in the empirical domain, the latter refers to a transcendentally *necessitated* element of every experience.

Although the scope of concepts is always universal (for Kant it is a 'mere tautology' to state as much), Kant contrasts two distinct modes of universality at work in his account of subsumptive judgments of objects of experience: on the one hand, that proper to pure concepts and, on the other, that proper to empirical concepts. The universality of the latter, whilst sufficient for differentially thinking some object as an *a*, is neither certain nor exhaustive in the sense of true lawfulness and so attains '*merely the form* of universality' in the generality of a common concept under which various particulars can be thought.[34] This is because subsumption under empirical concepts never determines an object of experience *qua object* (as is the case with subsumption under the categories), but rather produces an intellectual judgment *about* it or, in Kant's terms, 'only the *mode of reflection* concerning it, in order to attain its cognition'[35] (hence he will refer to these cognitions, from the *Critique of Judgment* onwards, as 'reflective' judgments). This generic universality, being without transcendental necessity, must therefore itself be *produced* through an ascent from the particulars to the general via 'comparison of objects of experience'. This involves three acts of the understanding: comparison, reflection and abstraction.

---

32   Kant 1998, A132–3/B171–2.
33   Kant 1998, A134/B173.
34   Kant 1992b, § 1, 3.
35   Kant 1992b, § 82.

I see, e.g., a spruce, a willow, and a linden. By first comparing these objects with one another I note that they are different from one another in regard to the trunk, the branches, the leaves, etc.; but next I reflect on that which they have in common among themselves, trunk, branches, and leaves themselves, and I abstract from the quantity, the figure, etc., of these; thus I acquire a concept of a tree.[36]

But because in this process the content of the concept must be derived from the content of experience itself, subsumption under these concepts yields judgments that have only *a posteriori* validity. Subsumption under empirical concepts, therefore, is a far weaker process than its transcendental counterpart, as it deals only with the distribution of objective identity rather than its constitution and furthermore 'has only *subjective* validity, for the universal to which it proceeds from the particular is only *empirical* universality – a mere analogue of the *logical*'.[37] Therefore, in empirical judgments the rule under which the object is subsumed is only *provisional*, and can never determine but only reflect upon the object. Nonetheless, for Kant these empirical concepts are 'useful and indispensable' for experiential cognition [*Erfahrungserkenntnis*]: They aggregate the essential elements of an entity or relation and formalise them as the necessary conditions for identifying it in experience. An empirical concept is, like any other concept, the 'consciousness of a unity of synthesis', thus making, for example, the towerness of a tower thinkable.[38] When subsumed under such an empirical concept, the represented objective unity of the manifold is accompanied by a representation of its specificity as a *particular* unity that consciousness recognises. In this way, empirical subsumption *adds* a further intellectual determination to the synthetic representation of an object, a determination which allows us to think its specificity and therefore to assign to it a taxonomic position within the entire domain of objects.

At the level of its genetic process, subsumption under empirical concepts, as in transcendental subsumption, is effected through a process of schematisation which generates a rule for connecting a concept to an image. The schema mediates between the two elements, which in themselves 'are never fully congruent': 'No image of a triangle would ever be adequate to the concept of it. For it would not attain the generality of the concept, which makes this valid for all triangles, right or acute, etc., but would always be limited to one part of

---

36   Kant 1992b, § 6.
37   Kant 1992b, § 81.
38   Kant 1998, A103.

this sphere.'³⁹ Likewise, the concept of a triangle does not explicate all of the properties of a triangle given to us in intuition (as for example the length of the sides). Here, once again a 'third thing' in the form of a schema is needed to bring the concept to an image (to be 'exhibited') and allow the image to be thought in the concept; with this tool, the understanding gives a rule to the imagination for uniting concept and object in a judgment by rendering each element as one pole of the universal-particular (i.e., subsumptive) relation. Empirical subsumption is distinct from its transcendental variant in that it is not a unilateral process of conditioning but a mobile, bilateral method for approximating a set of marks given in an object to a general concept. Schemata here are produced by a process which follows the same stages as that used to generate empirical concepts in the first place:

1. *Comparison* of representations among one another in relation to the unity of consciousness;
2. *Reflection* as to how various representations can be conceived in one consciousness; and finally
3. *Abstraction* of everything else in which the given representations differ.⁴⁰

In this case, (1) the comparison is not between multiple given objects (e.g., the three different trees) but between a singular object given in experience and a stockpile of empirical concepts explicable in the imagination (cat, dog, fox, rabbit, etc ...). (2) Reflection discovers the isomorphism between marks intuited in the object and marks thought in the concept, asserting their adequation. And finally, (3) abstraction subtracts all the superfluous determinations found in the object but not the concept, thus 'perfect[ing] it and enclos[ing] it in its determinate limits'.⁴¹

Schematisation is crucial for determining whether the rule for synthesis given in the concept fits the object or not. If successful, the synthesis is effected and produces a new representation in which the object is thought as a particular instance of the (empirical) universal. This is the moment of 'recognition *in* the concept' which subsumes a determinate but singular object under the concept of an ontically distinct entity. Once again, subsumption marks a point of transition between two orders of representation; this time, from the cognition of objects in experience to classification as empirical types. Kant makes clear that the latter operation is dependent on – and logically preceded by – the former because subsumption under empirical concepts is the product of

---

39  Kant 1998, A141/B180.
40  Kant 1992b, § 6.
41  Ibid.

an 'intellectual' synthesis which is itself only the analytic dissolution of an originary 'figurative' synthesis effected in cognition. It is this figurative synthesis which first renders the object *as* an object, that is, as a unity of marks that can be intellectually surveyed, compared and deconstructed:

> A representation that is to be thought of as common to several must be regarded as belonging to those that in addition to it also have something different in themselves; consequently they must antecedently be conceived in synthetic unity with other (even if only possible representations) before I can think of the analytical unity of consciousness in it that makes it into a *conceptus communis*.[42]

The process of schematisation essential to empirical concept formation and subsumption is always for Kant a kind of second-order productivity in which 'empirical affinity' is the 'mere consequence' of 'transcendental affinity'.[43] The priority of transcendental conditions remains present even in the case of empirical judgments because 'although we learn many laws through experience, these are only particular determinations of yet higher laws'.[44] Within the architectonic of reason, empirical subsumption thus marks a transition from a discourse of production to one of distribution and organisation. The act of bringing an object under the concept of its type effects an organisation *within* the experiential series, which is not strictly productive but rather an analytic management of its members.

## 1.3  'Reflective' Judgment and the Faculty of Judging

In the *Critique of Judgment*, Kant significantly extends and deepens the notion of reflective judgment sketched out in the *Critique of Pure Reason* in the context of subsumption under empirical concepts. Here, it is no longer defined within the language of determinative categorical judgment but is assigned its own terminology and demarcated space within the system of transcendental philosophy. Kant primarily does this through the association of reflective judgments with the action of a cognitive faculty in its legislative mode, suggesting that 'the reflecting power of judgment is that which is also called the faculty of judging'.[45] This power, although essential to the operation of reason in its the-

---

42  Kant 1998, B133.
43  Kant 1998, A114.
44  Kant 1998, A126.
45  Kant 2000, v. This is in contrast to Kant's earlier thinking where the functions later

oretical and practical use, had not before the *Critique of the Power of Judgment* been awarded the status of a 'higher' faculty, i.e., one capable of determining the relations between faculties in order to produce a specific type of judgment according to its own *a priori* principle.[46] Thus despite Kant's claim that 'philosophy as a system can only have two parts',[47] it is shown in the third *Critique* to be grounded in a tripartite division of cognitive faculties corresponding to the three moments of the syllogism:

> [F]irst, the faculty for the cognition of the general (of rules), *the understanding*; second, the faculty for the subsumption of the particular under the general, *the power of judgment*; and third, the faculty for the determination of the particular through the general (for the derivation from principles), i.e., *reason*.[48]

Accordingly, what were in the first *Critique* merely 'useful and indispensable' inferences for grasping the variety of objective forms in experience now become a fundamental element of Kant's system – one that bears the crucial reconciliatory task of 'mediat[ing] the connection' between the domain of natural law prescribed by the understanding and the sphere of freedom legislated by reason. Unlike the other faculties, however, the power of judgment in its legislative action in no way acts to determine objects of cognition; by contrast, it "is related solely to the subject and does not produce any concepts *of objects* for itself alone".[49] Reflective judgment thus emerges as another species of judgment whose import is equal to the determinative, so that at the most fundamental level of cognitive activity they denote two different modalities of thinking the particular under the universal, each of which figures the role of judgment power in a different manner:

> The power of judgment can be regarded either as a mere faculty for *reflecting* on a given representation, in accordance with a certain principle, for the sake of a concept that is thereby made possible, or as a faculty for

---

assumed by the faculty of judging were assigned to the understanding, e.g., note 1579, in Kant, 2010, p. 27. There is some equivocation on this matter in the first *Critique*, which we might see as a 'midway' text in which the transcendental role of the power of judgment appears without its '*a priori* principle' having yet been fully established.

46  Cf, Deleuze 2008, pp. 1–9.
47  Kant 2000, II.
48  Ibid.
49  Kant 2000, III, emphasis added.

*determining* an underlying concept through a given empirical representation. In the first case it is the *reflecting*, in the second case the *determining* power of judgment.[50]

This formalisation of the power of judgment opens up the problem of subsumption within Kant's thought in a number of highly important ways. The act of subsuming is no longer simply an aspect of theoretical or practical inferences but rather, through its identification with the faculty of judging, becomes one of the three basic cognitive operations of which the subject is capable. Furthermore, by directly explicating the reflective mode of subsumption, Kant expands his account of how the universal-particular relationship can be posited in a situation where the content of the universal pole (the major premise or 'function of unity') cannot be derived from an already given concept and must instead be found. Throughout the third critique, Kant's elaboration on the possibility of such a non-conceptual subsumption takes the form of a detailed account of the interaction between the power of judgment and the understanding in reflective judgments of taste and teleology.

The theoretical and practical occasions for subsumption outlined by Kant in his first two critiques saw the power of judgment, under the legislation of both the understanding and reason, play a primarily determining role as 'a faculty merely for subsuming concepts given from elsewhere'.[51] But in the case of reflective judgments, where no principle of determination (i.e., concept) is available, the power of judgment is commissioned to reflectively formulate the universal that is lacking. Thus it is shown to be 'not merely a faculty for subsuming the particular under the general (whose concept is given), but is also, conversely, one for finding the general for the particular'.[52] What is noteworthy in this mature conception of reflective judgment is the peculiar manner in which the understanding guides the power of judgment's activity: For while it contributes nothing to the content of the understanding (pure concepts), it is crucial as a *power* whose *a priori* principle is the prescription of *lawfulness* ('the general'). The role occupied by the concept-function in determinate judgment is, in reflective judgment, filled by a purely formal and indeterminate notion of generality derived from the understanding's generic power to posit lawfulness *per se*.

A significant problem emerges as a consequence of this conceptless account of subsumption, which concerns the initial requirements for a reflective judg-

---

50   Kant 2000, V.
51   Kant 2000, II.
52   Kant 2000, IV.

ment to be carried out. In objective cognition, determinative judgment is grounded in a given concept which acts as the *principle* for judgment, i.e., that on the basis of which the judgment can proceed, in other words, the major premise; here, category and principle are synonymous. By contrast, however, reflective judgment must 'produce' its concept through a series of comparative and analogical procedures; consequently, the *process* of reflection seems to logically precede the discovery of the conceptual *principle* by which, on the model of determinate judgment, it could take place. This generates an aporia at the level of the temporal structure of reflective judgment, which for Kant to solve requires *a non-categorial* principle that can set the concept-producing judgment into motion. This *a priori* principle, native to the power of judgment, is the *assumption* of an agreement between the products of nature and our discursive mode of reflection:

> If there is to be a concept or a rule which arises originally from the power of judgment, it would have to be a concept of things in *nature insofar as nature conforms to our power of judgment*, and thus a concept of a property of nature such that one cannot form any concept of it except that its arrangement conforms to our faculty for subsuming the particular given laws under more general ones even though these are not given.[53]

Through this principle, which Kant calls 'purposiveness', cognition attributes a discursive systematicity to nature for pragmatic purposes, assuming a 'general correspondence' between natural forms which makes reflection through comparison possible. Such a principle is necessitated because of the transcendental distinction between the *a priori* lawfulness of experience and the 'disturbingly unbounded diversity of empirical laws and heterogeneity of natural forms'; which means that 'it might be possible for us to connect perceptions to some extent in accordance with particular laws discovered on various occasions into one experience, but never to bring these empirical laws themselves to the unity of kinship under a common principle'.[54] So whereas experience is composed as a system, natural laws are merely aggregated and never attain a necessary unity. The principle of assumed purposiveness thus serves to bring nature into agreement with the form of experience, 'in order to be able to reflect in accordance with its own subjective law, in accordance with its need'.[55] Through this

---

53   Kant 2000, II.
54   Kant 2000, IV.
55   Kant 2000, V.

presupposition, purposiveness is invested in objects not at the level of their individuality, but 'only in general', at the level of the formal interconnectedness of natural representations *in* experience. So individual objects may not display objective purposiveness but insofar as they are part of nature, we think it in them; nature gives us 'not the least trace of a system' and yet we must constitute it as one. The notion of system that Kant has in mind here is manifestly subsumptive:

> The logical form of a system consists merely in the division of given general concepts (of the sort which that of a nature in general is here), by means of which one thinks the particular (here the empirical) with its variety as contained under the general, in accordance with a certain principle.[56]

Thus in reflective judgment, empirical particularity is formally (i.e., *a priori*) subsumed under the universal principle of nature as purposive. This posits the identity of nature and experience to make the content of experience fit for reflection, and ultimately, subsumption *in concreto*. While the particular laws that are thereby discovered and that play the role of the concept are found from amongst the products of nature, the application of the judgment always requires the *a priori* representation of generality (given by the understanding) in conjunction with the *a priori* principle of purposiveness (given by the power of judgment). In this way, reflective judgment, although undertaken without the aid of determinate *a priori* concepts, is nonetheless grounded in the transcendental accord between the power of the understanding and the power of judgment. The capacity to creatively generate concepts afforded by this accord is what leads Kant to distinguish determinate judgment, which he terms 'mechanical', from the subjective reflection on nature, which he calls 'technical':

> The reflecting power of judgment thus proceeds with given appearances, in order to bring them under empirical concepts of determinate natural things, not schematically, but *technically*, not as it were merely mechanically, like an instrument, but *artistically*, in accordance with the general but at the same time indeterminate principle of a purposive arrangement of nature in a system.[57]

---

56   Kant 2000.
57   Ibid.

## 1.4 Subsumption and Aesthetic Judgments

The discussion of reflection and purposiveness in the introduction to the *Critique of the Power of Judgment* paves the way for the sustained enquiry into aesthetic judgments that occupies the first part of the book. Aesthetic judgments differ from both determinate judgments of theoretical and practical objects and reflective judgments about natural forms, as their conclusions concern 'only the receptivity of a determination of the subject'.[58] The question which Kant seeks to address in his third critique is: How can *objective* judgments, which are 'always made by the understanding', be formed on the basis of reflection on purely *subjective* affections?[59] Of course, theoretical and practical cognitions are also determinations of consciousness in the broadest sense (as all cognitions are), but in these the judgment determines the relation *between the representation and the object*; by contrast, aesthetic judgments determine the relation *between the representation and the subject*:

> By the designation 'an aesthetic judgment about an object' it is therefore immediately indicated that a given representation is certainly related to an object but that what is understood in the judgment is not the determination of the object but of the subject and its *feeling*.[60]

Kant's introduction of the concept of 'feeling' here contradicts the account of judgment given quite consistently throughout the first two critiques as a solely discursive enterprise, that is, one based on cognition through concepts. For whilst objects are always determined conceptually, the subject can only be determined affectively, which is to say, in terms of feeling. The very notion of aesthetic judgment cannot therefore be based on the comparison of conceptual marks but has an entirely alternative measure for differentiating and connecting representations in consciousness. Some fifteen years before the publication of the third critique, in a lecture course on metaphysics, Kant intimated towards such a criterion, speaking of a 'special' and 'wholly other faculty' of the soul, for 'distinguishing things according to the feeling of pleasure and displeasure, or of satisfaction and dissatisfaction'.[61] This feeling of pleasure or displeasure is what is determined by an aesthetic judgment, and, as the 'one so-called sensation that can never become a concept of an object', is always attributed to the subject.[62]

---

58   Kant 2000, III.
59   Kant 2000, VIII.
60   Ibid.
61   Kant 2001, 28: 245.
62   Kant 2000, VIII.

But if it is only the subject's affective state that is thereby determined, and if, as a corollary, this determination is itself non-conceptual, is it legitimate for Kant to speak of aesthetic judgment as subsumptive, or even as judgment at all? It is not only the case that no concept is given for aesthetic judgments but, equally, that no concept could ever be found through reflection; pleasure and displeasure are 'felt, not understood'. This is the reason why aesthetic judgments cannot be expounded within the terms of the table of judgments, and, as Howard Caygill notes, are defined only negatively in relation to the four categorial groupings: They 'are in respect of quality *without* interest; they are universally valid *without* a concept; their relation is final but *without* an end; and their modality, necessary but *without* a concept'.[63] Each of the categories is effective only insofar as it gives determination to a representation on the basis of a fixed quantity, quality, relation or modality, but this is not possible when the 'object' of determination in question is the subject itself. How then, can the feeling of pleasure and displeasure act as a universal principle under which the particular aesthetic representation could be subsumed in order to render the judgment objective?

In characteristically Kantian fashion, the problem rests upon the dynamics of the subject's internal mediation. It is the subject itself rather than some putative 'external domain' that is for Kant the seat of objectivity and universality: We can recall how in the *Critique of Pure Reason*, the subjective particularity of intuition was rendered objective by subsumptive judgment, which articulated the sensory manifold according to the discursively thinkable, universal relations specified by the understanding. The transcendentally objective aspect of the subject is precisely what enables the individual to supersede the particularity of its own subject-ness when subsuming its perceptions under its rational, systematic intellect. (This is why subsumption is so central to Kant's entire project: It is the mediating act that brings all particularity into lawful and, most importantly, communicable form.) Similarly, in reflective judgments of natural forms, the attribution of purposiveness to nature makes the content of empirical experience fit for systematic cognition. But aesthetic judgment breaks away *before* the categorial determination of the manifold and follows a parallel path of discrimination not rooted in conceptual synthesis or analysis. So although Kant holds that we cognise the manifold as an object of experience, nothing we might say about it in this respect has any traction on our aesthetic judgment of it. This is because any such endeavour would involve defining the aesthetic (i.e., affective) character of the representation in

---

63    Caygill 1989, p. 299.

terms of *objective* attributes, thus de-subjectivising it: Size, texture, colour, etc. cannot be predicated of the subject.

It might therefore seem that, in bypassing conceptual determination, Kant relinquishes the possibility of universally valid aesthetic judgments. The feeling of pleasure or displeasure occasioned in the subject by the representation is entirely *particular*, what Kant calls a 'private interest'; in addition, the representation of the object to which this feeling is connected is equally particular: it is a pre-categorial 'image' [*Bild*] of which no generality can be thought. Therefore, if the relationship between terms in an aesthetic judgment is only ever one of particular to particular (of 'feeling' to 'image'), then it can never attain objective determination at the level of its *content* in the way a judgment of the understanding can. However, as we shall see, this is not an obstruction to aesthetic judgment but rather its unique quality, as such a judgment has a purely formal yet at the same time subjectively oriented validity: Its universality is derived only from the *form* of the judgment and remains indifferent to the content. (We might then add to the three forms of universality enumerated above – logical, transcendental, empirical – a further, fourth one, namely *subjective* universality.)

Just as with reflective judgments of natural forms, when no concept is given to the power of judgment, it must proceed on the basis of its own inner principle, which is that of purposiveness – or the assumed conformity of a representation 'to our faculty for subsuming the particular given laws under more general ones'.[64] However, as aesthetic judgments are not logically related to the cognition of the object but only to the effect of an intuition on the subject, this purposiveness cannot be cashed out in terms of the correspondence between empirical forms and cognition; instead, the aesthetic purposiveness of a representation denotes 'nothing but its suitability to the cognitive faculties that are in play in the reflecting power of judgment'[65] – in other words, a subjective rather than objective purposiveness. On the basis of this principle, the pure, indeterminate form of the object is constituted as the particular that is subsumed 'under a relation that is merely a matter of sensation, that of the imagination and the understanding reciprocally attuned to each other'.[66] Bizarrely, then, what is represented in the object is only the formal principle by which we reflect on it, 'the subjective, merely sensitive condition of the objective use of the power of judgment *in general* (namely the agreement of those two faculties [imagination and the understanding] with each other)'.[67]

---

[64] Kant 2000, II.
[65] Kant 2000, VII.
[66] Kant 2000, § 38.
[67] Kant 2000, VIII, emphasis added.

The perception *in the object* of a formal accord between the faculties of understanding and imagination is thus the result of the judgment; the latter generates a representation of the *general* (i.e., indeterminate) agreement of the powers of apprehension and presentation *as such*.

> If, then, the form of a given object in empirical intuition is so constituted that the *apprehension* of its manifold in the imagination agrees with the *presentation* of a concept of the understanding (though which concept be undetermined), then in the mere reflection understanding and imagination mutually agree for the advancement of their business, and the object will be perceived as purposive merely for the power of judgment, hence the purposiveness itself will be considered as merely subjective; for which, further, no determinate concept of the object at all is required nor is one thereby generated, and the judgment itself is not a cognitive judgment. – Such a judgment is called *an aesthetic judgment of reflection*.[68]

Reflection, which is based on the relation of the apprehending power of the imagination and the law-prescribing power of the understanding, is here set into free play. Whereas the activity of the imagination was determined by schematism in the first critique and by reason in the second critique (through the moral idea), in the *Critique of the Power of Judgment*, there is no heteronymous source of determination for the imagination. Consequently, whereas a judgment is habitually conceived of as the end result of a process which fixes the relation between two terms according to a rule or principle (for example synthesis or reflection), a judgment of beauty depends on the freedom of the very powers of determination: It is a determinate indeterminacy. That is, the judgment is determinate at the level of the relation between powers but indeterminate insofar as there is no rule by which the relation is given specific concretion – it has no determinate *content*. The free play of the faculties, which Kant also calls harmony, is a merely formal (i.e., indeterminate) purposiveness; and thus beauty is taking enjoyment in the form of purposiveness as such: form *becomes* the content.

With this, the *topos* of judgment is interrupted by an explosive instance of transcendental slippage. Despite the centrality of transcendental powers and conditions to Kant's critical project, their valence concerns only the grounds of *possibility* for most instances of judgment (cognitive, moral, natural). In the case of an *actual* judgment, these conditions remain however concealed; only

---

68  Kant 2000, VII.

the conditioned result appears to the conscious subject. This is not so with an aesthetic judgment of taste: What is judged in a predication of beauty (as opposed to 'agreeableness', which is never objective) is the pleasure resulting from the subject's *capacity* to feel its own life, to represent its own subjective state to itself: '[T]he faculty of making one's own representations the object's of one's thought'.[69] In other words, aesthetic judgment 'holds the given representation in the subject up to *the entire faculty of representation*, of which the mind becomes conscious in the feeling of its state'.[70] The condition of possibility for judgments thus becomes itself the 'object' of the judgment; the aesthetic judgment of taste 'has taken into consideration solely … the *formal condition* of the power of judgment, and is pure, i.e., mixed with neither concepts of the object nor with sensations as determining grounds'.[71] Therefore, through *feeling*, aesthetic judgments apprehend a pure determinability or formal purposiveness that expresses nothing but the transcendental structure of judgment-power itself in its harmonious operation, where it 'does not (as in theoretical judgments) merely have to subsume under objective concepts of the understanding and stands under a law, but where it is itself, subjectively, both object as well as law'.[72] This is the sense in which a judgment of beauty mediates the subject's self-affection and results in a feeling of the principle of life [*Lebensgefühl*][73] which accompanies the judgment. The pure formality of aesthetic reflection and the subjective involution that it precipitates are key to understanding how judgments of the beautiful are *universally* valid for Kant, in the sense that they are founded not on the peculiarity of the object which occasions them or the individuality of the subject who judges but on the universality of the structure of subjectivity manifest in the faculties whose harmony is apprehended:

> [Their] determining ground must lie not merely in the feeling of pleasure and displeasure in itself alone, but at the same time in a rule of the higher faculty of cognition, in this case, namely, in the rule of the power of judgment, which is thus legislative with regard to the conditions of reflection *a priori*, and demonstrates autonomy; this autonomy is not, however (like that of the understanding, with regard to the theoretical laws of nature, or of reason, in the practical laws of freedom), valid object-

---

69  Kant 'The False Subtlety of the Four Syllogistic Figures', §6.
70  Kant 2000, §1.
71  Kant 2000, §38.
72  Kant 2000, §36.
73  Kant 2000, §1. For an extended discussion of this principle, see Caygill 2000, pp. 79–92.

ively, i.e., through concepts of things or possible actions, but is merely subjectively valid, for the judgment from feeling, which, if it can make a claim to universal validity, demonstrates its origin grounded in *a priori* principles.[74]

Such a judgment is thus expressed with a 'universal voice' and makes an *a priori* claim on the community of subjects which demands agreement even if no such agreement can be reached in actuality, because the *principles* on which the subsumption of the particular is grounded are themselves valid for all judging subjects. The 'objectivity' of a subjective judgment of beauty is therefore derived from its 'universal communicability', a notion which arises from Kant's refiguring of the Aristotelian concept of a *sensus communis*:

> That in which the sense of human beings agree is the *universal* sense. But how can a human being pass a judgment according to the universal sense, since he still considers the object according to his private sense? The community amongst human beings constitutes a communal sense. Out of the intercourse among human beings a communal sense arises which is valid for everyone. Thus whoever does not come into a community has no communal sense[75]

In terms of the subsumptive structure of judgments of taste, particularity is brought to bear under a fully anthropological and vital principle of universality. This is not figured merely as an abstract, distributive unity but rather as an expression of the concrete community of rational beings, a collective unity. In this way, 'objectivity' is restored in the space of the aesthetic by virtue of the formal subjective universality of judgments of beauty. Through the critique of such judgments, Kant posits two registers of affection and discrimination that operate in parallel within the subject (or, more accurately, the *Gemüt*): that of *thinking* and that of *feeling*.[76] Thinking unfolds in the judicial relation of representation and object, be it comparative or determining, in which the subject (*qua* affect) is a silent partner; feeling, by contrast, emerges solely from the relation between the representation and the subject, meaning that here the object is held in stasis as the mere 'occasion' of the relation. In the former case, categorical subsumption determines a 'natural' economy of objective repres-

---

74  Kant 2000, VIII.
75  Kant 2001, 28: 249.
76  See Caygill 2000, p. 80.

entations; in the latter case, reflective comparison with the entire life of the subject determines an affective economy of purely subjective representations, to which the subject is either attracted or repelled. This attraction or repulsion is part of the vital movement of the promotion or hindrance of life. If a representation 'harmonises' with the principle of life, it produces pleasure, whereas if it resists the principle, it produces displeasure. However, given that the pleasure in a judgment of beauty results from the formal character of the judgment at the level of subjective powers, life must here be considered in its extra-individual mode: It is not 'my' life that is felt and promoted in a judgment of beauty but rational life *as such* (hence Kant's designation of *sensus communis* as the *universale in concreto*).[77]

## 1.6   Conclusion

The typology of judgment given throughout Kant's three critiques elucidates a series of possible relations that a subject can have to a representation. Underlying these relations is, in each case, a different technique of subsumption with different requirements and consequences.

In pure cognition, subsumption is a question of production and the point of distinction where a *process* of production (in this case synthesis) generates an individuated *product* (the object in general, =x). In the oscillation between synthesis and subsumption, we can see how the process is itself transformed or remodelled from the standpoint of the product, constituting a tension between (at least) two perspectives on the process. In subsumption under empirical concepts, as it is conceived in the first *Critique*, Kant deals with the question of distribution and the economy of 'types' within the domain of nature. Here, the account of subsumption bears more resemblance to the notion of a conceptuality which 'covers' the individuality of the particular that is thought under it, abstracting from its concreteness and repressing its unique identity. However, Kant demonstrates that this reflective mode of subsumption has only a superficial and pragmatic – what will later become purposive – relation to the object, which always depends on the prior operations of the understanding in categorically determining the manifold according to basic conceptual 'marks'. Once determined, the object can be reflected on and subsumed under the concept of its species. Neither of these processes of subsumption, however, simply take the particular as a mere *instance* of the universal, rather they elaborate techniques of synthesis which always have to be effected in order for the identity of particular and universal to obtain.

---

77   Kant 2010, p. 27 (note 1578).

Whereas cognitive and practical judgments operate through subsumption under concepts, in which the understanding and reason in turn legislate the power of judgment, by contrast, aesthetic judgments are peculiar in that they are grounded not in a concept but in the legislative action of judgment-power itself – i.e., the very capacity to subsume. Such judgments precipitate an involution of judgment power that generates *Lebensgefühle*: an affective representation of the subject's very power of representing. Here, the subject *qua* individual is brought under itself *qua* rational being, as it subsumes its particular representation act under its universal capacity to represent. Through this, the consistency of Kant's conception of the subject and its self-relation is disrupted, with the *a priori* structure of consciousness, which conditions but is itself never conditioned, suddenly entering the stage as an *a posteriori* element of experience (albeit one that is 'felt' rather than 'thought'). The consequences of this are explosive, and the third critique bears witness to a performative unravelling of the edifice which Kant has built up throughout his works on theoretical and practical reason. Perhaps most troubling for the Kantian enterprise is that such judgments convey a sense of the *whole* more than determinate, objective knowledge ever can; the subject, which can only be thought of as an 'aggregate' of powers, is from the vital standpoint of life a disjunctive unity capable of surveying its own state affectively.[78]

Most importantly, however, is the idea, quite consistent throughout Kant's critiques, that subsumption always implies – and indeed is operative at – points of transition between different orders of representation: between manifold and object, object and form, rule and law, representation and power, etc. What is so significant about aesthetic judgment in this respect, is that it implies a point of transition not just between two orders of representation, but between the order of representation taken *in toto* and a perhaps more fundamental order of vital powers (something also attested to in the 'analytic of the sublime'). That this transition always occurs through the mediation of a judgement of beauty,

---

78   Here the pleasure taken in a judgment of beauty (and its transgression of the structure of 'mechanical' subsumption) has a peculiar double-character that prefigures certain formal aspects of Marx's conception of communism in extremely illuminating ways. Its two aspects are (1) that the feeling of life that accompanies the free play of the faculties is a *self-expressive* representation of subjective powers, unleashed in creative modulation; (2) that the pleasure emerges from the generic *universality* of the powers that are felt, that they are shared amongst a community of equals disposed with shared capacities. In one and the same judgment, both the entirety of individual capacities and the generic universality of these capacities are expressed and explored – although crucially, not exhausted. It is not hard to see how elements of this model can be transposed into the context of sensuous activity rather than contemplative enjoyment.

however, establishes the problem of the finite manifestation of the infinite that would go on to become a central concern for both romanticism and speculative idealism.

## 2    Hegel's Critique of Subsumption

The significance of Kant's critique of theoretical reason for Hegelian philosophy lies not only in the former's quest to demonstrate which kind of judgments about objects are legitimate (taken here to mean *universally valid*, in the sense expounded above) but arises equally from its conclusion that these judgments have always already taken place when we experience an object. Kant discovered the conceptual mediation – in the form of *judgments of subsumption under 'pure' concepts* – implicit in all apparently immediate knowledge. This transition from immediacy to its mediating condition is a movement derived from Kant's pre-critical logic, where discrete concepts were shown to be the product of subsumptive judgment acts.[79] But whilst in formal logic, thought need only find agreement with itself in order to produce valid judgments, in the sphere of experience dealt with in the first *Critique* (transcendental logic), thought must find agreement with its other, that in the subject which is *not* a determination of thought – sensible intuition – in order for an object to be known. 'Transcendental logic' represents Kant's attempt to guarantee the correspondence of thought and object by enclosing them within a unifying, law-bound structure of subjectivity. On this account, to know an object is to *have specified* (subsumptively) the consistency of its empirical content according to the basic categorial determinations of the understanding. This is the epistemological context in which subsumption emerges in the *Critique of Pure Reason* as a condition of possibility for the experience of objects, which is equated with knowledge thereof.

For Hegel, Kant was correct to argue that thought is always implicit in the constitution of objectivity and that this involvement is a process entirely immanent and internal to consciousness. Hegel recognised that, in subsuming intuitions under concepts in this way, consciousness permeates them with itself, with its own unity and self-relation, sublating their particular imme-

---

79    Kant 1992a, § 2. It also corresponds to Kant's most general definition of reason, as orientation towards the unconditioned: '[T]he proper principle of reason in general (in its logical use) is to find the unconditioned for conditioned cognitions of the understanding, with which its unity will be completed' (Kant 1998, A307/B364).

diacy into the *universality* and *determinateness* that, for him as for Kant, constitute objectivity:

> The *comprehension* of an object consists in nothing else than that the ego makes it *its own*, pervades it and brings it into *its own form*, that is, into the *universality* that is immediately a *determinateness*, or a determinateness that is immediately universality. As intuited or even in ordinary conception, the object is still something *external* and *alien*. When it is comprehended, the being-in-and-for-self which it possesses in intuition and pictorial thought is transformed into a *positedness*; the *I* in *thinking* it pervades it.[80]

In accordance with critical philosophy's new understanding of the object as pre-constituted by the spontaneity of the 'I', Hegel holds that the determinations of the object emerge from the subjective process of its comprehension. Crucial to this conception is Kant's attempt in the transcendental deduction to reciprocally derive both the categories under which the manifold is subsumed from the *unity* of the 'I' and, simultaneously, the unity of the 'I' from the *act* of thinking the object under these categories. It is the equation of conceptual universality with the unity of the pure 'I' arising from this deduction that dissolves the opposition between truth and subjectivity and gives rise to a conception of the object as mediated. This forms the general structure of transcendental logic with which Hegel's philosophy engages; but despite his affinities with it, Hegel took issue with Kant's model of subsumptive cognition in three primary respects: (1) the modelling of the apperceptive 'I' – and therefore the transcendental subject – on the empirical, psychological individual; (2) the uncritical appropriation of the categories of the understanding from Aristotelian logic; (3) the limitation of *truth* to objects of experience alone, which left critical philosophy still mired in the sphere of empirical appearance.

Metacritically outlining these limits to Kant's model of cognition allowed Hegel to incorporate the basic movement of transcendental critique (from conditioned to condition) within a reconstructed outline of both the elements and the total structure of unity of Kantian thought. Neither of these two aspects, Hegel contested, was the product of a fully immanent philosophical derivation, and much extraneous and unjustified content had been smuggled into Kant's philosophy. But Hegel did not reject the basic structure of opposition between the *unity* and *determinateness* of self-consciousness; instead, he sub-

---

80  Hegel 1999, p. 585.

jected them to the dialectical critique that would produce (1) a phenomenology of spirit (in reference to transcendental subjectivity); (2) a speculative logic (in reference to the categories); (3) a new conception of truth as speculative totality. These transformations bear on the status of subsumption within Hegel's system, insofar as both the structured context of the subsumptive act and the specific determinations executed by it are subject to a new derivation that fundamentally alters their nature.

Hegel's modification of the concept of subsumption begins first and foremost with his critique of the constitutive divisions of transcendental logic, specifically those which precipitate the emergence of subsumption in the *Critique of Pure Reason*: that is, the basic opposition of *concepts of the understanding* and the *manifold of intuition* carried over from Kant's distinction between the 'empty' form of thought given in general logic and the content to which it is applied. The crucial consequence of this division is that Kantian philosophy takes the subsumed to be 'entirely unhomogeneous' to that which subsumes it, such that for Hegel the subsumption amounts to an *external* imposition on the matter given in intuition: '[T]he empirical *material*, the manifold of intuition and representation, first *exists on its own account*, and ... then the understanding *approaches* it, brings *unity* into it and by abstraction raises it to the form of *universality*'.[81] Thought thus pervades intuition to know it as its own but does so coercively, imposing its own relations and mediation upon it rather than drawing out the truth of those that are already present within it; the manifold neither has, nor develops, an inner, *concrete* universality and only obtains universality when the functions of unity given by the understanding have been determined in it subsumptively. For Hegel, this model is consonant with the worldview of Newtonian science, for which 'the universal (the genus etc.) contained in [the particular] is not determined on its own account, nor is it intrinsically connected with what is particular; but universal and particular are mutually external and contingent, just as much as the particularities that are combined are, on their own account, external to each other and contingent'.[82] On the basis of this standpoint, it appears that 'I possess [concepts] and the [Concept], just as I also possess a coat, complexion, and other external properties'.[83]

Despite their *a priori* interconnection, concepts and intuitions remain utterly distinct (and implicitly self-sufficient) 'sources' of cognition within the

---

81   Hegel 1999, p. 587.
82   Hegel 1991b, § 9.
83   Hegel 1999, p. 584.

Kantian system; indeed, it is precisely this difference that for Kant necessitates their mediation in a 'third thing', the transcendental schema. Hegel opposed this fixed externality of faculties, arguing that the difference between sensible intuition and concepts is one only of the 'forms' of 'a content that remains *one and the same*'.[84] In *Faith and Knowledge*, Hegel's early review of the 'reflective' philosophies of his time, the primary distinction between intuitive and conceptual syntheses appears simply in that the concept grasps the positedness of determinations *in distinction* from its own self: 'Synthetic unity is only concept because it binds the difference in such a way that it also steps outside of it, and faces it in *relative* antithesis'.[85] Whilst the centrality of synthetic unity would be reduced in Hegel's later works, the emphasis on a 'truly necessary, absolute, original identity of opposites' would be retained, in opposition to the Kantian idea of an original division of the faculties that 'constitute only an aggregate and not a system'.[86]

Hegel thus disparages the weakness of the subsumptive-synthetic relation between concepts and intuitions that is supposed to ground the truth of experience for Kant, describing it as a relation that unites the two elements of cognition in an 'external, superficial way, just as a piece of wood and a leg might be bound together by a cord'.[87] Such unity is not, for Hegel, a properly philosophical unity in which relations between elements and higher determinations are developed immanently out of those elements as their implicit conditions: '[T]he very expression *synthesis* easily recalls the conception of an *external* unity and a *mere combination* of entities that are *intrinsically separate*'.[88]

Kantianism, by asserting a model of 'mechanical' connection between independent elements, gives the opposition of thought and external reality held by 'normal consciousness' a philosophical articulation, reproducing it in the transcendental distinction between the object as it is *for us* and as it is *in itself*. Because our sensible mode of intuiting the 'external' object is deficient, lacks conceptual coherence and unity, it must be subsumed under an alien schema of universality, and this 'subsumption under the species alters what is immedi-

---

84  Hegel 1991b, § 3.
85  Hegel 1977, p. 70, emphasis added; See Hegel 2007, p. 205.
86  Kant 2000, 111. Insofar as Kant indicates the philosophical imperative to construct knowledge as a scientific system, it is still only on the basis of turning this aggregate into an architectonic whose unity does not shape but is built upon its contents. See Kant 1998, 'The Architectonic of Pure Reason'.
87  Hegel 1995, p. 441.
88  Hegel 1999, p. 589.

ate'.[89] Only the object *for us* – that which results from subsumptive judgment – is true for Kant, and yet this truth is paradoxically qualified as having no bearing on the thing as it might actually be, lost as it is in the process of its comprehension. For Hegel, this expulsion of the *in itself* from the realm of knowledge leads Kantianism to yield only a 'truth of the false':

> It seems absurd, if what we want is knowledge of external objects, to alter these external objects by our very [abstractive] activity upon them. Quite absurd to want to come to know things as they are [in themselves] and yet alter them, thus receiving things into our knowledge only as altered. The alteration consists in the fact that we separate off what is singular or external and hold the truth of the thing to lie in what is universal rather than in what is singular or external. Quite oddly, for Kant it is by altering things that we are persuaded we secure their inner truth.[90]

The one-sidedness of this structure of determination is, on Hegel's account, exactly what undermines the Kantian conception of truth, reducing it to a tautological affirmation of subjectivity that assimilates consciousness's other (the *in itself*) to itself, whilst simultaneously reducing itself (qua 'I') to the empirical. It thereby fails to recognise – in anything other than a nominal sense (that expounded in Kant's 'refutation of idealism') – the subject's own mediation in and through this other, with the process of subsumption effected unilaterally and mechanically (even by Kant's own admission) upon the sensibly given material.[91] 'The understanding is in this way an intrinsically empty *form* which, on the one hand, obtains a reality through the said *given* content and, on the other hand, *abstracts* from that content, that is to say, *lets it drop* as something useless'.[92] And yet in spite of this, transcendental subjectivity cannot entirely dispose of the *in itself* that stands beyond it; it remains beholden to precisely that which it repudiates. The conceptual identity produced by the understanding 'finds itself immediately confronted by or next to an infinite non-identity, with which it must coalesce in some incomprehensible way'.[93] The epistemological horizon of Kantian philosophy, the limit of comprehension implied by it, therefore 'remains entirely within the antithesis' between nature and reason,

---

89  Hegel 2008, p. 12 (§ 22).
90  Ibid.
91  Subsumption is mechanical for Kant, insofar as *determinative* judgments of objects are concerned. See the opposition of 'mechanical' and 'artful' subsumption in Kant 2000.
92  Hegel 1999, p. 587.
93  Hegel 1977a, p. 76.

subject and object, thought and being, willing and acting, finite and infinite, etc., precisely because of its original incapacity to know the object as it really is.[94] 'A formal idealism which in this way sets an absolute Ego-point and its intellect on one side, and an absolute manifold, or sensation, on the other side, is a dualism.'[95]

Kant does of course recognise the higher unity that would resolve these oppositions in the form of reason's orientation toward the unconditioned. However, this orientation, far from genuinely grounding the unifying movement of thought, has, in contrast to the objective universality of the understanding's 'fixed determinations,' only the inferior status of being responsible for, at best, the production of 'regulative principles' and, at worst, 'transcendental illusions'. The constitutive oppositions of Kantianism are therefore superseded only *subjectively* in the ideas, which have no objective, i.e., real truth content. Again, Hegel criticises the division separating the discrete concepts of the understanding and the unifying tendency of reason (what Hegel simply calls *the Concept*) as a characteristic limit of 'the reflective philosophy of subjectivity':

> Kantian philosophy declares finite cognition to be all that is possible ... it falls back into absolute finitude and subjectivity, and the whole task and content of this philosophy is, not the cognition of the absolute, but the cognition of this subjectivity.[96]

Because Kant aims at a critique of the finite intellect rather than knowledge of the absolute, his philosophy is resigned to a 'progression in finite determinations', accepting that 'an endless aiming at the concrete is required for thought, a filling up in accordance with the rule which completion prescribes' – albeit a completion never to be realised, only striven towards in the mode stipulated by its abstract universality:[97]

> [Kantian philosophy] leads knowledge into consciousness and self-consciousness, but from this standpoint maintains it to be a subjective and finite knowledge. Thus although it deals with the infinite Idea, expressing its formal categories and arriving at its concrete claims, it yet again denies

---

94   Hegel 1977a, p. 67.
95   Hegel 1977a, p. 78.
96   Hegel 1977a, p. 68.
97   Hegel 1995, p. 424.

this to be the truth, making it a simple subjective, because it has once for all accepted finite knowledge as the fixed and ultimate standpoint.[98]

It is precisely in the rejection of this finitude that Kant's critical differentiation between the truth of legitimate and illegitimate judgments of subsumption is called into question by Hegel. What we must ask then, is how the character and effects of subsumptive judgment are altered by Hegel's refutation of the static division between the aesthetic, analytical and dialectical moments of transcendental subjectivity, and what role subsumption plays in Hegel's reconfigured concept of the subject *as process*.

## 2.1   A New Derivation

Overcoming the empirico-epistemological boundary of Kant's philosophical claims – specifically the adherence to a structurally constitutive distinction of subject and object – is the task Hegel set out to achieve through his dialectical treatment of consciousness in the *Phenomenology of Spirit*. The *Phenomenology* deals with the development of the relation between consciousness and its object, progressing through the series of forms or 'shapes' of experience, each of which specifies a different relationship of knowledge to its object. This developmental process passes from the immediacy of sense-certainty, through the emergence of self-consciousness from relations of recognition between individuals to the social forms of spirit, arriving ultimately at the standpoint of absolute knowing, from which the opposition between subject and object (substance) is sublated into the unity of spirit with itself and the knowledge of experience is resolved into a pure ontology in the logic (i.e., not simply the determinations of the object as it appears to consciousness, but the pure determinations of the object as it 'actually' is). Hegel's initial rupture with Kant consists in the fact that, rather than attempting to ascertain the necessary content and structure of experience in order to then critically determine what counts as knowledge, for Hegel the process of reflecting on knowledge cannot be divorced from knowledge itself (as illustrated by his well-known metaphor, which likens Kants critical method to the desire to learn how to swim before getting in the water).[99] With this process, philosophy has already begun. It is thus not simply the final stage of consciousness taken in isolation that can be thought of as the 'true standpoint' of knowledge, but rather all the stages in the totality of their development

---

98   Hegel 1995, pp. 426–7.
99   Hegel 1995, p. 428.

that constitute the truth of knowledge – as a process: 'In this movement the passive subject itself perishes; it enters into the differences and the content, and constitutes the determinateness, i.e., the differentiated content and its movement, instead of remaining inertly over against it'.[100] Subjectivity cannot thus be reduced to a static aggregation of principles and powers but is instead grasped as the dynamic movement of the whole in its dialectical self-development.

This informs the status of subsumption in Hegel insofar as the Kantian 'I' is premised on precisely the fixed division of faculties that Hegel rejects, specifically the dualism of sensibility and intellect, whose heterogeneous contents have to be brought synthetically into relation. The overcoming of precisely this division by virtue of subsumption under concepts forms the basis for the reciprocal establishment of the *unity* of consciousness and the *consistency* of experience in Kant's first *Critique*. Hegel's dialectical critique of consciousness in the *Phenomenology*, however, transforms this oppositional structure into a *processual* concept of subject, as the organic self-development of an (in the last instance) objective process. The unity of consciousness is thus no longer a static structure of self-relation but the dynamic unfolding of knowing through its various shapes or moments. Integral to this movement is the supersession of the finite standpoint of *individual* consciousness and the development of the *social* concept of subjectivity emerging in the transition from subject-object relations to subject-subject and then subject-substance relations in the various forms of ethical life. Hegel's exposition attempts to demonstrate, in the first place, that interpersonal relations are an implicit condition for the existence of individual self-consciousness. At this stage, the problem ceases to have solely epistemological significance (i.e., of the correspondence between thought and object) and instead becomes a problem of *social recognition*, because the object that appears to consciousness is revealed to itself be another free self-consciousness – i.e., a subject. What is at stake here is the way in which objective structures of recognition produce contradictory relations – of *mis*-recognition – between individual self-consciousnesses. Not only is the subsumption of intuitions under concepts that is so fundamental for Kant thereby demoted to a partial and limited stage in this conceptual development, but the very constitutive limit of knowledge set out by Kant – individual, empirical experience – is superseded as consciousness 'leaves behind it the colourful show of the sensuous here-and-now'.[101]

---

100   Hegel 1977b, § 60.
101   Hegel 1977b, § 177.

Subsequently, at the point in Hegel's exposition where social relations emerge as *objective* structures rather than contingent relations between isolated individuals, that is, with the emergence of *spirit*, contradiction arises primarily at the level of the relation between individual self-consciousnesses – the 'I' which is subject – and the *forms* of social relations, or of ethical life, that unite them – the 'we' that is substance. Although Hegel does not explicitly discuss these contradictions in terms of subsumption, their conceptual structure is homologous with what he identified as two defining feature of Kantian subsumption: the weak synthetic unity of heterogeneous elements and the coercive determination of individual elements under an abstract universality. Insofar as subsumptive relations thus obtain at the level of structures of spirit, they are relations between individuals and the universality of the social form they exist within and are constituted by (in contrast to the simple case of domination of one self-consciousness by another described in the section on 'Lordship and Bondage'). This can occur in terms of the dominant universality of the social substance which subsumes individuals with antithetical desires (as in the case of 'ethical life') or of the alienated abstract universality of individual personhood under which the community proper is subsumed (as for example with private property in ancient Rome). Here, we find that the same structure of double determination that was operative in Kant's theory of subsumption, and which distinguished between (i) the individual representations that are bound together by concepts and (ii) the relation of these unified representations to the compositional totality in which they are unified, is reproduced at the level of (i) relations (of recognition) between individuals and (ii) relations (of recognition) between individuals and the community. Andrew Chitty draws attention to this in the following claim:

> [F]ully realised (or 'absolute') spirit is constituted only when this mutual recognition between individuals that brings into existence a universal self is supplemented by a *second* mutual recognition between this universal self and the individuals that compose it, or between individuals acting as members of this universal self and the same individuals acting as particular individuals.[102]

It is not necessary to give an in-depth analysis of all subsumptive relations (and their sublation) in the *Phenomenology*; what is pertinent to the problematic as a whole is the fundamental transformation of the concept of the subject

---

102  Chitty 2009, pp. 124–5.

that Hegel carries out. With Kant, the fixed, transcendental structure of subjectivity provides both the context and resources that give rise to subsumptive judgment acts. Hegel lauds the *Critique of Pure Reason* because in it, 'the unity which constitutes the nature of the *Concept* is recognised as the *original synthetic* unity of *apperception*, as unity of the *I think*, or of self-consciousness'; but if this conception of the I is expanded – as it is in the *Phenomenology* – then the context and resources for subsumption are thereby also altered.[103] Most important for the present inquiry is the aforementioned transition that occurs in the course of the process of the (subjective) development of spirit and leads to the exposition of properly social (as opposed to merely interpersonal) forms of self-consciousness. This transition (from *self-consciousness* to *spirit*) lays the foundation for the analysis of a concept of subsumption that pertains to individuals subsumed under objectively universal structures of sociality which constitute their collective and individual identities and practices. We are no longer dealing with *synthetic judgment acts* internal to an individual consciousness but with the development of *relational social forms* that determine individual identities and collective practices in terms of both their subjective and objective implications (as developed in the *Phenomenology* and *Philosophy of Right*). This is the first essential modification to the problem of subsumption that we can find in Hegel.

There is a second, related aspect of Hegel's critique of subsumption in Kant that follows directly from this new concept of the subject as process: the issue of the content of that process, i.e., its determinate stages or 'shapes' and their objective status once the phenomenological derivation of ontology (as logic) has been achieved. This consists, first and foremost, in a critique of the specific forms of conceptual universality under which subsumption can occur, as well as their status as *actual abstractions*, rather than determinations of the object whose validity is limited to its appearance *for us*. The exposition given by Hegel in the *Science of Logic* seeks to submit the categories of thought to a rigorous enquiry that does not depend on their belonging to an empirical consciousness (Hegel believed that he had already achieved the immanent development of self-conscious spirit into logic with the *Phenomenology*) but attempts to dialectically develop the determinations of thought out of their own immanent content and contradictions.[104] Hegel therefore introduces not only a new conception of subjectivity, but also of logic, in the course of which the conceptual form of subsumption will be posited with a 'higher' determinacy.

---

103  Hegel 1999, p. 584.
104  Hegel 1999, p. 48.

## 2.2   *From Pure Concepts to Dialectical Categories*

As we have seen, Kant believed formal logic to be devoid of specific content, merely describing the empty functions of thought as such,; yet when transcendentally adapted to the form of intuition as 'pure concepts of the understanding', such functions came to constitute the *a priori structure* of all objective experience. In this adapted form, the concepts enumerated traditional metaphysical categories such as quality, quantity, relation etc. *Transcendental logic* was the product of this logicisation of metaphysical concepts, which displaced these determinations of the object to the subject-structure itself and then reintroduced them into the cognised object via the subsumptive operation. Hegel was broadly in accord with the necessity of such internalisation and the explication of a subjectively mediated structure of objectivity. Concerning Kant's transcendental deduction of the subject-structure of consciousness, however, Hegel claimed that the specific thought-determinations – the categories of the understanding which specify the modes of organizing and relating the determinations of the object to the unity of the I – were, firstly, not the product of an immanent derivation (he accused Kant of having naively appropriated the formal logic on which they were based from 'ordinary' logic, a largely unmodified Aristotelian theory of judgments) and, secondly, attenuated by their epistemologically restricted validity:[105]

> First of all, the Critical Philosophy subjects to investigation the validity of the concepts of the understanding that are used in metaphysics, but also in the other sciences and in ordinary representation. This critique does not involve itself with the content, however, or with the determinate mutual relationship of these thought-determinations to each other; instead, it considers them according to the antithesis of subjectivity and objectivity in general. ... The more detailed forms of the *a priori*, i.e., of thinking which, in spite of its objectivity, is interpreted as a merely subjective activity, are presented ... in a systematic order which, it may be remarked, *rests only upon psychological-historical foundations*.[106]

> Now because the interest of the Kantian philosophy was directed to the so-called *transcendental* aspect of the categories, it treated them in such a way as to reveal nothing about what they are in themselves; what categories are without the abstract relation to the ego common to all and wherein

---

105   Hegel 1995, pp. 438–9.
106   Hegel 1991b, § 41, emphasis added.

their specific nature relatively to each other and their relationship to each other consists, such questions were not an object of consideration.[107]

Continuing the efforts of his Jena system, Hegel proposes in the *Science of Logic* to undertake a complete reconstruction of the categories of pure thought. One of the central premises of this project is the rejection of Kant's initially logical distinction between the *form* and *content* of thinking; an assumption that is problematically reproduced at the level of the relation of concepts and intuition, giving rise to the need for transcendental subsumption in order to establish their correspondence. Instead, Hegel proposes to take the categories of thought as simultaneously providing the content *and* form of a scientific enquiry into thinking:

> It is quite inept to say that logic abstracts from all *content*, that it teaches only the rules of thinking without any reference to *what* is thought or without being able to consider its nature. For as thinking and the rules of thinking are supposed to be the subject matter of logic, these directly constitute its peculiar content.
> 
> Far from [objective thinking] being formal, far from it standing in need of a matter to constitute an actual and true cognition, it is its content alone which has absolute truth, or, if one still wanted to employ the word matter, it is the veritable matter – but a matter which is not external to the form, since this matter is rather pure thought and hence the absolute form itself.[108]

By asserting the identity of the form and the content of thought within a single self-developing process (whose 'method' is also not be distinguished indistinguishable from its 'matter') Hegel was able to claim that his exposition constituted a systematic derivation, i.e., one in which each determination emerges immanently from the dialectical critique and determinate negation of the previous (something Kant never achieved, instead articulating his categories in parallel to one other). Furthermore, Hegel would claim that the results of this process, rather than being mere subjective forms of thought pertaining to individual consciousness in its opposition to the object, have objective validity, insofar as the determinations of logic are actual moments of a reality far more 'concrete' than the sensory show of empirical experience. Thus 'the science of

---

107   Hegel 1999, p. 63.
108   Hegel 1999, pp. 44; 49–50.

logic in dealing with the thought determinations which in general run through our mind instinctively and unconsciously ... will also be a reconstruction of those which are singled out by reflection and are fixed by it as subjective forms external to the matter and import of the determinations of thought'.[109] All such 'lifeless' determinations of the understanding, which had been reduced by the logic of the time to analytical, mechanical, that is, concept-less [*begrifflose*], irrational procedures, are in Hegel's logic enfolded within the systematic sequence of logical forms in their immanent development. It is by virtue of the speculative identity of *concepts* and *the Concept* that critical philosophy's antithesis between the limited, abstract universality of the conceptual content of thought and the distributed universality of its 'external' ground in individual consciousness is dissolved:

> The antithesis between form and content, which is given special validity when the Concept is supposed to be what is only formal, now lies behind us, together with all the other antitheses that reflection keeps fixed. They have been overcome dialectically, i.e., through themselves; and it is precisely the Concept that contains all the earlier determinations of thinking sublated within itself. Certainly the Concept must be considered as a form, but it is a form that is infinite and creative, one that both encloses the plenitude of all content within itself, and at the same time releases it from itself.[110]

The second essential modification of subsumption that we find in Hegel's philosophy is therefore the idea that those determinations of the object through which subsumption might occur can only be understood in the fullness of their truth by grasping their place and *actuality* within the systematic totality of determinations in which externality and synthesis are sublated in the course of the organic development of mediating conditions.

These two aspects of Hegel's critique of Kant therefore articulate the unity of the processual subjective totality and, with it, the function and implications of subsumption on an entirely new conceptual plane. On one hand, it is the development of the process as a whole that gives unity and meaning to the various moments of its existence. On the other hand, the categories themselves, in their dialectical interrelation and development out of one another, are precisely what constitutes the determinate moments of the process. In this way,

---

109  Hegel 1999, pp, 39–40.
110  Hegel 1991b, §160.

the basic Kantian structure of apperception has been retained, but the scope of the 'I' and its moments have been both expanded and given a higher degree of conceptual coherence. An important question arises at this point, namely how subsumption fits within the general movement of the Concept as both a constitutive feature of the movement as such and, simultaneously, as a part of one of its determinate stages or moments, which as a partial and thus inadequate moment will be abolished in the course of its development. Is this a repeat of the tension between synthesis and subsumption we found in Kant, i.e., of that between *process* and *act*? And is this tension resolved in Hegel's speculative repositioning of subsumption at a specific moment in the exposition of the concept as whole?

## 2.3  Subsumption's Place in the Exposition

A consequence of Hegel's speculative re-founding of logic is that subsumption, like any other logical determination, cannot simply be grasped as an abstractly self-sufficient conceptual relation that is applied to a content independent of it. Instead, its truth and meaning must be established by virtue of its place within the concrete totality. Subsumption's conceptual determinacy therefore emerges at the stage in the concept's self-development at which it is 'posited', although it should be noted that it is not for Hegel a logical category proper in the way that 'quality', 'ground' or 'the judgment' are. Hegel's discussion of subsumption arises in the 'subjective' logic, i.e., that part of the *logic* which deals not with the 'ontological' determinations of objects but with the forms of subjective thinking taken at the same time as the concept's own object. Such forms broadly correspond to the traditional entities of logic: the *concept*, *judgment* and *syllogism* – those that originally gave rise to the problem of subsumption from Aristotle onwards and, notably, in Kant. The treatment of these forms emerges in the logic once the essential determinations of the object have been developed to their highest form as 'substance', but the subjective side of thinking that grasps such determinations remains only implicit, such that the antithesis between *concepts* and *the Concept* (what for Kant would correspond to understanding and reason) has not been overcome (even if it has been methodologically alluded to). This is what 'The Doctrine of the Concept' undertakes to do by developing the various functions of unity which relate the determinations of being with the reflected determinations of essence, leading to the freedom of the concept in its externalisation and return to self (resolving *concepts* into *the Concept*).

Structurally, Hegel's exposition mirrors the Kantian treatment of subsumption in the latter's lectures on formal logic in that it begins with the immediacy of the concept, then demonstrates its mediation through acts of judgment and finally places these discrete acts within the syllogistic form that can then be extended to produce chains of inferential or mediated reasoning. However, Hegel's critique of the subjective forms of the concept from the standpoint of his transformed conception of the subject-structure and the systematic derivation of its determinate content provides a new perspective on the conceptual structure, content and most importantly the limits, of the subsumptive relation. For Hegel, the first shape of the subjective concept is its discreteness as *a* concept (rather than *the* Concept), which in its first mode of appearance is associated with the abstract universality of concepts of the understanding: 'The [Concept] in the guise of immediacy constitutes the point of view for which the [Concept] is a subjective thinking, a reflection external to the subject matter'.[111] Here, the concept is statically self-identical and bears only an external relation to any content which might be contained subsumptively under it; it therefore lacks concreteness. But it is precisely the specific determinacy of its content that contradicts the universality of its form (as concept), revealing it to be only a limited form of universality – a 'particularised' universal:

> [The simple concept's] abstract determinations are eternal essentialities only in respect of their form; but their content is at variance with this form; therefore they are not truth, or imperishable. Their content is at variance with the form, because it is not determinateness itself as universal; that is, it is not totality of the Concept's difference, or not itself the whole form; but the form of the limited understanding is itself the imperfect form, namely, abstract universality.[112]

The simple concept therefore splits into two moments: *universal* and *particular*. These are 'diverse' and 'opposed' moments of the concept, which, as John Burbidge points out in his commentary to the logic, 'function as particulars vis-a-vis each other, even though one of the particulars is called the universal'.[113] Finally, these two antithetical aspects are united in the singular [*einzeln*] concept, which constitutes the third moment, and the unity of the Concept as such in all its moments: 'as the second negation, that is, as negation of the negation, it is absolute determinateness or singularity and concreteness'.[114] A higher form of universality that incorporates these differentiations is thereby posited over and above the initial abstractness of the 'simple' concept.

---

111  Hegel 1999, p. 597.
112  Hegel 1999, p. 610.
113  Burbidge 2006, p. 83.
114  Hegel 1999, p. 603.

*Universality, particularity* and *singularity* are thus for Hegel the 'genuine distinctions' or 'types' of the Concept. Yet to think of them as discrete existences apart from each other is still to grasp them via 'external reflection', which marks the limit of the singular concept's universality in the sense that 'the Concept as such does not abide within itself, without development (as the understanding would have it); on the contrary, being the infinite form, the Concept is totally active'.[115] Hegel therefore goes on to develop the implicit condition for the existence of these moments of the Concept in their concreteness, which is the *activity* of their 'immanent distinguishing and determining ... in the *judgment*', the movement of thought that generates their distinctness and then holds it together. It is in this sense that Hegel asserts, much like Kant, that 'to judge is to determine the Concept'.[116] It is here, in the active articulation of the relations between conceptual determinations, that Hegel's main discussion of subsumption arises.

For Hegel, judgment always and necessarily 'particularises' the concept by explicitly positing the relations between its 'independent extremes', *universal* (predicate) and *singular* (logico-grammatical subject), each of which is itself already a concept. It thus develops the Concept's own reality out of itself and its own essential determinations: 'The judgment can therefore be called the proximate *realisation* of the [Concept], inasmuch as reality denotes its general entry *into existence* as a *determinate being*'.[117] Judgment is the Concept's actualising activity, and its significance points beyond the subjective emptiness of its formal logical character. At first, however, it takes the 'subjective' form of an 'external unity' posited between the two concepts that occupy the positions of subject and predicate:

> The judgment has in general for its sides totalities which to begin with are essentially self-subsistent. The unity of the [Concept] is, therefore, at first only a *relation* of self-subsistents ... From this *subjective* standpoint, then, subject and predicate are considered to be complete, each on its own account, apart from the other: the subject as an object that would exist even if it did not possess this predicate; the predicate as a universal determination that would exist even if it did not belong to this subject.[118]

---

115  Hegel 1991b, § 166.
116  Hegel 1991b, § 165.
117  Hegel 1999, p. 621.
118  Hegel 1999, p. 625.

Thus, whilst the *relating* of subject and predicate has been posited explicitly, the *relation* remains abstract. The judgment is characterised by the antithesis of *subsumption* and *inherence*, which mirrors the tension we have already developed between the two universalities of the subject-structure and its determinations. The abstractly universal property inheres in the subject, whilst the subject is subsumed under the predicate.

> Since the predicate is thus distinct from the subject, it is only an *isolated* determinateness of the latter, only *one* of its properties; while the subject itself is the *concrete*, the totality of manifold determinatenesses, just as the predicate contains one; it is the universal. But on the other hand the predicate, too, is a self-subsistent universality and the subject, conversely, only a determination of it. Looked at this way, the predicate subsumes the subject; singularity and particularity are not for themselves, but have their essence and substance in the universal. The predicate expresses the subject in its Concept; the individual and the particular are contingent determinations in the subject; it is their absolute possibility. When in the case of subsumption one thinks of an external connection of subject and predicate and the subject is conceived of as a self-subsistent something, the subsumption refers to the subjective act of judgment above-mentioned in which one starts from the self-subsistence of both subject and predicate. From this standpoint subsumption is only the application of the universal to a particular or an individual, which is placed under the universal in accordance with a vague idea that it is of inferior quality.[119]

Because of their initially presupposed externality, subject and predicate attain only an abstract, 'differenceless identity' – that posited in the 'is' of the copula – yet at the same time this 'is' asserts the supersession of this external relation, insofar as it posits an identity of being between the two extremes: '[T]he *copula* indicates that the predicate belongs to the *being* of the subject and is not merely externally combined with it'.[120] The contradictory structure of judgment is that it renders explicit both the self-subsistence of the independent extremes *and* their abstract identity in the copula, whilst their sublating into a higher unity is only implicitly contained in the form as a whole and remains undeveloped. The relation is truly antithetical: On the one hand, the discrete identity of each

---

119   Hegel 1999, pp. 628–9 (translation modified).
120   Hegel 1999, p. 626.

is constituted by its relation to the other, on the other, their posited identity is undermined by their mutual externality. Each absorbs the other from the standpoint of its own abstract universality (*subsumption* of the subject under the predicate, *inherence* of the predicate in the subject), but at this stage no standpoint of higher unity that would sublate these oppositions is posited concretely.

Subsumption first arises as one side of the judgment in general, but it is in Hegel's exposition of the 'judgment of reflection' that it emerges as the dominant or characteristic logical shape of the judgment as a whole and is treated in detail. Here, rather than the determination of the predicate as just one of the subject's multiple properties, as was the case in the judgment of existence, 'it is the subject rather that is alterable and awaits determination' by the predicate, which 'no longer inheres in the subject; it is rather the implicit *being* under which this individual is subsumed as an accidental'.[121] In these *reflective* judgments, the predicate unilaterally 'constitutes the *basis* by which, and in accordance with which, the subject is to be measured and determined', so that it receives a concrete identity only as a manifestation of the conceptual richness of the predicate.[122]

Hegel goes on to develop the various modes of subsumption of the subject under the predicate, in which the subject develops itself into a progressively universalised form: from the singular judgment ($x$ *is* $y$), to the particular judgment (*these* or *some x's are* $y$), to the universal judgment (*all x's are* $y$) in which subject and predicate reach apparent equality. Yet even at this developed point, the universality of the relation is only

> the external universality of reflection, *allness*; '*all*' means *all individuals*, and in it the *individual* remains unchanged. This universality is, therefore, only a *taking together* of independently existing individuals; it is the *community* of a property which only belongs to them in *comparison*. It is this community that is usually the first thing that occurs to subjective, unphilosophical thinking when universality is mentioned. It is given as the obvious reason why a determination is to be regarded as universal that it *belongs to a number of things*.[123]

The distinction between this 'allness' and the true universality of the Concept clearly demonstrates that subsumptive judgment has not overcome the anti-

---

121   Hegel 1999, p. 645.
122   Hegel 1999, p. 644.
123   Hegel 1999, p. 647.

thesis holding subjectivity and determinateness apart; it is only a one sided relation in which the subject is the 'essential *appearance*' of the predicate's implicit universality. This is because both predicate and subject remain abstract extremes:

> [I]f the abstract universal which is the predicate falls short of constituting a Concept, for a Concept certainly implies something more, and if, too, a subject of this kind is not yet much more than a grammatical one, how should the judgment possibly contain truth seeing that either its Concept and object do not agree, or it lacks both Concept and object? On the contrary, then, what is impossible and absurd is to attempt to grasp the truth in such forms as the positive judgment and the judgment generally.[124]

This, then, is the constitutive limit of the subsumptive relation for Hegel: Its universality is stunted at the point of 'allness' – it can only determine its own being in the subject unilaterally and externally, and has no deeper reach that would establish an explicit unity with that which it subsumes. As Hegel goes on to show, this 'allness' will develop its implicit universality into the '*genus*', 'the universality which is in its own self a concrete'.[125] The genus holds both the richness of determinations and the ground of unity together, such that it 'does not *inhere* in the subject ... but it is no longer *subsumed* in its predicate' either.[126] By rendering explicit the immediate identity of subject and predicate, the very character of the judgment has become objective, and, crucially, the antithesis between the poles has been sublated into a diverse unity: '[W]hen the predicate is determined to *objective universality*, it ceases to be subsumed under such a determination of relation, or comprehensive reflection'.[127] Now it is the copula, rather than either of the extremes, that constitutes the true universal. At this point, the identity of subject and predicate is rendered explicit and their difference is dissolved:

> Subject and predicate are therefore identical, that is they have coalesced into the copula. This identity is the genus or absolute nature of a thing. Insofar, therefore, as this identity again sunders itself into a judgment it

---

124   Hegel 1999, p. 595 (translation modified).
125   Hegel 1999, p. 649.
126   Ibid.
127   Ibid.

is the *inner nature* through which subject and predicate are related to one another – a relation of *necessity* in which these terms of the judgment are only unessential differences.[128]

With this, the antithetical relation between conceptual determinations has been sublated and 'the form of the judgment has perished … because subject and predicate are in themselves the same content', a content which is now unified in the syllogism.[129]

The subsumptive relation taken as self-subsistent has therefore in the course of the exposition been shown by Hegel to only ever determine a limited form of universality, which does not properly belong to the subject. This concludes Hegel's critique of subsumption as such (as a logical form) because once the relation of difference between conceptual determinations has resolved itself into a truly universal identity, the relation between universal, particular and singular is no longer subsumptive – each moment is equally universal and the relation becomes that between universal, universal and universal. Subsumption therefore falls away in the movement from fixed and simple immediacies to the living dynamic totality, which incorporates all of these putatively self-sufficient moments into the whole.

## 2.4  Conclusion

The 'critical' concept of subsumption is first developed by Kant in response to the problem of how distinct cognitive orders and elements can be related and unified in the absence a self-evident or naturally given taxonomy of species and genera. In his attempt to establish the truth of experience, Kant's critique of apparently self-sufficient forms of objectivity reveals them to be conditioned by a complex series of form-determining processes that synthetically unify the sensibly given manifold according to a dominant order of rational consistency. In this 'critical' sense, subsumption expresses a relation of determination or belonging between two essentially heterogeneous elements or orders: a relation that is made possible by their common ground in a unified medium of composition, which at the same time is given consistency only by virtue of the subsumptive judgments that it enables. Emerging from this new conception is a kind of reflexive circuit or *self-grounding structure*, a reciprocity between the act of subsumption and its subjective ground or compositional totality. One direct result of this, which bears on the basic logical scheme of universal,

---

128   Hegel 1999, pp. 649–5.
129   Hegel 1999, p. 663.

particular and singular, is of special interest here because it will be crucial for thinking about subsumption in Marx's writings. It is that, on this account, there can be no unmediated subsumption of singularity by a universal that stands outside it. Instead, subsumption can only occur through a mediation that has its basis in the unifying structure in which both the singular and the universal are 'composed'. To put it another way: Particularity is always a mediated *result*. (Logically, this suggests that subsumption is better thought as a syllogistic process rather than a form of judgment.)

Hegel devotes little explicit discussion to subsumptive relations, and it certainly does not play a central role in his system in the way that it does for Kant. Nonetheless, his engagement with the broader aspects of the problematic laid out above have important consequences for the development of the concept of subsumption, in many respects opening the way for Marx's theorisation of it. For Kant, the transcendental subject is a fixed structure of unity within which both concepts and intuitions are composed (and can therefore be related subsumptively). Hegel not only recognised the importance of such a unity in which heterogeneous elements could be correlated, but he criticised Kant for not developing it far enough, for not producing a properly 'philosophical' unity at the level of this structure. In the first place, Hegel decries the weakness of the subsumptive-synthetic relation between concepts and intuitions, which for him consists in uniting the two elements of cognition in an 'external, superficial way'. Hegel subsequently takes issue with the relation posited by Kant between concepts of the understanding and the 'I' in which they are grounded. In contrast to Kant, Hegel says that sensible intuition and concepts are forms of 'a content that remains *one and the same*'. Instead of conceiving of the subjectivity of consciousness as a static aggregation of principles and powers that are unified in a structure of reflexive closure, Hegel attempts to grasp it in the *Phenomenology* as the dynamic movement of knowing passing through the various stages of its immanent self-development. From this perspective, the basic structure of Kantian subjectivity only represents a partial moment in a larger process, given that, for Hegel, no single structure or 'shape of consciousness' taken in isolation can be thought of as the 'true standpoint' of knowledge, but it is rather all the stages in the totality of their development which constitute this truth as a unified movement.

The reflexive closure that defines the relation between form and totality in Kantian philosophy is thereby transformed into a *processual* concept of subject (and totality), which is no longer indifferent to the determinations of universality that it employs but rather only exists in and as the unity of these determinations. This also indicates a transition from a *synchronic* set of universals or faculties – a fixed 'field of categories' – to a *diachronic* sequence of subjective structures – each with their own 'set' or 'field' – that are immanently connected in their dialectical development rather than related through the mediation of their common abstract and fixed grounding. What Hegel thus achieves is a new conception of how acts of relational determination (such as subsumption) interact with the structure of unity in which their *relata* are situated. From the standpoint of this unity, the subsumption of particulars under the universal (or universals) is not an infinitely self-identical act but takes on a fundamentally different character and produces vastly different effects depending on the stage of development at which it occurs, while at the same time driving that development onwards. Thus Hegel opens the structure of fixed determinations that defined Kantian subjectivity and makes it part of a process of dynamic dialectical *development*. The act of subsuming some particular under a universal can at any given stage of this process only constitute a partial and limited shape of the whole – meaning that it does not have the same degree of immediate reciprocity as it did in Kant, for whom the whole was grounded in a single structure of determination. The subject (of knowledge) now represents a developmental rather than simply reflexive or structural unity: not just a closed set of relations but an immanent movement in which any such closure is negated. What this means is that the significance and effect of any act of subsumption can only be grasped with reference to its place within the systematic totality of determinations – the only standpoint from which it could be determined as *actual*.

In the *Phenomenology*, this processual concept of subjective development results in the supersession of the finite standpoint of an isolated *consciousness* and the development of the *social* concept of subjectivity that emerges with the transition from subject-object relations through subject-subject and then subject-substance relations in the various forms of ethical life. Hegel's exposition attempts to demonstrate, in the first place, that interpersonal relations are an implicit condition for the existence of the individual self-consciousness that provides the standpoint of Kant's philosophy. Not only is the subsumption of intuitions under concepts that is so fundamental for Kant thereby demoted to a partial and limited stage in this conceptual development, but the very constitutive limit of knowledge set out by Kant – individual, empirical experience – is exploded (to use Adorno's phrase) as consciousness 'leaves behind it the colourful show of the sensuous here-and-now'.[130] The resulting emergence of social relations as *objective* structures of spirit generates contradictions at the level of the relation between individual self-consciousnesses – the 'I' which is

---

130   Adorno 1993, p. 3; Hegel 1977b, §177.

subject – and the ensemble of social relation within which they are united – the 'we' that is substance. Subsumptive relations thus appear within structures of spirit as that which binds particular individuals to the universality of the *social form* they exist within and are constituted by. This is hugely important for Marx's thinking on subsumption, as it lays the foundation for an analysis of processes through which individuals are subsumed under objective structures of sociality which constitute their identities and practices at a collective and individual level. We are no longer dealing with *synthetic judgment acts* of an individual consciousness but with the development of *relational forms* that determine the practical action of 'individuals' in a collective context.

Yet despite the complexity Hegel introduces into the critical concept of subsumption and his demolition of the reflexive closure of apperception underpinning the coherence of Kant's account of determining subsumption, he too introduces a form of theoretical closure which overdetermines the scope of subsumptive relations. Hegel imprisons the relation between conceptuality and objectivity, universality and particularity, the 'field of categories' and the elements to which they give form, within a speculatively totalised developmental series. The full truth of any discrete element as well as any synchronic 'shape' or configuration of categories within this series can only be registered with reference to the (speculative) unity of the process as a whole. This ultimately leads Hegel to criticise – entirely correctly – the logical relation of subsumption on the basis of its immanently contradictory character and to derive its truth from the dynamic mediation of the syllogism at the apex of the *Logic*. But the logical 'completeness' of this derivation and the total series of the system within which it is inscribed endows it, as a compositional medium, with a self-grounding and self-sufficient quality similar to that of Kant's transcendental subject. Both accounts of subsumption are therefore marked by a theoretical closure of the totality, as *reflexive* closure of the structure or *speculative* closure of dialectical development respectively. This establishes the limit point of the critical-philosophical concept of subsumption, given that it is a *theoretically* bound totality that circumscribes the limits of relation, form and composition. What remains to be considered are the possibilities and qualities of subsumptive relations whose truth and meaning cannot be determined within a purely theoretical context.

CHAPTER 2

# Materialism, Social Form and Reproduction

> Vulgar criticism ... discovers contradictions everywhere. ... a truly philosophical criticism of the present constitution does not content itself with showing that it contains contradictions: It explains them, comprehends their genesis, their necessity. It grasps their particular significance. This act of comprehension does not however consist, as Hegel thinks, in discovering the determinations of the concepts of logic at every point; it consists in the discovery of the particular logic of the particular object.[1]

∴

This chapter traces the development from a critical-philosophical to a critical-social concept of subsumption through a general reconstruction and extension of what can in the most general terms simply be called Marx's 'materialism'. This materialism emerges from Marx's critique of philosophy (in both its idealist and 'traditional' materialist variants), finds its first iteration in his famous eleven *Theses On Feuerbach* and acts as a consistent – although progressively more sophisticated – theoretical framework right through to *Capital*, where key elements are introduced to conceptualise it in its most developed form: as a *materialism of the social reproduction process*. This reconstructive endeavour draws heavily on the work of Mexican-Ecuadoran philosopher Bolívar Echeverría, who from the 1970s onwards emphasised and sought to elaborate upon the originality and richness of Marx's discourse on materialism and its centrality – however textually implicit – to Marx's later work. In addition to its more general scope and effects, this account of materialism acts as the key theoretical mediation between the philosophical accounts of subsumption presented by Kant and Hegel and what is normally considered to be a strictly socio-economic theory of 'subsumption under capital' outlined by Marx in his 'mature' works. Whilst the turn to human practice and history ostensibly represents a break with the limitations of philosophical discourse, it is crucial to note that this

---

1  Marx 1992, p. 159.

occurs, at least in part, as a critique of and through the categories of that discourse, which are not thereby jettisoned altogether but rather 'refunctioned', as Hans-Georg Backhaus argued:

> Upon examination of the Marxian conception, already at first sight it becomes visible that it is based on a large number of refunctioned conceptual pairs and problems of philosophical provenance. Yet two complexes of problems dominate: On the one hand, the problem of universals, i.e., the problem of the synthesis between the general and the particular or the individual respectively; on the other hand, the subject-object problem. Moreover, there are the relations between being and semblance, essence and appearance, being and significance, being and becoming, substance and relation, premise and result, act and entity, concept and existence.[2]

We can identify a persistent relevance of the central problems and motifs of subsumption developed at a philosophical level – form-determination, compositional totality, reciprocity and subjectivity – to their new theoretical context: the 'real life' of 'social humanity' and the subsumption of individuals 'under social production'. Thus in contrast to interpretations which emphasise an alleged break between an early 'humanist' Marx and a late 'scientific' or 'economic' Marx, our focus on the status of the key conceptual coordinates of the problem of subsumption enables us to pursue a coherent line of thinking that not only relates Marx's early critique of philosophy to his critique of political economy but also connects the latter back to former. This exploration of its underlying conceptual structure and premises allows for a richer theorisation of what is at stake in capitalist subsumption than in Marx's own cursory treatment of this problem.

Two principal questions emerge as we survey this line of development from philosophy to Marx's materialism. The first is: What *kind* of 'logic' is employed by Marx's materialist critique and what is the logical *structure* of that critique?[3] The second question is: How is the very idea of logic itself transformed as 'we pass from the problem of knowledge, where Kant and Hegel principally situated and treated it, to the problems linked with the constitutive and constituent phenomena of social reality resulting from dynamic and complex capitalist social relations'?[4] The relation between these two questions,

---

2  Backhaus 1997, p. 26.
3  See on this question Zeleny 1980.
4  Castillo Mendoza 2002, p. 5.

and what ultimately establishes the condition of intelligibly for them both, turns on Marx's understanding of history and the dialectical interpenetration of thought and being it stipulates. It is the introduction of historical openness that explodes the theoretical closure of totality which in Kant and Hegel's philosophies overdetermine the relations between subjective activity, actuality and form. By grasping this relation as 'natural-history' and, in its processual realisation, as 'reproduction-development', Marx's materialism develops an entirely new perspective on the problem of subsumption that is able to grasp it as operative beyond a strictly ideal context, namely as subsumption to social forms.

1      Critical Beginnings

In a condensed but illuminating set of 'Introductory Notes on the Subsumption of Labour under Capital', Carlos Castillo Mendoza identifies the first of three periods in which the concept of subsumption is used by Marx as the one coinciding with his *Critique of Hegel's Philosophy of Right* in 1843: 'Here, subsumption appears as a logical operation with which Hegel conceals a political operation'.[5] If apparently immediate forms of logical identity were criticised by Kant and Hegel to reveal active processes of synthesis, mediation and form-determination, then this much is also true of Marx's earliest use of subsumption. But where Kant and Hegel discovered further subjective processes and ideal relations subtending the subsumption of particulars under universals, thereby deepening and enriching the philosophical logics they employed, the radicality of Marx's orientation consists in the fact that what he critically exposed beneath an apparently harmonic subsumption was not further philosophical mediations but pertained to a political dimension and 'real', that is, non-ideal processes. At its most profound level, this indicates an entirely new articulation of logical relations with social being that signals the development of Marx's materialism as an original theoretical standpoint. In its initial form, established in Marx's writings from 1843/4 onwards, this theoretical orientation is already grounded in a new plane of engagement that marks a shift beyond the critique of philosophy to the critique of social reality, a new object for theory (a new sphere of 'actuality') that at the same time assigns to theory a new role and, concomitantly, introduces an entirely new mode of conceptualising what a subsumptive process entails (*of what, by what, under what*). Insofar as the

---

5   Ibid.

conceptual focus guiding Marx's thought retains from Kant and Hegel's work the centrality of the question of *form-determination*, it differs from those previous philosophies as to the ultimate grounds from which this act originates and, as a consequence, its adequate theoretical expression: *revolutionary, practical, historical materialism*.

Crucial in engendering this theoretical reorientation was the inescapable historical need, in the wake of Hegel's thought, for post-Hegelian philosophies to take up positions – affirmative, revisionist or critical – in relation to the 'total system' (a system marked, as we have seen, by the structure of speculative closure). The debates that arose in this context centred primarily on the problem of the relation of the system to the existing world – the Europe of the 1830–40s – and, above all else, turned on the question of how to interpret Hegel's famous double-dictum from the *Philosophy of Right* that 'what is rational is actual and what is actual is rational'.[6] Whilst the self-sufficiency and completeness ('rationality') of Hegel's philosophy might have been acknowledged at a theoretical level *qua* philosophy, the 'left' and 'young' Hegelian critics that followed in his wake nonetheless perceived an inadequacy in its 'actuality' [*Wirklichkeit*] and, contending that the rational was *not yet* actual in world-historical terms, claimed that there was still a need for its *actualisation* or *realisation* (both alternate renderings of *Verwirklichung*). The divergent positions within post-Hegelian thought therefore split on the basis of how they conceived of the unity or disunity of the 'rational' and the 'actual' and of the philosophical and political implications that followed from their assessment of that relationship. Which is to say, they differed over how, if it was indeed deemed necessary, this realisation was to be undertaken. Such differences were not merely the product of divergent political 'applications' of an uncontested Hegelian philosophy but had their basis in fundamentally conflicting interpretations of the system as a whole, as Emmanuel Renault points out:

> The Right conceived of realisation as 'Realisierung', through the model of the transition of the Science of the Logic into the Philosophy of Nature. On the contrary, the Left conceived of realisation as 'Verwirklichung', through the model of the realisation of freedom in the world historical process. According to Left-Hegelian interpretation of the double dictum, contemporary culture and society was not yet rational but still in a process of rationalisation.[7]

---

6   Hegel 1991a, Preface.
7   Renault 2012, p. 5.

What would it mean for the rational to be actual or, as the 'right' Hegelians claimed but the 'left' Hegelians disputed, for the system to have been realised? For Hegel, actuality indicates not simply that something *is* (actuality is not mere existence) but that it *is* in the highest sense as free, *self-subsistent* existence, the 'unity of particularity and universality' or 'essence and existence': '[I]n it, *formless* essence and *unstable* appearance, or mere subsistence devoid of all determination and unstable manifoldness have their truth'.[8] Something therefore attains actuality for Hegel, much as for Aristotle, through the manifestation of its *inner* essence in an *outer* existence, in 'particularising itself' in a determinate material content, actualising its potentiality:

> That which exists for itself only, is a possibility, a potentiality; but has not yet emerged into Existence. A *second* element must be introduced in order to produce actuality – viz. actuation, realisation; and whose motive power is the Will – the activity of man in the widest sense.[9]

Hegel expresses this idea of actualisation through externalisation most forcefully in the *Science of Logic*, in the lapidary formulation 'What is actual *can act*' [*was wirklich ist, kann wirken*], going on to qualify the act in terms of its power to produce (systemic) effects: 'Something manifests its actuality *through that which it produces*'.[10] This production, finally, 'proves' the actuality of a being insofar as it manifests itself outwardly in an other that nonetheless remains identical with it (a relation Hegel describes in the *Phenomenology of Spirit* as 'pure self-recognition in absolute otherness'), rendering this other a moment of its self-expression, its *freedom*: '[W]hat is actual can preserve itself in otherness, i.e., objectify itself.'[11]

This unity of inner and outer constitutes a self-subsistent totality, a singular composition that encompasses all of its various determinations within itself. Actuality is therefore always the product of a dialectical process that totalises its constituent conditions, the multiplicity of determinations through which it passes or is made up of. As Beatrice Longuenesse states: '[A]ctuality is not something that is ontologically given, but the ultimate moment of reflection', it is a *result* rather than a starting point; this is crucial to our investigation because it is one of the foundational speculative principles that Marx would come to

---

8   Hegel 1999, p. 546.
9   Hegel 2004, p. 22.
10  Hegel 1999, p. 546.
11  Hegel 1991a, § 82.

overturn.¹² Yet for Hegel actuality is not only this result taken in isolation, it is also the *process*, the activity of the system itself in and as each of these determinations: '[A]ctuality is self-movement'.¹³ The actual is thus the truth of the dialectical whole in its various moments of posited particularity; this is why Hegel associates it with both the 'idea' and 'living spirit', that which is: '[N]ot an essence that is already finished and complete before its manifestation, keeping itself aloof behind its host of appearances, but an essence which is truly actual only through the specific forms of its necessary self-manifestation.'¹⁴ For the system of speculative philosophy to be actual, then, its inner rationality – its freedom – would have to be proven outwardly in and as a forming and ordering of the substance of world-spirit; it would have to have *actualised* itself, to have made the world rational and itself worldly by subsuming or sublating the irrational elements of external existence to its comprehensive order of being.

Repudiating the accomplishment of this theoretically described unification of the ideal and existent, and thus contending that the project of actualisation was still underway, left Hegelianism asserted that philosophy had an active rather than contemplative role to play in this process: It bore the ongoing task of *criticising* the irrational aspects of the contemporary world whilst highlighting its rational dimensions, thereby guiding the course of its historical progression. However, from the perspective of 'young Hegelians' such as Ruge, Feuerbach, Bauer and Marx this 'left' Hegelian posture was insufficiently radical, For although it contested speculative rationality's actuality it remained largely committed to the methodology and objectives of the Hegelian system as a whole, departing only from the Hegelian right in asserting the need for and demanding its 'immediate application'.¹⁵ The young Hegelians interpreted such demands as an 'accommodation' to the system's *structural* irrationality, which they sought to break free from altogether; they declared, in Ruge's words, 'a war of liberation against the limitations of the system'.¹⁶ These limitations were first and foremost those of speculation and the project of overcoming them marked the beginning of a genuinely post-Hegelian theoretical discourse

---

12   Longuenesse 2007, p. 113.
13   Hegel 1977b, § 23.
14   Hegel 1971, § 378 (*Zusatz*). It is interesting to note the resemblance between this passage and Marx and Engel's famous statement in the *German Ideology* that 'Communism is not for us a state of affairs, which is to be established, an ideal, according to which actuality has to be set aright. We call communism the actual movement, which transforms [*aufhebt*] the current state of affairs' (Marx and Engels, 2014, p. 93).
15   See Renault 2012.
16   Ruge cited in Renault 2012.

that attempted to undermine the systematic self-sufficiency of philosophy.[17] In theoretical terms, this implied challenging not only the degree of actuality which the system could be said to possess but also the idealist methodology that determined the measure of that actuality itself; this challenge called into question what, precisely, the inward essence to be actualised and the 'outwardness' that could register such actualisation consisted in, the former as the active subject and the latter as the passive substance that was acted upon or subsumed.[18]

The kernel of this criticism, in which the first aspects of a practical-materialist outlook can be discerned, takes issue with the fact that actuality, as conceived by speculative idealism, determines the quality of outer objectivity on the basis of its correspondence to an inner rationality ('the concept') in a manner that leaves little room for comprehending the being of living (i.e., 'existent') individuals beyond their status as bearers – or *predicates*, for Feuerbach – of philosophical world-spirit.[19] If for the idealist discourse that culminates in Hegel's work the critical comprehension of actuality is not *simply* a theoretical problem, then it nevertheless, as Marx and the 'young' Hegelians perceived it, fails to transcend the limits of an ideally registered process, to which 'objective' being (which includes, crucially, human life in its 'natural form') stands in more or less adequate correspondence, an inevitable fate given that 'its essence is something other than itself'.[20] The need for a subjective will to 'prove' its actuality through the objective manifestation of its action, so central to Hegel's thought, has meaning only in an ideal sense here because such objectification can only be recognised as the 'positing' of conceptual determinations that characterises the basic mode of actualisation on the speculative plane. In this sense, true knowledge (Kant) or rational actuality (Hegel) is delimited by the format-

---

17 'Kant suspected he had initiated a revolution in the conception and resolution of metaphilosophical problems. In that way Kant established – before Feuerbach and Marx – that traditional metaphysics was at an end. However in response to Kant's views on the destruction of pre-critical ontology there arose philosophical systems in which Feuerbach and Marx recognized the culminating defence of metaphysics. For post-Hegelian thinkers the end of metaphysics means the end of speculative philosophy' (Zeleny 1980, p. 193).

18 As Patrick Murray notes: 'In his dissertation notes, Marx states that, to make real progress beyond what the Young Hegelians saw as Hegel's accommodation to an unreasonable social and political actuality, it will be necessary to reveal the accommodation latent in his basic principles through an immanent critique' (Murray 1988, p. 25).

19 In this sense Althusser was correct when he wrote that 'for Hegel, history is certainly a process of alienation, but this process does not have man as its subject'. Althusser 2003, p. 238.

20 Marx 1992, p. 400.

ive activity of a subject upon the mute matter that it thereby legitimates as properly objective or rational, in distinction to the representationally phantasmatic or 'merely existent' (which lacks *actuality*). This implies a unilateral arbitration of the worldly by the intellectual (or of reality by philosophy, as Marx would claim), a selection from amongst the empirically present, which singles out that sector of the object or of activity admitted to the rational order, distinguishing it from that to be re-formed and that to be neutralised or abolished. (Indeed, this process of selection, negation and formation within a subjective totality is exactly what subsumption, taken in its critical sense, involves; as an act, subsumption indicates not simply inclusion under a definition – logical predication – but subsumption under a *function* of the subject by means of which both the subject and subsumed entity are reciprocally, although unevenly, constituted.)

The distinctly post-Hegelian problematic raised by these criticisms supersedes the question of how it is that philosophical consciousness can or should comprehend the relation between its own rationality and the existent world (whether positively or negatively) and instead contests the adequacy of both this rationality (speculative logic) and this relation (philosophical comprehension) to the task of making the real truly rational. This shift leads beyond the question of the authoritative legislation of philosophy over the actual, as Paul Marshall Schafer argues:

> The basis of Marx's evaluation is that Hegel does not demonstrate the rationality of the real, as he claims in the Preface, but is methodologically restricted to developing the rationality of the ideal in the form of the real. The method of speculative idealism, in other words, leads only to the illusion of substantiality, for it is incapable of grasping reality in terms other than those offered by its own logic. Consequently every form of reality – whether natural, moral, political, or historical – is subsumed to the determinations of speculative logic.[21]

Breaking with Hegelianism, then, means decoupling actuality from a philosophical ideal to which the movement of the existing world can only ever correspond as a manifestation or derivative: '[S]ince abstract thought is the essence, that which is external to it is in essence something merely external ... a defective being'.[22] In prioritising the ideal aspect of development as the

---

21  Schafer 1999, p. 198.
22  Marx 1992, pp. 399–400.

actuality of all processes, Hegel had slipped back into the transcendence and one-sidedness he claimed to have overcome. Shattering the speculative closure of the idealist system was thus for Marx the condition for developing, simultaneously, an autonomous 'logic' of actuality and an immanent critique of its irrationality that would not be determined by a correspondence to philosophical reason and which would treat outer objectivity as equally essential to the constitution of the actual as its inner, subjective structure. But the criticism levelled here does not only apply to Hegelian philosophy, it places the valence of philosophical discourse as such into question and marks the beginning of a period of intense critical engagement during which Marx, along with Engels, attempts to 'settle accounts' with philosophy, asserting that 'with the exposition of actuality, self-sufficient philosophy [*die selbständige Philosophie*] loses its medium of existence'.[23]

But what is the content of this alternative conception of reality? What is it, if not the idea, that is in the process of actualisation and determines the rational content against which reality must be measured? Initially for Marx, following Feuerbach, it is a *human reality* constituted in a *human community*. In negating what he and Engels would later dismiss as 'philosophical illusions of the sovereignty of general conceptions', Marx took up and developed the idea of an inversion of subject and predicate formulated by Feuerbach in his critique of religion: '[T]he exchange of that which determines or that which is determined' whose consequence is that 'real man and real nature become mere predicates, symbols of this hidden, unreal man and this unreal nature.'[24] Against this idealist conceit, it would not be the life of the idea but the life of 'real humanity' (in its relationship to 'real nature') that actualises itself in the world-historical process, such that the former has to be grasped as an effect of the latter. By contrast, measuring the being of man against the purity of reason or the idea was, for Marx, a defining characteristic of the mystifying philosophical-theological worldview that blocked the way to a genuine comprehension of real (human) conditions and, by proxy (in light of this 'actual irrationality'), their revolutionary transformation. However, deconstructing the 'fantastic realisation' offered by religious consciousness, with which Feuerbach was primarily concerned, was only the first stage of Marx's program and, most importantly, functioned as a precondition for developing a far more radical 'criticism of the earth', of the really existing political (and, ultimately, socio-economic) forms of human existence.

---

23    Marx and Engels 1998, p. 43, translation modified.
24    Marx and Engels 2014, p. 34; Marx 1975a, p. 130; Marx 1992, p. 396.

Initially, Marx's confrontation with Hegelianism on the issue of the actuality and content of rational relations expressed itself most concretely in the guise of political questions surrounding the state's relation to civil society. Norman Levine notes that 'in 1841–1843 Marx stood in total agreement with Hegel regarding the universality of the state and like Hegel he applied an organic image to the state as a whole, a universal, which subsumed parts, particularities, into the totality.'[25] But by the time of writing his commentary on Hegel's *Philosophy of Right* in 1843, Marx's attitude toward the theory and reality of the state had changed radically. Whilst not entirely contradicting this earlier vision and indeed continuing to make use the Hegelian 'universal-particular logical apparatus', Marx had come to profoundly different conclusions about the social effects and political meaning of this subsumption of particulars on the part of the state.[26] Crucially, Marx rejected Hegel's positive view of the Prussian state as necessary, as *actual*, as universality and freedom manifest; instead of producing unity and cohesion through its subsumption of the conflicting interests of civil society, this activity was instead taken by Marx to be a source of contradiction and antagonism through its suppression of the truly universal community, the 'species-essence' [*Gattungswesen*]. For Marx, Hegel was unable to grasp the depth of this opposition because he presupposed the universality and positivity of the state in a manner that obviated the need to justify, or even assess, the particularities of its concrete action and relation to really existing society; he proceeded rather, by deriving its ideal form from speculative logic and then projecting this onto the existing institutional apparatus of his time, which could thereby be declared to possess 'actual rationality/rational actuality'. Holding that 'what matters is to recognise in the semblance of the temporal and transient the substance which is immanent and the eternal which is present', Hegel failed to grasp the necessity of actively shaping the temporal and the transient by any means other than a form of comprehension that is speculatively predisposed toward reconciliation.[27] Marx criticised this methodologically idealist

---

25  Levine 2012, p. 153. See Marx 1975b, p. 193: 'The state itself educates its members in that it makes them into state members, in that it converts the aims of the individual into universal aims, raw drive into ethical inclination, natural independence into spiritual freedom, in that the individual enjoys himself in the life of the whole and the whole [enjoys itself] in the disposition of the individual.'

26  Levine 2012, p. 153.

27  Hegel 1991a, preface. Whether Marx's reading of the *Philosophy of Right* as a whole and his charges against the Hegelian theory of the state are accurate or fair is not to be decided here, the point is rather to understand the limits of the particular critical-theoretical method for comprehending social actuality employed by idealism and how Marx superseded these limits with the development of his materialist treatment of the social process,

account of political institutions for starting out from the necessity of logical relations and functions, and then proceeding to find an existing content in which to embody them, a charge that finds one of its clearest and most concentrated expressions in a well-known passage repudiating Hegel's assertion that the executive embodies the logical act of subsuming the particular under the universal:

> Hegel does not inquire whether this mode of subsumption is adequate or rational. He simply holds fast to the one category and contents himself with searching for something corresponding to it in existence. *Hegel thus provides his logic with a political body; he does not provide us with the logic of the body politic.*[28]

Marx here sets out *in nuce* the content of his new conception of actuality. It is the immanent logic of the 'body politic' that Marx seeks to uncover and critique as 'the truth of this world', rather than demonstrating, as Hegel sought to do, the identity of a preordained rational order with the extrinsic world-surface in which it is objectified. In displacing the problem of truth from the logical essence *in* its appearance to the logical essence *of* the apparent, a new understanding of actuality becomes possible: one that inverts the determining relation between rationality and social being. Marx both establishes the theoretical task to be achieved and at the same time breaks (if only at this point naively, on *political-representational* terms) with Hegelian idealism by setting actuality firmly on the side of 'the world of man, state, society': It is that upon which conceptual activity must mould itself (and indeed already does, if initially only in a mystified, ideological form) rather than that which is moulded by conceptual activity in its spontaneous self-activity.

Human finitude and particularity is not, therefore, a deficiency to be resolved by the 'estranged mind' of philosophical reason or, as in its Hegelian political corollary 'objective spirit', as the activity of the state in shaping the substance of civil society; by contrast, it is the source of the dynamic historical force of human social being, that which confers upon men and women the capacity and urgency of positing their own subjective content *in action*, as self-activity [*Selbsttätigkeit*]. History is thus no longer the medium of a monolithic reason, but reason in its concreteness is the expression of humankind's histor-

---

which would in turn come to shape his understanding of capitalist domination. On the topic of Marx's misprisions in his critique of Hegel, see Fine 1995, pp. 84–109.
28  Marx 1992, p. 109, emphasis added, translation modified.

ical being and struggles, as shaped, limited and motivated by the latter. Whilst in Marx's early work this conviction fixated on the contradictions of Prussian political and legal institutions and their ideal expressions, the revolutionary implications this work raised opened the way for a more comprehensive and wide ranging re-centring of critical-theoretical activity in which human practice functions as the motive force and compositional medium that displaces the foundational primacy of the self-actualising idea, albeit, as we shall see, at different levels of conceptual and historical determinacy.

## 2   The Actuality of Practice

Holding that 'man is the highest being for man', Marx assumed the theoretical task of developing a concrete notion – a science [*Wissenschaft*] – of what exactly this 'highest being' consisted in, and, if 'the Concept' was no longer to be the measure or source of its movement, how this being could both register and produce the revolutionary actualisation demanded of it, of abolishing the irrational and instituting the (humanly) rational. This meant not simply affirming the human in the abstract against the idea (as it did for Feuerbach) but developing a comprehensive and determinate account of what exactly constituted the actuality of the human as the concrete subject of the world-historical process. An account was needed of how real humanity, 'the body politic', rather than an ideal intellect, 'acted', and of the content that would 'actualise itself' through this activity.

At the heart of this problematic was an awareness of the inadequacy of the idealist conception of action as the unilateral effectivity of an absolute subject that constituted actuality (or, in its weaker variation, of an ideal subject engaged in the process of its self-absolutisation). For the idealist tradition against which Marx and his contemporaries were reacting, rational free-willed subjectivity was the source of reality, the driving motor of the historical process: Hegel believed that 'the will was a special way of thinking, it was thought translating itself into reality'.[29] The challenge for critical post-Hegelianism in all its diversity was to move beyond the act of thinking to the primacy of the act or action itself, conceived in its most general, 'human' sense. This marked a break with the monopoly conferred upon thought over the individual's embodied, active relation to reality, as it meant that this relation would no longer be reducible to an intellectual operation or conceptual

---

29   De Ridder 2008, p. 294.

representation but would instead subsume thinking under itself as a partial and limited moment of a 'real' or 'material' idea of action – what Marx conceptualised as *practice*. In the conflict between rational and irrational elements of actuality, the task demanded of a practical standpoint was not only to identify and criticise its irrational elements but also, crucially, to supersede them through *real* (i.e., non-theoretical) action. This inversion relegates the function of *positing* in the medium of thought to the status of a secondary or derivative moment in relation to *actualising* in the medium of *practice*, which is thereby established as a new index of form-determination, registering action in relation to the material life of *men and women* and its *revolutionary transformation*, rather than the *Concept* and its intellectual development.

The concept of practice at work here, central to Marx's conception of a properly human form of action, has its antecedents in a number of different positions within 'left' and 'young' Hegelian thought, aspects of which were drawn upon synthetically and intensified by Marx in his polemic against idealism and socialism. The term practice ('praxis') itself was taken from August von Cieszkowski, who in 1838 asserted that:

> The future fate of philosophy in general is to be practical philosophy or, to put it better, the *philosophy of praxis*, whose most concrete effect on life and social relations is the development of *truth in concrete activity*.[30]

This was echoed by Moses Hess, a contemporary of Marx and influence on his early thinking, whose 1843 *Philosophy of the Act* emphatically rejected speculative philosophy's attenuated and parochial grasp of activity:

> Not being but action is first and last ... Now is the time for the philosophy of spirit to become a philosophy of activity. Not only thinking but the whole of human activity must be lifted to a plane on which all oppositions disappear.[31]

Such assertions were essential in formulating the specific problem of human action in its relation to actuality which would shape Marx's theoretical orientation towards extra-theoretical activity. But despite the boldness of their claims, both Cieszkowski and Hess still subscribed to a broadly Hegelian vision of the

---

30   Cieszkowski 2010, p. 77.
31   Hess 1964, translation modified.

process of actualisation, as driven by the autonomous act of a subject upon its other, the object, or nature. Hess, for example, claimed that:

> Life is activity. But activity is the recovery of an identity through the establishment and transcendence of its opposite, the producing of its likeness, its likeness to itself, through the breaking of the barrier within which the 'I' is 'not-I'. Activity is, in a word, self-creation, the law of which is perceived by the spirit through its own act of self-creation.[32]

Cieszkowski and Hess were unable to break with idealism in any profound theoretical sense because despite having replaced cognition by 'practice' or 'activity' in name, it remained unclear how this 'self-creation' differed in its putatively human form from the labour of the Concept; it remained an act of intellectual willing, mediated by a 'worldly' process. What is at stake in these philosophies of action, then, is still very much the realisation of philosophy as a singular, absolute reason that stands over and against the irrationality of the objective world.

It was in response to this residual theological-idealist vision of realisation that Marx drew critically on Feuerbach's materialism of the human, which rejected a singular vision of the rational and sought to ground the struggle for actualisation beyond the sphere of intelligibility delimited by philosophical comprehension, locating it instead in the particular 'real being' of the species, in human 'flesh and blood'. For Feuerbach, this sensible, human standpoint opened the possibility for the realisation of philosophy (or at least the ideals posited by it) whilst being 'also its negation': It was, in Renault's words, 'an attempt to redefine the philosophical principles at the very level of the concrete existence of humans, that of the human existence in its sensitive and particular reality'.[33] The reality of sensuous human existence was to determine the conditions to which actuality and its comprehension would have to adhere. This stood in stark contrast to idealism's reduction of human reality to the predicative expression of an all-encompassing world-spirit that overdetermined the significance of human experience by situating it within a schematic philosophy of historical development:

> [T]otality or the absoluteness of a particular historical phenomenon or existence is vindicated as predicate, thus reducing the stages of devel-

---

32  Ibid., translation modified.
33  Renault 'The Early Marx and Hegel'.

opment as independent entities only to a historical meaning; although living, they continue to exist as nothing more than shadows or moments, nothing more than homoeopathic drops on the level of the absolute.[34]

Marx recognised that Feuerbach's critical re-orientation of humanity and history could break through the idealist reduction of activity to which other post-Hegelian philosophies remained committed: 'Feuerbach's great achievement is', Marx claimed, 'to have founded true materialism and real science by making the social relation of "man to man" the basic principle of his theory'.[35] This anthropological materialism offered Marx a critical standpoint from which to grasp the meaning of domination and the necessity of revolution as immanent to the experience and struggles of real, living humanity. As Gopal Balakrishnan highlights, 'the appeal of Feuerbach's naturalism to Marx at the time, even as he noted its apolitical and indeed ahistorical limitations, was its identification of the human essence with suffering.'[36] But because Feuerbach's analysis remained at the level of an abstract notion of the human in general, which in turn depended on a mechanistic or intuitive conception of matter (the human essence conceived in terms of its 'natural organic qualities') it could only function, in Marx's view, as an equally reductive materialist inversion of the idealist exaggeration of subjective freedom, one that Marx would use as a foil in order to produce his own original conception of the relation between human activity and actuality: a 'new' materialism of practice.

Marx's critical *Theses On Feuerbach* aphoristically condense the essential co-ordinates of this new materialism which, beyond the polemical displacement of an idealist vocabulary of the absolute into the worldly language of the human community ('all mysteries that turn theory towards mysticism find their rational solution in human practice and in the comprehension of this practice'), sketches out a radical new conception of the relationship between subject and object, between materiality and ideality, and between actuality [*Wirklichkeit*] and activity [*Tätigkeit*], shattering the structure and limits of 'traditional' theoretical discourse and opening the way for a new form of revolutionary or 'critical' discourse adequate to the 'communist problematic' of revolutionary transformation.[37] In spite of their brevity, the *Theses* propose an entirely new mode of theoretically grasping actuality at its most fundamental

---

34  Feuerbach 1972.
35  Marx 1992, p. 381.
36  Balakrishnan 2014, p. 125.
37  Marx in Suchting 1979, pp. 21–22.

level, which is to say that they elaborate – in a rudimentary outline – an entirely new account of the process within which *the constitution of objectivity* and its reciprocal condition, the *actualisation of subjectivity*, occur. Within the context of transcendental or dialectical critique, this double-process is, as we have seen, the foundation of actuality as a plane of objective presence and universal reference upon which a formal lawfulness or coherence (a 'logic') determines the structure of an order of being within which something can be qualified as intelligible, actual. As Bolívar Echeverría recognises in his reconstructive interpretation, it is at this level of depth that the *Theses* operate:

> The most elementary and fundamental, the determining 'in' the ambit of a theory is the manner in which it gives an account of the irreducible experience of the presence of sense in the real, of the presence of the real as endowed with sense and not as an ineffable chaos or as an absolutely undefined in-itself; or, what is the same, the manner in which it gives account of the proper capacity to affirm something – that would be simple existence – of the object, of the proper capacity to produce significations.[38]

With this in mind, the radicality of Marx's proposition can be appreciated: Idealism and traditional materialism do not simply constitute two distinct systems, discourses or 'philosophemes' within which human action and existence might be registered (and between which one must choose), but there is also, at an even more fundamental level, an implicit reciprocity between them, insofar as their antithesis constitutes the horizons and possible limits of comprehension characteristic of what Echeverría terms the dominant 'modern theoretical discourse', the broad discursive field that includes both and which demarcates the 'problematic region' within which Marx's critique is operative. In opposition to this antithesis – and precisely through a critique of its two poles that demonstrates the points at which each slips into the affirmation or presupposition of its other – Marx is able to theoretically postulate a new ground of actuality that overcomes the mystifying opposition between 'abstract thinking' and 'sensuous intuition', proposing instead a unifying concept of *practical materialism*.

For Marx, as we have seen, idealism sought to grasp the true nature, actuality, or objectivity of its object through the comprehension of its full determinateness, as a dialectically (or transcendentally) articulated series of ideal determ-

---

38   Echeverría 1986, p. 25.

inations or marks – representations in the most general sense. This bringing forth of the object's truth attained reality or objectivity only as a process of *conceptual* development enacted unilaterally by the subject (and through which the subject is reciprocally actualised), thus negating the object's materiality or immediate external presence in favour of a logically determined representational form. By reducing the constitution of objectivity, the order of the real, to 'a process emanating from the act in which the subject "posits" the object', as Echeverría puts it, idealism remained within the age-old philosophical dualism of thought and being, even as it sought to suppress (or supersede) being by reducing it to a mere effect of thought.[39] Marx's intervention in thesis II exposes the insufficiency of this merely ideal and one-sided idea of development through which objectivity or actuality could purportedly be captured theoretically and constituted actively, contending instead that the object's mediations and potential development, its *truth*, must be both comprehended and transformed through a different kind of activity, one that is not reducible to the effect of an ideal subject alone.

Conversely, however, neither can this objectivity be reduced to the passive materiality of sensible intuition, the object [*Objekt*] with which Feuerbach had identified the human essence:

> The chief defect of all hitherto existing materialism – that of Feuerbach included – is that the thing [*Gegenstand*], actuality, sensuousness, is conceived only in the form of the *object* [*Objekt*] or of *intuition* [*Anschauung*], but not as *human sensuous activity* [*sinnlich menschliche Tätigkeit*], practice, not subjectively. Hence it happened that the active side, in contradistinction to materialism, was developed by idealism – but only abstractly, since, of course, idealism does not know real, sensuous activity as such. Feuerbach wants sensuous objects [*Objekte*], really distinct from the objects of thought [*Gedankenobjekten*], but he does not conceive human activity itself as *objective* [*gegenständliche*] activity.[40]

The double-critique at work in this passage, which identifies the insufficiencies of both poles of the idealism-materialism antithesis, is strikingly clear in Marx's novel conjunction that equates 'thing' [*Gegenstand*], 'actuality' [*Wirklichkeit*], and 'sensuousness' [*Sinnlichkeit*]. Marx not only refutes the idealist account of the 'abstract' process of objective constitution/subjective actualisa-

---

39   Echeverría 1986, pp. 25–6.
40   Marx 1978b.

tion but also rejects the possibility of reverting to an account of actuality founded on the primacy of an inactive, intuitive notion of objectivity, circumscribed by the same 'traditional' discursive horizon: that adhered to positively in the opposing materialist-empiricist perspective, the dumb counterpart to living, active subjectivity that Marx refers to in *Capital* as the 'abstract materialism of natural science'.[41] So whilst *contra* idealism, the object retains a *degree* of self-sufficiency and is not constituted by the intellect *ex nihilo*, neither does it have an intrinsic 'sense' or 'reality' *independent* of its relation to a subject (to *practice*) such that objectivity would be an intrinsic feature of the object as 'matter', a 'pure presence' or 'metaphysical substrate' preceding subjective mediation, as Echeverría puts it. This implies a dissociation of materiality and matter (a 'materialism without matter', in Etienne Balibar's somewhat polemical expression), without which 'traditional' materialism lapses back into a special kind of idealism, a danger that Sartre drew attention to:[42]

> In order to grasp materiality as such, it is not sufficient to discuss the word 'matter'. ... There is a materialist idealism which, in the last analysis, is merely a discourse on the idea of matter; the real opposite of this is realist materialism – the thought of an individual who is situated in the world, penetrated by every cosmic force, and treating the material universe as something which gradually reveals itself through a 'situated' praxis.[43]

Yet conversely, just as the objective cannot be reduced to a mere externality devoid of sense, neither can the subjective be taken as an immaterial source of the rational operability of the actual: The 'situatedness' of practice dissociates subjectivity as process from the abstract activity of the independent intellect. This is alluded to in thesis III, when Marx attests to 'the coincidence of the changing of circumstances and human activity'.[44]

Marx's discourse therefore breaks with the underlying structural antithesis between an *active* ideal subjectivity (exemplified by Hegelian absolute spirit) and a *passive* material objectivity (the immediacy of external, intuited otherness) that supports the seemingly counterpoised theoretical perspectives of idealism and 'traditional' materialism. Instead, *practice* will form the content (at least in this initial iteration) of a discourse on actuality that recognises both

---

41  Marx 1976, p. 494 (fn).
42  Balibar 1995, p. 23.
43  Sartre 2004, p. 29.
44  See Suchting 1979, pp. 12–3: 'practice changes not only the 'object' but also the 'subject' of practice, and indeed the two changes are simultaneous.'

its active and material aspects as constitutive dimensions of one and the same process; of a *concrete subjectivity* and an *active objectivity*, an ongoing process of 'sensible human practice' that is at once mediated (as object) and mediating (as subject) – hence its designation as a *gegenständliche* practice. Echeverría elaborates this dual aspect of objective activity as the basic foundational moment of Marx's materialism:

> In order to adequately problematise that which distinguishes objectivity as such it is necessary to consider it *'subjectively'*, that is, as a process in motion, and as a process that affects essentially and equally both the subject and the object that appear in it; to consider it *'as activity'*, as praxis that founds every cognitive [*cognoscitiva*] subject-object relation and that therefore constitutes the sense of the real.[45]

In this conception of practice, object and subject attain a new articulation in which neither is given a privileged role as the 'organising principle' of the actual, such that neither corresponds simply to one pole of the opposition between idealism and ('traditional') materialism; the antithesis has been scrambled. Instead, both subjectivity and objectivity are grounded in the unity of a 'practico-critical' process of active world-constitution. By 'materialising' subjective activity as in itself already 'objective', and thereby making the objective active, its truth – its *actuality* – now consists in the production of directly 'material' (i.e., practico-objective) effects rather than the sublimation of these into their spiritual or representational results – a conversion that speculative philosophy must always undertake. For any kind of determination to take place in this sphere of practical composition, it must therefore result from and be grasped as 'sensible human activity' [*menschliche sinnliche Tätigkeit*]; willing, conscious action that 'proves its truth' by shaping the objective reality that confronts it, materially, rather than just theoretically (thesis XI).

Marx thereby dissolves the distinction between the mute objectivity of a passive matter and its formative mediation or synthesis in a pure, active intellect, as exemplified in both Kant's and Hegel's respective compositional totalities.[46] In his 'new' materialism, Marx posits an original *unitary medium* for subject and object, in which they figure as dialectically unified aspects of a

---

45  Echeverría 1986, pp. 25–6.
46  In keeping with the line of enquiry set out at the beginning of the book in relation to Kantian philosophy, I will call them 'compositional' totalities to at this point remain agnostic about the causal relation between structure and expression, although Marx's conception of social reproduction outlined further below will resolve the question of this relation.

*process* which neither can ultimately claim a monopoly to. The action of a (practical) subject no longer stands outside, opposed, or retrospectively related to a passive material dimension (however essential it might have been to the constitution of that dimension in transcendental or dialectical terms) but is now inscribed within the same medium of objectivity, as a coterminal aspect of it, as its 'active side'. As Karel Kosík put it:

> Reality stands out to man not primarily as an object of intuition, investigation and theorising, whose opposite and complementary pole would be an abstract cognitive subject existing outside and beyond the world, but rather as the realm of his sensuous-practical activity, which forms the basis for immediate *practical intuition* of reality.[47]

The practically conceived conjunction of materiality and subjectivity thus reassumes from idealist philosophy the centrality of the subject's capacity to give concrete form to objective reality, to shape reality according to its own conscious will and plan – 'men themselves change circumstances', in Marx's famous assertion – but this transformative activity occurs as an immanent moment of a *practical* totality that delimits the possibilities for realising such a capacity.

## 3   Theory of Practice and the Practice of Theory

The radicality of Marx's elaboration of practical materialism in the years 1845–6 had effects not only in terms of the substantial content of its theoretical proposition; it also essentially modified the status of theoretical discourse as such, establishing incipiently the possibility of its properly critical character, in the sense that, as Echeverría claims, 'the necessity of thinking the revolutionary process turns out to be, simultaneously, the necessity of revolutionising the process of thinking'.[48] Through his 'new' materialism, it becomes possible for Marx to designate, in a manner not available to the idealist account of actuality – for which, as Etienne Balibar has noted, subjectivity and representation were fundamentally bound together – a new relationship between the practice of theory and the theory of practice.[49] Theory here becomes merely a partial moment or region of the concrete practical totality, the conditions of social

---

47   Kosík 1976, p. 1, emphasis added.
48   Echeverría 1986, p. 23.
49   Balibar 1995, p. 24.

being that come to legislate over its possibilities and exigencies. After materialism, knowledge is 'not a purely theoretical, internal process' but 'stands in the service of life', such that the 'logics of science ... are embroiled in the logics of practical material life'.[50] This reduction of theoretical activity to a mere species of practice has a double effect, both negative and positive. On the one hand, it undermines the immediate revolutionary capacity of criticism; this had been central to the young Hegelian vision of actualisation, in which the critique of illusory ideas was the key to the emancipation from irrational conditions: '[N]ot criticism but revolution is the driving force of history'.[51] On the other, however, it allowed for the development of a new role for critique that would be consistent with its own materialist premises, as self-conscious of its function within a broader practical-revolutionary process. Jindrich Zeleny alludes to this when he claims that 'an integrating aspect – not to be neglected – of that revolutionary process is scientific activity, above all the "conception of praxis" as positive science – the science of practical activity, the practical process of development of men'.[52]

This reconfiguration of the theory-actuality relationship is crucial for grasping what occurs with the concept of subsumption in the course of Marx's development of a theory of practice, insofar as it is understood in terms of its foundation of a new relationship between the abstract and the concrete. By reconstructing actuality in theory, Marx's discourse seeks to dissolve mystified or ideological connections and replace them with concrete concepts that not only represent actual conditions but are also effective, in practical terms, in circumscribing a particular relationship between theoretical activity and actuality.[53] This does not simply mean negating conceptual abstractions as such but also, crucially, implies identifying the presence and effects of actually existing abstractions or logical forms – such as subsumption – within the practical structure of reality.[54] In this sense, the critique of philosophy (as well as 'tra-

---

50  Schmidt 1971, p. 95; Murray 1988, p. 72. It is important to note that the concept of 'life' at work here is *not* the Hegelian one, in which 'organism' 'refers to a logical order of things and not to 'biology', even if the model to which [Hegel] refers is the living organism' (Tombazos 2014, p. 147).

51  Marx and Engels 1998, p. 61.

52  Zeleny 1980, p. 194.

53  'The Marxian terms "mirroring" and "image" – though seldom together – are used to characterise epistemology as subordinate to a new conception of theory as an aspect of praxis. This has an anti-ideological function which emphasises the non-identity of thought and reality within a unity of active, hence perceiving thinking individuals and their relations' (Zeleny 1980, p. 154).

54  'Practice must be seen not only as contributing to the constitution of objectivity but as

ditional' theory more generally) is realised as and forms a particular moment of the critique of ideology – the 'destruction of the pseudoconcrete' – insofar as it seeks to break the mystified connection between the object of scientific or critical enquiry and the conditions under which it is carried out (and indeed motivated); that is, it seeks to clarify and potentialise the former by grasping the essence, or truth, of the latter. The duplicitous world must therefore be 'both understood in its contradiction and revolutionised in practice'.[55] As Marx had already established in 1843, the task of revolutionary science is first and foremost to comprehend the logic of real conditions and their transformation. Yet if this is so, Zeleny asks:

> How is a positive science which 'grasps praxis' possible? With Marx there is no question of founding such a science – in the sense of a Kantian critique of reason – since Marx would consider the very question of a standpoint for practical materialism to be uncritical, a return to speculative philosophising.[56]

The problem of an absolute or rational beginning that would found science, which was a primary concern for both Kant and Hegel, is therefore dissolved as a merely ideological one, one that obscured the fact that the determinants of thinking were given by the real conditions of humanity under which thought is realised and to which it must ineluctably respond. ('The dispute over the reality or non-reality of thinking – that is isolated from practice – is a purely *scholastic* question.')[57] Whereas in Hegel's philosophy, the development of the thing in thinking *is* the development of the thing in actuality (as a consequence of the speculative identity between thought and being) Marx's materialist inter-

---

the basis of our assessment of the truth or otherwise of our thinking about it' (Suchting 1979, p. 7).

55   Marx in Suchting 1979, Thesis IV. Even so, this picture still remains somewhat simplistic in its differentiation of a general practical sphere and a specific discursive domain of it, within which communication occurs exclusively. Bolívar Echeverría has complicated this model by giving an account of the dialectical relation between the process of material production and consumption (praxis) and the process of the production and consumption of significations (communication). In this account, due to primarily to the characteristic 'transnaturalisation' that occurs in the human reproduction process (elaborated upon below), every act of material production and consumption is equally and necessarily an act of signification or interpretation. See Echeverría 2014, pp. 24–38, and Echeverría 1986, pp. 38–50.
56   Zeleny 1980, p. 194.
57   Marx in Suchting 1979, thesis II.

vention dissolves this identity, such that conceptual development is restricted to the theoretical *reconstruction* (rather than retrospective *construction*) of an objectivity that is developed in reality through praxis. This is a point expressed most emphatically in Marx's 1857 'Introduction':

> The concrete is concrete because it is the concentration of many determinations, hence unity of the diverse. It appears in the process of thinking, therefore, as a process of concentration, as a result, not as a point of departure, even though it is the point of departure in reality and hence also the point of departure for observation [*Anschauung*] and conception.[58]

Although in thinking it is the result, the concrete is the actual [*wirklich*] point of departure: Thus thought activity strives to reach the actual in order to develop a materialist self-consciousness within and in relation to the actual as totality and horizon of *all* activity. In positing this critical relation between the concrete in thought and the concrete (practical) actuality from which it derives, Marx supersedes the opposition between ideal (and therefore 'unreal') conceptions and 'real' humanity that defined Feuerbach's post-Hegelian humanism. Instead, ideal conceptions are registered within the terms of practice, making it possible to grasp their concrete origins and 'real' effects. As Balibar notes:

> The point is no longer to *denounce* the abstraction of 'universals', of 'generalities', of 'idealities', by showing that that abstraction substitutes itself for real individuals; it now becomes possible to *study* the genesis of those abstractions, their production by individuals, as a function of the collective or social conditions in which they think and relate to one another.[59]

A science of praxis does not therefore depend on a beginning principle (e.g., the 'I', which in its universal validity could only be derived idealistically) but on those 'material' conditions and practices that support and motivate the production of ideal forms. As Marx and Engels assert in the *German Ideology*, the premises are always already in existence. Comprehending these practical premises therefore becomes the basic task of theory, but because it is practice itself that constitutes actuality in its fundamental form and that produces the

---

58   Marx 1993, p. 101.
59   Balibar 1995, p. 36.

relation between subject and object, this theoretical task produces a unique mode of self-relatedness, a self-conscious reflexion on human actuality in its active unfolding (as idealism already recognises it to be, albeit in a distorted, one-sided form). This holds not only for forms of ideal abstractions identified by the critique of ideology but also for the actual forms of abstraction that constitute the material conditions of practice, the inner 'logic' of the practical social body in which relations such as subsumption are key. Marx's critical discourse therefore takes practical activity as its theoretical object whilst at the same time constituting a central aspect of this activity, precisely insofar as it deliberately supersedes its status as a *merely* theoretical discourse and is instead grasped as a form of praxis.

But given that this conception of practice is still a reconstruction in thought, how close does it come to the actuality it refers to and reflects? If it is to be the 'real reality' of a radically original critical discourse, simply negating the primacy of the ideal in favour of practice as such is insufficient, as such a discourse remains, at worst, constrained by an idealist framework, or provides, at best, no more than a truncated critique of philosophy that fails to transcend its particular concerns and posit a new 'problematic region' proper to the revolutionary project. The concept of activity outlined in the *Theses On Feuerbach* does not sufficiently determine the processual objectivity of the relationship between thought and activity. It remains discursively located in the opposition between the two as abstract essences, valorising one over the other on the grounds of a higher degree of actuality or a richer quality of being. The *Theses* therefore set out the task to be achieved and the critical framework for doing so but do not themselves achieve this; they mark a point of departure, a critical axis upon which the possibility of articulating critical discourse with a higher degree of determinacy is possible. But this further specification remains to be given. The *idea* of practice remains abstract or at least underdetermined in relation to its conditions and therefore nothing more than the mere notion of a potential to act whose actualisation can only occur under given conditions or, what is the same thing, in specific forms without whose elaboration the actual is reduced to, and remains constrained by, the abstractly possible. Therefore, beyond the idea of practice as such (as 'human sensuous activity'), a more developed conception of the conditions structuring this activity and its resultant forms is required to satisfy the demands of the revolutionary problematic posed by Marx. The broader question here, one that results from the abolition of the self-sufficiency of the *idea*, is: What are the *subjective* and *objective* dimensions of practice? What is the structure of practice as an active process?

## 4 From Practice to Natural-History

### 4.1 *Material Subject: 'Trans-individuality' and Social Constitution*

Whilst it will be necessary to go beyond the *Theses* in order to respond to the second aspect of the inner structure of practice – specifically that of the *objective* moment in the process of activity – to which they provide no substantial answer, we can nonetheless find in the *Theses* (VI, VII, IX and X) the basic theoretical conditions for thinking this structure, namely that of the *subjective* articulation of the process as a socially constituted totality or 'ensemble' of inter-individual relations. These relations make up the sum total of practical interdependencies between the agents of 'sensuous practice', determining their possible action, uniting them within a social totality and singularising their efficacy as a collective subject. The idea of 'a certain social body, a *social subject*' is not novel to Marx and is established paradigmatically by Hegel in the transition from self-consciousness to spirit that takes place in the *Phenomenology*.[60] It is this concept of collective constitution, placed into dialectical tension with elements of Feuerbach's anthropological materialism that allows Marx to explicate the subjective dimension of practice as at once social *and* material (with each aspect reciprocally giving content to the other). Marx himself had been thinking against an abstract conception of the human individual as early as his doctoral dissertation ('Abstract individuality is freedom from being, not freedom in being'), but the *Theses* represent a progression beyond the conception of subjectivity previously held by Marx, e.g., in 1843, when he claimed that 'subjectivity can exist only as a corporeal individual' and on that basis argued that collective politics ought to struggle for a radically democratic version of *representational* actuality, i.e., the political form that corresponded most adequately to the real *individual*.

In the *Theses*, Marx begins to elaborate the properly dialectical mode of comprehending how it is that social relations between individuals determine the realisation of practice and thus constitute the 'real essence' of humanity that is to be subjected to critique. The idea of social relationality is synthesised with the first moment of the *Theses* – the negation of the primacy of the ideal in favour of the practical – in order to assert that 'all social life is essentially practical' – implying, reciprocally, that all practice is essentially social. This is the most developed result of the *Theses* (VIII), one that combines their two principle arguments. Humanity is therefore redefined as a collective subject realising itself by means of a 'trans-individual' practice (to use Balibar's

---

60  Marx 1993, p. 86; See chapter 1 of this thesis.

term), determined by the totality of cooperative relations through which the active capacity of each individual can be realised in process. Crucially for Marx, this totality of relations through which the practical essence of humanity is realised is not fixed but variable in its concrete actuality, rendering the identity of the individuals dependent on historically specific structures of sociality: '[T]he *abstract* individual ... belongs to a *definite form of society*'.[61] The Individual cannot thus be the starting point of a critical account of practice, as it has its genesis in the variable conditions of that practice (social relations). The theoretically undetermined content of practical individuality posits only a negative essence characteristic of the human species and, in doing so, breaks with a second antithesis presented by the traditional theoretical discourse, in many ways derivative of that between idealism and materialism – that between 'individualist' and 'holist' conceptions of human constitution.

Marx refutes, on the one hand, the idea that humanity and the objective activity proper to it emerges principally in and through a transhistorical form of individuality – either as the empirical aggregation of isolated persons (society as the 'result' of isolated egos, *pace* Stirner) or the naturalist reduction of individuals to mere exemplars of the genus (the generic conception of humanity adhered to by Fichte and Feuerbach and criticised by Hegel and Hess), both of which are capable only of grasping human activity as what Lukács disparages as a Kantian 'pseudo-practice' of the individual that is unable to alter the 'object-forms' of reality – that is, of its own fixed identity – and must simply be reconciled to operating within them.[62] Marx associates this outlook with 'old materialism', insofar as it treated individuals as passively dislocated and thus failed to grasp their practical interconnection as constitutive of their identities, needs and capacities. He argued that this view corresponded to a politics of abstract, juridical relationality:

> The highest point attained by *intuiting* materialism, that is, materialism which does not understand sensuousness as practical activity, is the outlook of single individuals in "civil society."[63]

Inversely, however, Marx's insistent critique of the notion of 'society' as a unilateral force that stands over and against real individuals – ubiquitous, as we have

---

61  Marx in Suchting 1979, thesis VII, emphasis added.
62  Lukács 2014.
63  Marx in Suchting 1979, thesis IX, translation modified.

seen, in his commentaries on Hegelian philosophy and in the *German Ideology* manuscripts – equally demonstrates a refusal of the reduction inherent in any deterministic holism or structuralism that would stamp individuals as mere effects of the social form to which they belong, as constituted by it without in any significant sense also constituting it.

In contrast to these polar reductions, Marx states that the standpoint of his new materialism, or, what is the same, the subject 'of' practice (or 'as' practice) is 'socialised humanity', the 'social' aspect of which must be taken as dialectically opposed to and intended to displace what would be a merely *natural* determination of the human as a fixed essence (located either in the individual or the totality) abstracted from the 'historical process'. By contrast, human actuality consists in praxis, and the conditions and form of praxis are determined socially, according to historically variable forms.

As a result, it is the logic of this process of formation/forming that becomes the central object of critique for Marx rather than a putative separation or alienation between an underlying essence and a phenomenal reality. (Methodologically, we can discern here a similar move to the first thesis' rejection of the opposition between traditional materialism and idealism; Marx does not adhere to the antithesis between them but inscribes both within a dialectical relation of determination grasped as a unified process.) Balibar emphasises the importance of the suspension of this antithesis in opening the path to a new mode of theoretical enquiry in Marx's thought:

> For the discussion of the relations between the individual and the genus, it substitutes a programme of enquiry into this multiplicity of relations, which are so many transitions, transferences or passages in which the bond of individuals to the community is formed and dissolved, and which, in its turn, constitutes them.[64]

The refutation of the idea that there is a fixed form of practice, Marx's negative essentialism, therefore turns out to be the condition for thinking the historical development and transformation of human existence – and therefore the revolutionary problematic to which Marx's discourse responds – in materialist terms, that is, in accordance with the idea that it is the *particular* conditions and structure of social activity (rather than an invariable essence) that determine the practical possibilities and limitations of the realisation of humanity's social being.

---

64  Balibar 1995, p. 32.

A continuity, and indeed a radically original response, can be discerned here with the problem posed by Kant in his second critique (although the theological provenance of this problem stretches far back before him): that humanity is the site of a conflict or tension between natural ('pathological') and rational determination that must be resolved practically. Marx takes up this problematic in an entirely novel manner. Its novelty lies, firstly, in the form in which this conflict plays out, which, as the subjectivity of the human, is not generically present in each individual (who *ought* to choose rational over pathological action) but depends on the collective mode of life within which individuals exist and realise themselves, as parts of the social subject; secondly, in that, if this totality of social individuals is not united 'naturally', according to a preconceived image, then the primary theoretical problematic of a revolutionary science must be the processes through which individuals come to relate to each other in specific historical forms and, in turn, how these forms might be subject to transformation. The concrete existence of humanity thereby attains a higher determinacy than that of mere action in the abstract: Individual practice is realised socially, and the social is realised in the collective, coordinated activity of an organic totality of individuals united in a singular subject that exists (and is capable of changing) in the process. Marx thus establishes a dynamic of reciprocal determination between individuals and the (total) social subject: '[J]ust as society itself produces man as man, so is society produced by him'.[65] Although a certain degree of reciprocity between individuality and the collective totality can be found in Hegel's works on spirit – albeit with well-known speculative deformations – the mode of relationality constituting this circuit remains ideal and consists in merely representational or logicised connections, whereas for Marx the circuit is articulated practically in real human activity.

### 4.2   Practical Object: The 'Mediating Instrumental Field'

In the terms of Marx's theoretical orientation and method, the enquiry into the logic of the 'body politic', the political structure of the social subject with which he began, has become an enquiry into the global structure and functional logic of the *practical relations* governing the realisation of objective activity within a collaborative totality. But beyond the social interconnections between individuals enabling and giving form to this activity – the threshold of comprehension delimited by a theory of 'trans-individual practice' – its *objective* structure, the external, 'natural' conditions that confront the social subject and its relation to these conditions, remains to be determined, even as a general, trans-

---

65   Marx 1992, p. 349.

historical form, before it is grasped in its historical concretion. We must then ask: in what do the objective *conditions* that constitute practice and that are in turn transformed by it consist? Social relations are obviously also conditions of practice and possess a certain degree of objectivity for the individual inscribed within them. They are however not purely self-constituting and the practices that they structure are not enacted directly upon those relations (that is, they may pertain to *objectivity*, but they are not as such *objective*). Instead, praxis is an activity *mediated through the practical relation to the object, to externality*.[66] It is the manuscripts written jointly by Marx and Engels in 1845–6, historically known as *The German Ideology*, which, complementary to Marx's *Theses On Feuerbach*, offer an initial explication of this relation to the object of praxis by reintroducing one of the key themes dealt with in Marx's 1843–4 writings: *the relation between humanity and nature as the basis for 'life'*, as the *'real reality'*, the *actual in process*. If the dialectical recognition of the subject's mediation through the object is entirely in keeping with Hegel's philosophy, it is the irreducibly 'natural' status of the object (as well as, ultimately, the subject) that is speculative idealism's undoing, as Marx recognised in his early critique of that philosophy:

> Abstraction comprehending itself as abstraction knows itself to be nothing: It must abandon itself – abandon abstraction – and so it arrives at an entity which is its exact opposite – at *nature*. Thus, the entire logic is the demonstration that abstract thought is nothing in itself; that the absolute idea is nothing for itself; that only *nature is* something.[67]

The residual exteriority of the object to the subject that is in the *Theses On Feuerbach* retained from 'old materialism' (and equally acknowledged – if only implicitly – by idealism) has an underlying correspondence in the realm of *nature*, of *natural being*. What the practical subject-object relation thus consists in is a relation of the *living* subject to the natural conditions that confront it as its object. But – and again Marx's scrambling of the idealism-materialism antithesis is key here – the object as nature is not conceived of as dumb matter,

---

66  'These *natural conditions of existence*, to which he relates as to his own inorganic body, are themselves double: (1) of a subjective and (2) of an objective nature. He finds himself a member of a family, clan, tribe etc. – which then, in a historic process of intermixture and antithesis with others, takes on a different shape; and, as such a member, he relates to a specific nature (say, here, still earth, land, soil) as his own inorganic being, as a condition of his production and reproduction' (Marx 1993, p. 490).
67  Marx 1992, p. 397.

as *intuited*, any more than the subject could be taken to be an immaterial, self-grounding will; rather, owing to its mediation through the subject in the unity of practice (just as much as the subject is itself mediated through this natural relation), it must be grasped as a *practical object* – a concept first introduced by Sartre but given a more developed theoretical articulation by Echeverría.[68] The practical object is exterior to the subject (and in this sense 'natural') but endowed with 'sense' or a specific determination of being according to its functions (symbolic and 'real') within the practical totality encompassing them both, and defined by its capacity to respond – either immediately or through its practical transformation – to the historical needs of that subject, regardless of whether it is a product of previous praxis or an untransformed natural material. The object of practice therefore always, necessarily, has a socio-practical objectivity that transcends and is irreducible to its purely 'natural' – which is to say, empirically intuited – qualities. This objectivity [*Gegenständlichkeit*] is the 'general form' or global context within which anything can appear in opposition to the subject as the possible object of its activity:[69]

> Whichever element of nature, be it physical, chemical, vital, psychic; whichever fact, be it material or spiritual, etc., whichever parcel of exterior or interior reality, whichever section of material, of whichever materiality it may be, when it is integrated into a social process of production and consumption, of the reproduction of a social subject, constitutes that which we could call a practical object, or an object that has a social natural form.[70]

The only possible mode of being in which nature can confront the social subject is therefore already mediated by it, so that, as Lukács puts it in *History and Class Consciousness*, 'nature's form, its content, its range and its objectivity are all socially conditioned'.[71] (This has important effects, for example, in terms of the relation between individual members of the social body and the objective world that confronts them, as the objectivity of the world may be mediated and stamped with a particular practicality at the level of the social totality, but this practical significance may escape or be denied to individuals – herein lies the basis for the 'fetish character' of capitalist commodities.) Marx differenti-

---

68 See Sartre 2004, p. 45; Echeverría 2014, pp. 30–32.
69 It is then deployed by Marx in the context of specific historical forms of objectivity, such as 'value-objectivity' [*Wertgegenständlichkeit*].
70 Echeverría 1998a, p. 15.
71 Lukács 1971, p. 234.

ates between two principal forms of practicality: the *object* and *instrument* of practice, the former being that which is worked upon and the latter that which facilitates the work, augmenting the productive powers of the human body by functioning as its 'inorganic body'. The practical object, taken as the totality of individual objects and instruments operative and available within a society (just as the social subject incorporates all of its individual members), as well as the techniques proper to them, articulates external nature as 'an objective totality gifted with a distributive intentionality'.[72] It is this practical object, the 'mediating instrumental field' of all practice, that provides the *objective* 'premises' of human actuality, which a logic of social actuality must analyse and critique (in conjunction with the subjective aspect) if it is to be a science of 'actual historical man' rather than mere 'man'.

### 4.3  *Natural-Historical Being: Practice as Production*

Practice, as the foundational process through which human existence attains its concrete actuality, is therefore constituted in the active relations between the *practical object* and the *social subject*: '[A] certain mode of production or stage of industry is always conjoined with a certain mode of social interaction or stage of society', Marx and Engels assert.[73] The former corresponds to a natural totality that is given sense according to its 'instrumental operativity', that is, incorporated (or 'totalised', in the Sartrean sense) within a practical context that determines its objective character, the latter to a collaborative community 'in their given social connection'.[74] There is an important dialectical mediation at work between these two poles or totalities in their concrete connection. On the one hand, the intensive relational composition of the social subject depends on and responds to the structure of the 'mediating instrumental field' and the techniques through which its praxis is realised, on the other, the very 'practicality' of that field is an expression and result of the relations and objectives posited by the social subject. Thus whilst nature is socialised by its incorporation within a specifically human process of activity, human social existence is itself 'naturalised' by its incorporation within the broader physiological functioning of natural life as *reproduction*. Marx had already noted this reciprocity in 1844, although in much more general terms:

---

72  Echeverría 2014, p. 30.
73  Marx and Engels 2014, p. 71.
74  'Marx indicates how bourgeois political economists transformed the properties of things, which are formed by their relation in a particular whole, by their roles and functions in a particular process, into fixed, substantial properties, independent of relations in a historically transitory whole.' Zeleny 1980, p. 25.

> An objective being acts objectively, and it would not act objectively if objectivity were not an inherent part of its essential nature. It creates and establishes only objects because it is established by objects, because it is fundamentally nature. In the act of establishing it therefore does not descend from its 'pure activity' to the creation of objects; on the contrary, its objective product simply confirms its objective activity, its activity as the activity of an objective, natural being.[75]

Even in Marx's early texts, 'consistent naturalism' was the 'unifying truth' of both materialism and idealism that superseded their theoretical separation. The 'consistency' at stake here would be precisely the recognition of a dialectical interpenetration between humanity's 'natural' and 'socio-historical' being: The human cannot be abstracted from nature – '[as if] man is not always confronted with a historical nature and a natural history' – but is rather realised in and through it, as part of it.[76]

> Man lives from nature – i.e., nature is his body – and he must maintain a continuing dialogue with it is he is not to die. To say that man's physical and mental life is linked to nature simply means that nature is linked to itself, for man is a part of nature.[77]

If the medium of this 'dialogue' is the active conjunction of social subject and practical object, its language or code is established by Marx and Engels through their association of the natural materiality of 'the human body' (Feuerbach's 'flesh and blood') with the practical form of its expression in *'needs and labour'*.[78] These are categories which fall neither on the side of the social or the natural but must be grasped dialectically as socio-natural, or more precisely, natural-historical.[79] Corporeality, humanity's natural or objective being, is given an immediately historical dimension, insofar as it is only ever expressed in the form of the particular needs and capacities driving and realising social life; at the same time, human subjectivity, in whichever historical and social circumstances it is operative and in spite of whichever specific higher goals and projects it might posit, is bound to its necessary mediation through the

---

75  Marx 1992, p. 389.
76  Marx and Engels 2014, p. 51.
77  Marx 1992, p. 328.
78  Marx and Engels 2014, p. 34, emphasis added.
79  'Natural history is not a synthesis of natural and historical methods, but a change of perspective' (Adorno 2006, p. 261).

'natural' processes sustaining its biological existence. The concrete totalisation of this double-process is therefore grounded in the unity of the reproduction of natural life through historical means: that cyclical movement which fulfils the vital needs of the social subject on the basis of the resources, techniques and knowledges available to it in its given circumstances (geographically, ethnically, culturally, etc.). In their famous passage on the natural foundations of history, Marx and Engels declare that:

> We have to make a start with the Germans, who are devoid of premises, by setting forth the first premise of all human existence, and therefore of all history, namely the premise that men have to be in a position to live in order to be able to "make history". But living requires above all else eating & drinking, shelter, clothing & yet other things. The first historical act is therefore the production of the means to satisfy these needs, the production of material life itself, & indeed this is a historical act, a founding condition of all history, which must be fulfilled today, on a daily & hourly basis, just as it was thousands of years ago, simply for men to stay alive.[80]

This passage is crucial and marks the point at which human activity, *practice*, is designated in its specificity as 'production', which takes place according to the demands, and as the realisation of, a specifically natural process of life. Even where critical and post-Hegelian philosophies acknowledged the constitutive role of nature or the natural dimension of human existence, it was in almost all cases – with Schelling perhaps being the notable exception – restricted to a merely secondary status in terms of the determination of the actual, having no effective presence other than as an expression or objective product of subjectivity, which, conversely had to pay no such conceptual tribute to nature. The subject was given monopoly over every process (for example in Kantian philosophy, where the lawfulness of nature is a product of subjectivity) and even the concept of 'life' was considered in terms of rational consistency or development (eminently for Hegel). Here however, this unilateral primacy is disrupted because any possible process of subjective development, that is, all *history*, has its premises and actuality in the 'mundanity' of those everyday processes that are the basis for natural life. This natural basis of social being is not an incidental fact, but forms the essential and irreducible content of the totality of practices, objects and relations that constitute the 'production of material life', which in any particular configuration, however culturally or

---

80  Marx and Engels 2014, p. 63.

technically mediated, nonetheless remain delimited by the 'regularities proper to matter' in its natural functioning.

What exactly is Marx's account of these 'regularities'? And how do they inform what remains the horizon and object of his theoretical engagement, the modes of historical existence and their transformation? From the mid-1840s onwards, Marx not only developed a far more sophisticated conception of how the reciprocal process of subject-object constitution was structured socially and materially, but also came to a unique and decisive perspective on the natural-objective structure of its unity. Alfred Schmidt claims that 'when he engaged on his analysis of the social life-process, thus concretising the concept of appropriation, Marx went far beyond all the bourgeois theories of nature presented by the Enlightenment'.[81] Marx developed his ideas of the natural basis grounding the realisation of the social production process through his close interest, along with Engels, in new discoveries and theoretical innovations in the natural sciences.[82] Energetics, in particular, was one of the most important fields of scientific enquiry at this time, and Marx drew on one aspect of this broad theory, making use of the concept of *metabolism* [*Stoffwechsel*], which describes the circulation of energy or matter between an organic system and its environment. As John Bellamy Foster defines it:

> It captures the complex biochemical process of exchange, through which an organism (or a given cell) draws upon materials and energy from its environment and converts these by various metabolic reactions into the

---

81  Schmidt 1971, p. 79.
82  'We knew that Marx and Engels had both filled multiple notebooks with extracts from, and commentaries on, the leading natural science writers of their time. We also knew that these notebooks covered a wide range of scientific fields – physics, chemistry, biology, physiology, geology, and agronomy – in each of which the analysis of energy dynamics occupied an important if not central position. In fact, as we studied the matter further we discovered that Marx and Engels had some familiarity with and in some cases had closely studied the works of many of the scientists involved in the development of thermodynamics (both the first and second laws) – including Hermann von Helmholtz, Julius Robert Mayer, James Prescott Joule, Justus von Liebig, Jean-Baptiste Joseph Fourier, Sadi Carnot, Rudolf Clausius, William Thomson, Peter Guthrie Tait, William Grove, James Clark Maxwell, and Ludwig Eduard Boltzmann. In addition, we knew that Marx had attended numerous public lectures on natural science in the years leading up to and following the publication of Capital, Volume I in 1867, and that among these was a series of lectures by the English physicist John Tyndall, author of *Heat Considered as a Mode of Motion*. Tyndall, a major figure in the developing physics in his own right, was the principal advocate of the ideas of J.R. Mayer – one of the co-discoverers of the conservation of energy (the first law of thermodynamics)' (Foster and Burkett 2006, p. 112).

building blocks of growth. In addition, the concept of metabolism is used to refer to the specific *regulatory processes* that govern this complex interchange between organisms and their environment.[83]

Marx appropriated this notion of material interchange and its 'regulatory processes' and began to incorporate it, from the 1850s onwards, as an essential aspect of his theory of praxis that would explain its structure as a natural process, as 'part of nature', with a greater determinacy than had previously been possible. As a metabolism, the interaction between the subjective and objective factors of the practical process denotes an active and transformative relation to nature delimited by a conservationist economy, a process of working upon the object through an *exchange* of material (or energy) between an organic and inorganic totality which, as Carlos Oliva points out, is the basis for every process of organic life, 'the form in which the primary [natural] relation is given, common not only to the animal and the human being, but, we could presuppose, to every being that exists and reproduces itself.'[84] At the same time, however, the metabolic aspect of praxis is for not Marx reducible to the merely quantitative fact of a purely energetic transfer but also implies, *qualitatively*, a change of form on the part of the interacting totalities and the matter exchanged, brought about by, or borne out of, this interchange.[85] This leap from the quantitative to the qualitative – characteristically associated with dialectical development – is essential in unifying Marx's multi-layered analysis of the reproductive process and transforms the function and meaning of the metabolic concept in Marx's discourse, which 'for all its scientific air, is nonetheless speculative in character'.[86]

As a generalised process, systematically foundational to the functioning of the natural world, metabolism carries out, or rather carries with it, what the naturalist philosopher and physiologist Jacob Moleschott described as the 'eternal circulation of material' through its various forms.[87] For Marx, human practice also participates in and is bound by the laws of metabolic interchange

---

83   Foster 2000, p. 160, emphasis added.
84   Schmidt 1971, p. 76; Oliva Mendoza 2013, pp. 189–90.
85   'Marx follows Hermann and Liebig in declining to reduce the content of the energy income and expenditure to pure energetic terms.' 'For Marx and Engels, the emphasis was on irreversible change and qualitative transformation' (Foster and Burkett 2006, pp. 121, 111).
86   Schmidt 1971, p. 76. See also Foster 2000, ch. 5.
87   Jacob Moleschott, cited in Schmidt 1971, p. 87. Critical of Schmidt's account, Foster downplays the influence of Moleschott on Marx's appropriation of the metabolic concept, see 2000, p. 161.

in that it 'can only proceed as nature does ... can only *change the form of the materials*' through, in Pietro Verri's terms, 'composition and division' rather than 'acts of creation'.[88] 'Forms' here denotes the practicality of the object, an objectivity, as we have seen, determined entirely by its specific function in the practical process of production and consumption, by the functional position it occupies there: As its function changes, so do its determining characteristics, i.e., its form (as the unity of these characteristics). In identifying this form-determining and -altering activity with a metabolic basis, Marx's theory of praxis is imbued with a basic physiological dimension – 'the everlasting nature-imposed condition of human existence ... common to all forms of society in which human beings live' – that functions to mitigate any residual presence of the ideal productivity and 'ghostly battles' which mark its philosophical genesis, binding the form giving and consuming process to an underlying physical substrate which possesses its own processual 'logic'.[89]

## 5  Against Nature

But whilst the human metabolism with nature conforms to the general functioning of physiological reproduction, it does so in a distinctive and singular manner by means of which it 'transcends' its status as a purely 'animal' process. This transcendence emerges as a result of the characteristic underdetermination of the 'regulatory processes' governing the *form* of the interaction between human activity and its natural-practical object. Human reproduction cannot be mapped onto any *instinctually* given image of the sociality or technique that would constitute the praxis through which it is realised – a corollary of the negative essentialism already established in thesis IV and the *German Ideology* manuscripts. There is no generically fixed form of the metabolic interaction itself, nor, resultantly, of the forms given to natural material in the labour process or the social subjects produced by consumption. The human life process may of necessity obey certain basic bio-physical conditions, but, as Echeverría argues, the 'determination of its concrete figure is nevertheless delivered over to the side of freedom' such that 'the reproduction of its *animal* materiality is the bearer of a reproduction that transcends it, that of its *social* materiality'.[90] This moment of transcendence that lacerates the natural order and '*trans-*

---

88  Marx 1976, p. 133, emphasis added; Pietro Verri, cited by Marx in a footnote to the previous comment.
89  Marx 1976, p. 290.
90  Echeverría 2014, p. 27.

*naturalises*' human reproduction (to take Echeverría's term) from an animal to socio-natural process was identified by Georg Simmel as the foundational basis for the subject-object distinction:

> The fact is that, unlike animals, humanity does not integrate itself unquestioningly into the natural facticity of the world but tears loose from it, confronts it, demanding, struggling, violating and being violated by it and it is with this first great dualism that the endless process between the subject and the object arises.[91]

It is precisely here, with the idea of a constitutive trans-naturalisation of human reproduction, that the connection is established between the two essential moments of Marx's theory of praxis – its natural and historical dimensions – that are the dialectically interpenetrating poles of a single 'socio-natural' process. If, up to this point, Marx's thought appears to be susceptible to the criticism levelled against Kant in relation to the subsumptive relation between concepts and intuitions, which Hegel could only displace with recourse to a speculative operation of closure – namely, that it provides only a progressive elaboration of the constituents of actuality (nature and history) that draws them together asymptotically without ever being able to resolve them into a definitive unity – their hypostatised heterogeneity is overcome at this point. In bringing the development of each aspect to the point of its mediation through the other, as *already* the other, Marx is genuinely able to repose this opposition between form and content as one between substance and form, which is to say that of a unified self-acting *process*, a disjunctive synthesis in an open movement of self-explication.[92] This is also, then, the precise moment that discloses the possibility of a *material subjectivity*, promised in the first of the *Theses On Feuerbach*, one that transcends the objective closure of the metabolic process as a purely physical one whilst vindicating the materialist consistency of freedom and necessity on the basis of Lucretius' dictum that 'out of

---

91  Simmel 1997, p. 55.
92  'If the question of the relation of nature and history is to be seriously posed, then it only offers any chance of solution if it is possible *to comprehend historical being in its most extreme historical determinacy, where it is most historical, as natural being, or if it were possible to comprehend nature as a historical being where it seems to rest most deeply in itself as nature.*' Adorno 2006, p. 260; See Echeverría 1983, p. 3: 'If already in the *Grundrisse* of 1857 [Marx] saw the labour process "incorporated" as "matter" into the capital "form", in the 1861–3 manuscript he tried to see it, not as a reality *in-itself untouched* by a (capitalist) mode of operation external to it, but as a "substance" affected essentially by the capitalist "form" that, formally or really, it allowed to exist.'

nothing, nothing comes'.[93] The trans-naturalised condition of human activity summons a subjectivity, both necessitated and potentialised by the lack of a natural or instinctive schema guiding the reproductive process, to select a concrete social form for human existence that recodes or re-totalises the merely natural 'first nature' of its animal life. In exercising this capacity and producing new forms for its own existence according to the complex historical interplay between natural limits and social boundaries, the human supersedes its status as a *particular* animal and instead lays claim to the universality of organic being, which it takes as a substance that it can manipulate in a (theoretically) limitless manner, although only as a horizon of historical possibility (and on somewhat ambiguous terms):

> Whereas the animal is bound, in his appropriation of the world of objects, to the biological peculiarities of his species, and hence confined to definite regions of the world, the universality of man is signified by the fact that he can appropriate, at least potentially, the whole of nature.[94]

As Kant established, the possibility of such a universal activity and selective development is conditional upon the effective presence of an *autonomous* source of will-determination guiding praxis, whose exercise Marx locates primarily in the act of labour.[95] As 'an exclusively human characteristic', labour is distinguished from organic activity as such by its unique temporal structure, in which the spontaneous and conscious positing of a *telos* precedes and determines its concrete actualisation. The anticipatory conceptualisation of the results of labour, the projected ideal that propels and guides the process in the absence of an instinctive schema, is for Marx what 'distinguishes the worst architect from the best of bees' and is, at a more fundamental level, the condition of possibility for the subjective capacity that ultimately determines the form given to human reproduction, the historical actuality of the social pro-

---

93  This motto appears twice in *Capital*: 1978a, p. 408; 1976, p. 323. See also in the context of capitalist production Marx 1993, p. 304: 'Nothing can emerge at the end of the process which did not appear as a presupposition and precondition at the beginning.'
94  Schmidt 1971, p. 80.
95  'As the sole being on earth who has reason, and thus a capacity to set voluntary ends for himself, he is certainly the titular lord of nature, and, if nature is regarded as a teleological system, then it is his vocation to be the ultimate end of nature; but always only conditionally, that is, subject to the condition that he has the understanding and the will to give to nature and to himself a relation to an end that can be sufficient for itself independently of nature, which can thus be a final end, which, however, must not be sought in nature at all' (Kant 2000, § 83).

cess *in toto*. This capacity emerges in the course of labour, as 'a process by which man, *through his own actions*, mediates, regulates and controls the metabolism between himself and nature' in order to give a new form to the worked-upon matter.[96] The 'subjective' moment of praxis therefore emerges when a practical intentionality (that we cannot call rational or 'free' in an unqualified sense, but whose functioning is unintelligible on the basis of purely biological determinations alone) intervenes to direct the metabolic process according to its own pre-conceived goal:

> At the end of every labour process, a result emerges which had already been conceived by the worker at the beginning, hence existed ideally. Man not only effects a change of form in the materials of nature; he also actualises [*verwirklicht*] his own purpose in those materials. And this is a purpose he is conscious of, it determines the mode of his activity with the rigidity of a law, and he must subordinate his will to it. This subordination is no mere momentary act. Apart from the exertion of the working organs, a purposeful will is required for the entire duration of the work.[97]

The effective presence of a 'spontaneous' purposive intentionality within the labour process is therefore what displaces the purely natural determination of human reproduction, and establishes in its place what Echeverría calls, following Sartre and Heidegger, 'an autonomous dimension of being: that of human existence'.[98] The autonomy at stake here is, however, neither pure nor final nor absolute in the sense established by Kant in his practical philosophy, where there was 'in man a power of self-determination, independently of any coercion through sensuous impulses'.[99] For Marx, autonomy from natural determination is by contrast relative rather than absolute and should be taken to indicate the opening of an interstitial phase that suspends the ontological continuity of the natural life process, and in which the realisation of vital functions is carried out according to an independent logic, irreducible to the behavioural principles encoded in the biological structure of the human animal. It is this *socio-historical* logic that constitutes, in its transcendence of the regulatory order of biological being, the conditioned form of freedom proper to the practical subjectivity of the social individuals and the historical content of its multiple realisations. If a 'principle' of determination could be singled out as

---

96   Marx 1976, p. 283.
97   Marx 1976, p. 284, translation modified.
98   Echeverría 1995, p. 76.
99   Kant 1999, A534/B562.

that which guides (and limits) the exercise of this autonomous willing, it would have to be derived immanently from a global practical context delimited by a conjunction of the subjective and objective factors of the reproduction process as a whole (in any particular 'socio-ethnic' instance).

In labour, practical subjectivity 'proves the truth' of this autonomy by externalising or objectivising its ideal in a concrete product – a practical object or *use-value* – and thereby effects a transition from subjective into objective form, *actualising* itself. For Marx, labour is 'the manifestation of [the worker's] personal skill and capacity – a manifestation which depends on his will and is *simultaneously an expression of his will*.'[100] This expression does not only appear in the course of the labour process but also subsists in the intentional form given to the product. The fluid subjectivity of labour in process – what Marx, recalling Hegel's negative, refers to as 'pure restlessness' – metabolically undoes and transforms the fixity of objective conditions, it 'must seize on these things, awaken them from the dead' and infuse them 'with vital energy for the performance of the functions appropriate to their concept and to their vocation' (i.e., the end that subjectivity assigns to them). Labour consumes the object (both as *raw material* and *instrument of labour*), dissolving the hard fixity of its objectness, *subjectivising* it, whilst at the same time fixing its own free subjectivity in an external form, congealing its motility and *objectifying* itself in the product:[101]

> This form-giving activity consumes the object and consumes itself, but it consumes the given form of the object only in order to posit it in a new objective form, and it consumes itself only in its subjective form as activity. It consumes the objective character of the object – the indifference towards the form – and the subjective character of activity; forms the one, materialises the other.[102]
>
> Labour is not only consumed, but also at the same time fixed, converted from the form of activity into the form of the object; materialised; as a modification of the object, it modifies its own form *and changes from activity to being*.[103]

Through the labour process, subject and object therefore permeate one another, neither is what it was before the process began, formally *or* physically: Each has given and taken from the other. Every instance of transformative or

---

100  Marx 1988, p. 93, emphasis added.
101  Marx 1976, p. 289.
102  Marx 1993, p. 301.
103  Marx 1993, p. 300, emphasis added.

practico-critical activity conforms to this doubly determined structure of the human metabolism, realised through a complex series of transformative interactions.

Considered only from the perspective of the first phase of the social process, *production*, labour functions as the medium of actualisation through which the subject shapes the external objectivity of the world, imposing its own will and creative freedom upon actuality by virtue of its formation of the object that it subsumes under its own practical *telos*. But given that this *telos* is nothing but a function of its own reproduction process, of its anticipated self-constitution, the act of subsumptively determining the object also reciprocally determines – just as it determined the Kantian and Hegelian subject – the actuality of the social subject, realised in the second phase of the social process with the *consumption* of the object:

> Not only do the objective conditions change in the act of reproduction, e.g., the village becomes a town, the wilderness a cleared field etc., but the producers change, too, in that they bring out new qualities in themselves, develop themselves in production, transform themselves, develop new powers and ideas, new modes of intercourse, new needs and new language.[104]

In the moment of consumption, the practical intention that was expressed in labour and objectified in the form of the product is 'actualised':

> A product becomes an actual product only by being consumed. For example, a garment becomes an actual [*wirkliches*] garment only in the act of being worn; a house where no one lives is in fact not an actual [*wirkliches*] house; thus the product, unlike a mere natural object [*Naturgegenstand*], proves itself to be, *becomes*, a product only through consumption. Only by decomposing the product does consumption give the product the finishing touch; for the product is production not as objectified [*Tätigkeit*] activity, but rather only as object for the active [*tätige*] subject.[105]

The product is therefore not only determined by its purpose or role insofar as it is inscribed within a practical totality, as something *for* the active subject, a *potential* practical object, but reaches its highest degree of actuality in the

---

104   Marx 1993, p. 494.
105   Marx 1993, p. 91.

moment of its destructive absorption or transformation by the subject. The object's status as 'for the subject' (its practicality) is realised and affirmed *in actu*, when it 'steps outside this social movement [of circulation] and becomes a direct object and servant of individual need, and satisfies it in being consumed.'[106] For Marx this too is a trans-naturally determined process, realised under a particular socio-historical form which 'produces, both objectively and subjectively, not only the object consumed but also the manner of its consumption'.[107] Consumption is then ultimately an *affirmation* of the form of the object, of the intentional practicality given to matter in the course of the labour process (although not, of course, in every case). This is so, not only in terms of its *direct* effect in the satisfaction of a need that would affirm its immediate practical functionality, but also *indirectly* in that in being consumed, the object is 'subjectivised' and gives form to the consumer whose vital subjectivity is reproduced by means of it: '[I]t alone creates for the products the subject for whom they are products.'[108] This is the same social subject that will then collectively re-enact the first phase of the cycle, so that the form given to the subject in the moment of consumption shapes the possibilities of its future productive activity. Consumption therefore 'reacts in turn upon the point of departure and initiates the whole process anew.'[109] Stuart Hall emphasises the centrality of this mediation in the generation of new historical needs and capacities:

> Consumption produces production by creating the need for '*new* production'. It is crucial, for the later discussion of the determinacy of production in the process as a whole, that what consumption now does, strictly speaking, is to provide the 'ideal, internally impelling cause', the 'motive', 'internal image', 'drive' 'purpose' for *re*-production. Marx stresses '*new* production'; strictly speaking, and significantly, it is the need to *re*-produce for which consumption is made mediately responsible.[110]

There is thus a second aggregate effect borne by the reproductive process across its cyclical realisations. Viewed globally, in terms of the general effects and functionality of production and consumption as a whole, the basic autonomy at work in productive labour expresses and enacts not only the immediate repro-

---

106  Marx 1993, p. 89.
107  Marx 1993, p. 92.
108  Marx 1993, p. 91.
109  Marx 1993, p. 89.
110  Hall 2003, p. 123.

duction of the social subject but also the creative constitution of its concrete identity, what Echeverría refers to as a 'project' of self-construction, where:

> [T]he form that a good that has been produced has is never neutral or innocent; it always has a concrete use-value that determines, in turn, the form that the subject that will consume it should have. Labour has a *poiétic* dimension; its giving form is a *realisation*, Marx says. It is an invention and the carrying out of a project; a project that is only immediately the construction of a thing, which indirectly but ultimately is the construction of the subject itself.[111]

When the social process is grasped as a totality, as a process of socio-natural reproduction, we can see how praxis gives form not only to the objects and in turn the subjects of practical life, but also to the very form of the process itself, how reproduction is a mediating form of 'self-activity' [*Selbstbetätigung*]. The true activity of the social subject is consummated in this reproductive process of production/consumption, as that through which it gives form to its own sociality, to its 'socio-natural form' of existence. This forms the consistent materialist basis of Marx's thinking, even at its most historically specific, as for instance in *Capital*:

> Whatever the social form of the production process, it has to be continuous, it must periodically repeat the same phases. A society can no more cease to produce than it can cease to consume. When viewed, therefore, as a connected whole, and in the constant flux of its incessant renewal, every social process of production is at the same time a process of reproduction.[112]

## 6   Reproduction-Development

The *differentia specifica* of the human metabolic relation, of its reproduction process as a whole, is its constitutive underdeterminacy in purely 'animal' terms and the corresponding genesis of a socio-historical subjectivity that prosthetically undertakes this determining function. This account of 'transnaturalized' reproduction, elaborated by Marx and presented schematically

---

111   Echeverría 2014, p. 29.
112   Marx 1976, p. 711.

by Echeverría in his 1984 essay 'La Forma Natural de la Reproducción Social' ('The Natural Form of Social Reproduction'), is the most developed 'general' account of the structure of the practical process and its social structure, conceived as a totalising but mobile relationship between subject and object.[113] It is the basic theoretical framework through which a materialist account of social actuality can be developed. In his reconstructive account of this 'general form', Echeverría transposes Marx's conception of the specificity of human labour into a conception of the specificity of human reproduction, arguing that because human practice is not bound to any pre-established instinctual image – and, indeed, is distinguished by the lack of such a 'natural support' – its concrete content must always be given form according to the particular 'political' organisation that governs practical life. This is the 'basic politicity' inherent in the 'socio-natural form of reproduction'. The social subject must therefore consciously and necessarily subsume the natural ('animal') life process under a socio-historically determined form of political community in order to realise it. At the same time, because such a form is always inscribed within a cyclical temporality of biological reproduction (production/consumption) that must continually – and metabolically – re-establish its own validity, that is, the functional correspondence of the 'system of productive capacities' and the 'system of needs for consumption', the social process of establishing and modifying the form of human existence is always 'in play' and subject to change through the practical, collective action of its individual members in these two basic phases (it is therefore, necessarily, a *dynamic* politicity with a disjunctive structure). This contestability and dynamism is what distinguishes the socio-natural form of reproduction from purely natural being, which, according to Hegel, knows only repetition.[114] The active relation is determined, on the one hand, by its productive or creative moment as labour or production – the moment of *objectification* – and, on the other, by its receptive, affirmative or destructive moment as consumption or enjoyment (*Genuss*) – the moment of *subjectivation*: 'The person objectifies himself in production, the thing subjectifies itself in [consumption]', Marx states in the *Grundrisse*.[115] They form the *two modalities* of the metabolic relation to nature as it is conceived in process: in a first moment, as the realisation of the subject through the production of the object, and in the second as the realisation of the object in consumption that (re)produces

---

113  Echeverría 1984. Echeverría 2014 is based on a slightly revised version of the same text.
114  Hegel 1953.
115  Marx 1993, p. 89, translation modified in accordance with the German, Nicolaus instead gives 'the person'.

the subject. The realisation of the human's animal reproduction is therefore necessarily and exclusively tied to the reproduction of a socio-political order, while, conversely, the socio-political order is bound to the fulfilment of the basic physiological reproduction of the social subject. Not only are the natural and social aspects of human existence therefore mediated through one another in spite of their non-identity, but, as Echeverría points out, humanity re-establishes – precisely in its capacity 'to take the sociality of human life as a substance to which it can give form', to 'trans-naturalize' its 'animal' existence, and thus act as a 'subject' – the general lawfulness of nature at the same time as it transcends it.[116] This is also why, ultimately, for Schmidt, 'the different economic formations of society which have succeeded each other historically have been so many modes of nature's self-mediation.'[117]

At least three principal levels of systematic functioning are dialectically interwoven in this conception of the reproductive process as the most general structure of social materiality. Each of these acts as a delimiting condition of the subsequent one, but is nonetheless underdetermined in relation to it, and re-signified or rearticulated by the one that follows, giving it a greater concretion in its specification of the actuality of the process as a whole. These are, firstly, the *mechanical* processes occurring within space and time, the basic interaction of physical objects within a closed system as a whole (intuitive materiality or the general lawfulness of nature); secondly, the *physiological* reproduction process of organic life in the cycle of metabolic transformations, of the integration and expulsion of matter/energy through which an organic totality is able to maintain its vital functioning, that is, animal reproduction; thirdly, the *historically* determined but radically open collective and technical form of the activities and objects that make up the specifically human realisation of the reproductive process, namely, 'culture', 'mode of life', or what Echeverría calls the 'socio-natural form' of reproduction. Each successive process must meet the basic conditions set by the previous, more ontologically basic order, but at the same time supersedes the possibilities of signification or ontological registration (i.e., *actuality*) proper to that systemic level. Each process is thus subsumed and re-coded by principles of unity and coherence given by the higher one without at the same time abolishing its determining presence or internal logics of organisation and action. This recalls Marx's assertion that 'properties of a thing do not arise from its relation to other things, they are, on the contrary, merely *activated* by such relations' and reaffirms

---

116   Echeverría 1998b, pp. 77–8.
117   Schmidt 1971, p. 79.

the sense in which social existence is defined as a process of natural-history, where the realisation of natural functions has no independent 'sense' outside of its distinct historical forms of concretion and the social context enabling them.[118]

This grounding of the historicity of praxis in the socio-natural reproduction process is, ultimately, the distinguishing feature of Marx's materialism in its most developed 'general' structure, where the reproduction process is conceived of as a theoretical totality. It has the unique form of a constitutively underdetermined totality that escapes the closure of idealist philosophical systems because it displaces the process of the production of actuality – the reciprocity of the subject as act and of the object as its product – from its enclosure within both the circuit of consciousness (Kant) and the speculative development of absolute (Hegel), rendering it no longer the exclusive doing of a subject that would be produced or affirmed *a priori* (process as tautology for idealism) and locating it instead in the *historical* process in its – as yet to be determined – concrete 'density' and variability. It is now a genetic subjectivation as much as an immanent objectivation, an active and incidental production of a subject that acts through the praxis in which it loses it pure character as a 'prime mover' and is instead mediated and co-constituted by the objective forms of its realisation, thus suffering the continual and simultaneous loss and re-assumption of its power to give form to the object, itself and the total reproductive process. The process of constitution is no longer the sovereign work of a will that would be merely in contradiction with itself, but is instead mediated through the objective forms of its realisation, so that the quality of being a subject (in what would be its critical-idealist conception) is only a *possible* and *partial* predication of the individuals that enact the practical process: hence Sartre's assertion that praxis is 'an experience both of necessity and of freedom'.[119] In terms of a realisation of the rational – however ambivalent such an ideal is rendered by the critique of an ideality independent of non-ideal, practical actuality – a self-determining or genuinely free subject is only the horizon of the revolutionary process, not its premise.

---

118    Andrew Sayer articulates this in terms of 'emergent powers': 'Just as water has powers irreducible to those of hydrogen and oxygen; just as human beings as organisms have powers irreducible to the chemical processes which constitute them, so certain combinations of material and social relations produce social structures which have emergent powers. And it's in virtue of these emergent powers that "higher stratum objects" intentionally or unintentionally react back upon lower strata, not by "breaking" natural necessities, but by exploiting contingency at the lower levels' (Sayer 1998, p. 131).

119    Sartre 2004, p. 79.

This underdeterminacy not only leaves Marx's theory of social reproduction open to the possibility of historical concretion but in fact *demands* this concretion if it is to attain a properly critical character. By itself, a theory of reproduction in its general form is insufficient to account for the specific 'logics' or 'forms' of the different structures of socio-natural being and their transformation in the process because the unity of its moments do not form a self-concretising subject capable of establishing substantial form (this would be to reinstate Hegel's idealism of immanent development). As Hall points out, production and consumption are

> linked by an 'inner connection'. Yet this 'inner connection' is *not* a simple identity, which requires only the reversal or inversion of the terms of the syllogism into one another. The inner connection here passes through a distinct process. It requires what Marx, in his earlier critique of Hegel, called a 'profane' history: a process in the real world, a process through historical time, each moment of which requires its own determinate conditions, is subject to its own inner laws, and yet is incomplete without the other.[120]

The problem that follows from this – and that will form the basis for an engagement with the concrete actuality of the capitalist mode of reproduction and the role of subsumption within it – is that of how the abstract freedom of labour and the disjunctive temporal structure of the *reproduction* process act as the bearer of this 'profane' historical *development* (supra-cyclically), and, conversely, how the ongoing process of historical *development* and transformation penetrates the cycle itself, stamps its concrete character (both subjectively and objectively), and determines the horizons and mediations of form-determining activity within the immediate context of *reproduction*. In its developed processual form, the idea of natural history taken up from Marx by Adorno can be thought of as 'reproduction-development': The process of social reproduction 'bears' within it an (at least potential) dynamic of historical development, whilst historical development always occurs through the necessary realisation of the reproduction of individuals and their social relations. The significance of this dialectical couplet lies in the fact that by mediating both reproduction and development through one another, the dual process of their reciprocal realisation and determination remains theoretically open. As Read emphasises, it cannot be specified *a priori* or speculatively with reference to either one of

---

120   Hall 2003, p. 124.

the poles alone. Nor can it be specified according to a fixed configuration that would overdetermine their open possibilities:

> [T]he interrelations of production, consumption, and distribution could be considered as the exposition of a thought of immanence in that it is opposed to both the theoretical assertion of a transcendental scene of determination that remains exterior to that which it determines (as in most forms of economism) or the assumption of a concealed transcendental foundation (as in the anthropological ground of classical economics). A thought of immanence requires that all of the relations (production, distribution, and consumption) must be thought both as effect and cause of each other.[121]

The social reproduction process forms a dynamic totality to which all social relations and determinations are internal, and from which they ultimately derive their systemic 'meaning'. Much like the subject for Kant and Hegel, this 'structure in process' constitutes the compositional totality that defines Marx's developed materialism. For Marx, however, the totalisation of the reproductive process remains effective without thereby implying a theoretical closure or structural overdetermination by which the form and meaning of those internal relations and determinations would be established *a priori* in virtue of the process grasped in its abstractly general structure. Instead, the historical specific conjunction between the elements of reproduction and their ongoing development is a necessary supplement to the theory if it is to produce critical knowledge. The idea of a 'general form' of reproduction does not rest on any naturalistic (i.e., fixed) conception of needs and capacities. Nor does it intend to indicate an original, final or ideal state any more than 'simple commodity circulation' denotes a discrete historical stage in the development of capitalism – it is a 'layer' or phase in a process of conceptual concretion that specifies only minimal conditions but not their realised form. Marx is thus able to think history *through* reproduction without resorting to its totalisation, completion or abortion, which in Hegel's philosophy 'closes' the possibilities of form, composition and development. As Schmidt highlights:

> For Hegel, as well as Marx, reality is a process: 'negative' totality. In Hegelianism, this process appears as a system of reason. That is as a closed ontology, from which human history sinks to the level of being its derivat-

---

121  Read 2003, p. 50.

ive, a mere instance of its application. By contrast, Marx emphasises the independence and the openness of historical development, which cannot be reduced to a speculative logic that all beings must forever obey. Hence 'negativity' comes to refer to something which is limited in time, while 'totality' implies the whole of the modern relations of [re]production.[122]

To reach a concrete conception of this totality, the general theory has to pass through the synchronic multitude of particular forms and grasp their total articulation, not only statically, but as a living dynamic unity: 'Production in general. Particular branches of production. Totality of production' (following the logical schema: universality, particularity, singularity).[123] In doing so, the transhistorical scope of the categories on which this materialism of the social reproduction process is based must be mediated through their historically specific forms of concretion and *vice versa*, as Joseph Fracchia writes:

> Such categories depict transhistorical constants, crucial aspects of all historical epochs and, therefore, essential to the analysis of any given epoch. But it is precisely their 'transhistoricity' that renders them abstract. In order to reach the level of historical specificity, the particular content of these categories within a given socio-economic form must be determined, as must the categorial constellation that is peculiar to that form and consists of both transhistorically abstract *and* historically specific categories.[124]

This dialectical tension between transhistorically abstract and historically specific categories is absolutely fundamental for the critical effectivity of Marx's materialism, allowing it to distinguish between, for example, 'the *universal determinants* of ... labour, which it has in common with every other manner of working' and specific form taken by labour under capitalist conditions.[125] The historically transient character of this latter form – *value* – is obfuscated by bourgeois political economy, which naturalises it as an inherent aspect of all productive human activity. Marx's deconstruction of the apparent naturalness of value works precisely by contrasting it against the 'universally necessary' – but at the same time negative and insubstantial – categories of reproduction,

---

122  Schmidt 1981, p. 31 (modified translation given in Bellofiore and Riva 2015, p. 28).
123  Marx 1993, p. 86.
124  Fracchia 2004, p. 128, emphasis added.
125  Marx 1988, p. 64, emphasis added.

demonstrating the centrality of this materialist framework to his critique of political economy: It establishes 'the relation between the synchronic study of the capitalist mode of production and the diachronic reflection required to delineate capitalism's historical specificity – the relation, that is, between social critique and historical theory'.[126] In this sense, reproduction in general 'is an abstraction, but a rational abstraction', and even though, like labour, it 'makes a historic appearance in its full intensity only in the most developed conditions of society', its critical validity is no less forceful and integral to the comprehension of actual social forms.

## 7  Conclusion

Beginning with the contradictions of the idealist account of actuality, in which conceptual and subjective relations function to speculatively enclose and overdetermine activity or process, Marx (along with Engels in many important respects) adopts a series of increasingly coherent and comprehensive conceptual frameworks uniting actuality, activity and social being, moving from *praxis* to *production/consumption* and finally to *social reproduction*, as the most determinate general structure within which the production of actuality and the role of subsumption within that production can be thought. How does this materialism of the social reproduction process impact upon the problem of subsumption as it is inherited from idealist philosophy? Firstly, Marx's materialism challenges the sovereignty of concepts taken independently of their practico-social mode of existence, placing the status of conceptual categories into question on the basis of their non-conceptual conditions. At the same time, however, Marx does not simply install a new conception of the relationship between conceptuality and practice that would transcend the particularity of every context in which it exists; he goes further, abolishing the possibility of a universally valid configuration between these two spheres that could be grasped theoretically. In doing so, he displaces the problem of knowledge into the sphere of critical-historical analysis, opening the way for a multitude of socio-historical *logics*. A limited autonomy of the intellectual sphere is nonetheless preserved, whilst it is simultaneously grounded on the socio-practical forms from which it must ultimately derive its meaning and validity. The task of criticism must be to develop the relation between any sphere of partial truth (i.e., region of specific practicality) and the combined and living totality or

---

126  Fracchia 2004, p. 128.

force-field within which it moves. It is precisely from the unique shape of this relationship that the meaning and actuality of any form or practice must be established (rather than simply being able to reduce it to the totality unilaterally, as 'economism' does). This relationship between specific social forms, be they intellectual or 'manual', and the totality of composition can only be developed in the basis of a historically specific 'categorial constellation' defining the configuration and development of reproductive moments:

> In all forms of society there is one specific kind of production which predominates over the rest, whose relations thus assign rank and influence to the others. It is a general illumination which bathes all the other colours and modifies their particularity. It is a particular ether which determines the specific gravity of every being which has materialised within it.[127]

It is through subsumption under the historically specific categories of (re)production that the determinate forms and 'logic' of social being proper to a society are generated. Subsumption under conceptual categories is thus supplanted within Marx's materialism by a far broader and more dynamic theory of subsumption under social categories. It is from here that a theory of capitalist subsumption emerges as the historically specific logic of domination in the bourgeois epoch. Even as Marx progresses to this concrete level and focuses his theoretical energies on the system of economic categories, the critical force of this transhistorical framework is not lost but condensed into two decisive concepts: 'use-value' (or 'natural form') and 'concrete labour'. It is these that are subsumed by the abstract categories of capital and that adopt specific social forms as a result, as well as generating a specific set of conflicts and tendencies immanent to both production and reproduction. But even in spite of the systematic and expansive character of that subsumption, retaining the core coordinates of Marx's materialism is vital in affirming the critical insistence that 'society is no solid crystal, but an organism capable of change, and constantly engaged in a process of change'.[128]

---

127    Marx 1993, pp. 106–7.
128    Marx 1976, p. 93.

CHAPTER 3

# Capitalist Subsumption: Abstraction in Action

When Marx begins to outline the idea of a 'subsumption of labour under capital' in his critique of political economy, he explicitly draws together two discourses that have a crucial but unresolved relationship in his work. These were the subject of the first two sections of this thesis. The first, the philosophical-critical concept of subsumption, describes a relation and process of *logical* form-determination through which heterogeneous elements are integrated and unified within a self-sufficient totality (paradigmatically the transcendental or absolute subject). The second, Marx's materialism of the social reproduction process (which emerges from the first via a critical negation of its ideal and subjective character) establishes an account of *social* form-determination grounded in collective human activity and 'the sum of relationships and conditions' that constitute that activity as a historical 'structure-in-process' at the same time as being constituted by it.[1]

Capitalist subsumption (or 'subsumption under capital') involves a peculiar synthesis of these two ideas of form determination: the logical and the social. Not only, as we have established, do logical or abstract relations form a specific moment of the socio-practical life world (the domain of thinking, science and ideology), but, where capitalist relations of production prevail, a certain mode of abstract conceptuality (the abstraction of economic value) develops a pseudo-autonomous social existence – a 'purely social' or 'spectral' objectivity – that comes to shape that world, becomes its dominant principle of organisation and movement, as well as forming the basis for one of the primary modes of exercising power within it. Hans-Jürgen Krahl pointed towards this distinguishing aspect of capitalism when he argued, commenting on Marx's 1857 'Introduction', that 'Marx tries to demonstrate that, precisely in capitalist society there exists a determinate connection between abstraction and reality'.[2] The 'determinate connection' alluded to here is subsumptive: in capitalist societies, the concrete (i.e., the material life of society in its practical process of reproduction) is mediated, determined, unified and repressed by the abstractions of capital. These abstractions, or social forms,

---

1   I take the term 'structure-in-process' from Zeleny 1980, p. 217 (fn). Schmidt alights on a similar formulation – 'system in process' – in Schmidt 1981, p. 47.
2   Krahl 1978, p. 15.

come to act as the 'functions' by which individuals and their activity are related, brought into community and realised. It is in this sense that, in capitalist society, we find reproduced at the level of material practice and social relations the subsumptive structure of form-determination and conceptual incorporation expounded in the philosophical systems of Kant and Hegel. Abstract universals (value-forms) give shape and order to concrete reality by subsuming distinct elements (social individuals, natural objects) – the 'particulars' synthesised according to the concept or function which they are subsumed under.

Capital thus comes to fulfil a form-determining function at the level of the material life and historical existence of the human. Once capitalist economic relations take hold of the circulation and production of social wealth in human communities, pre-existing practices, identities and forms of sociality are transformed by their subsumption under its peculiar logics of commodification, quantification and accumulation. 'The strength of capital', Richard Gunn notes, 'is its capacity to re-form pre-capitalist relations as its own mediations and thereby to translate them into modes of existence of itself'.[3]

This particularising internalisation is the subsumptive procedure *par excellence*: Capitalist economic relations have a logical and 'impersonal' character and subsumption under them involves integration along a vector of abstract universality rather than through singular or arbitrary modes of interpersonal valuation and domination. Thus when Marx claims in the *Grundrisse* that 'individuals are now ruled by abstractions, whereas earlier they depended on one another', it expresses the qualitative transition in the form of political subordination brought about by capitalist relations.[4] At the same time, however, despite their abstractness, the apparently 'egalitarian' social relations and 'impersonal' power through which the forms of value operate and under which individuals are subsumed 'are very far from being an abolition of "relations of dependence"; they are rather the dissolution of these relations into a general form'.[5] Despite its concrete-abstractness (and despite a number of 'progressive', or at least politically ambivalent tendencies that can pertain to it), subsumption under capital must therefore be recognised as a new historical figure taken by domination and exploitation in the modern epoch: 'catastrophic violence in the latest

---

3  Gunn 1987, p. 61.
4  'The definedness of individuals, which in the former case appears as a personal restriction of the individual by another, appears in the latter case as developed into an objective restriction of the individual by relations independent of him and sufficient unto themselves' (Marx 1993, p. 164).
5  Ibid.

form of injustice', to use Adorno's formulation.⁶ As the mediating economic relation which acts as the 'automatic subject' of social production, capital is not simply a process of abstract domination (as Moishe Postone would have it) but also the mystified form through which the social power of the dominant class is exercised and reproduced.⁷

This chapter sets out the conditions, structure and effects of this 'general form' of abstract relationality in terms of the specific manner in which it comes to rule over and 'subsume' individuals and the social process of production. It is the practical processes and forms through which the abstractions of value are *actualised* that are at stake here and taken as the object of enquiry rather than a critique of their status as abstractions. Marx is clear that it is not simply the abstractness of capitalist relations, but rather their social autonomisation – the fact that they are 'intellectual [*geistige*] relations that take on a life of their own', as Adorno puts it – which is the source of their socially oppressive character as well as their (practical) truth.⁸ For Marx, 'those who consider the autonomisation [*Verselbstständigung*] of value as a mere abstraction forget that the movement of industrial capital is this abstraction in action.'⁹ Abstraction *per se* is thus not the critical issue here.¹⁰ Instead the primary concern is to grasp capital 'in action' as an economic abstraction in the process of becoming concrete, and, as a result, the concrete becoming a 'perverted' [*verrückte*] reality that is not 'ruled by reason' or collective interest but by the logic of boundless accumulation such that 'in modern bourgeois society all relations are *in practice* subsumed under the one abstract monetary and commercial relationship'.¹¹

Subsumption under the 'repressive abstraction' of the value-form and its expanded reproduction reveals itself to be the defining aspect of capitalist

---

6   Adorno 2003, pp. 93–94. Marx's comments on the wage-relation also affirm this: 'The constant sale and purchase of labour-power, and the constant entrance of the commodity produced by the worker himself as buyer of his labour-power and as constant capital, appear merely as forms which mediate his subjugation by capital. ... This form of mediation is intrinsic to this mode of production. ... It is a form, however, which can be distinguished *only formally* from other more direct forms of the enslavement of labour and the ownership of it as perpetrated by the owners of the means of production' (Marx 1976, p. 1063).
7   Postone 1993.
8   Adorno 2018 p. 154; Krahl affirms this: 'Abstraction, as Marx understands it, is repressive abstraction. Capitalist production, as production for production and not for consumption, forces upon individuals an abstraction defined by Marx as abstraction from interests, needs and use-values' (Krahl 1978, p. 30).
9   Marx 1978a, p. 185.
10  Osborne 2004, p. 21.
11  Marx and Engels 1998, p. 433, translation modified, emphasis added.

power and, furthermore, names the *process* of subordination specific to capitalism (such that subsumption and subordination in the context of capital are at times used synonymously by Marx) as well as distinguishing the form of social reproduction corresponding to it from all other previously (and currently) existing forms of social organisation and class oppression. It is therefore precisely through an understanding of capitalist subsumption that we can most comprehensively grasp the nature of the domination that arises on the basis of capitalist social relations.

This view, and the importance it ascribes to the concept of subsumption, represents a departure from typical accounts of both capitalist power and capitalist subsumption, including, in a certain sense, Marx's own account. Marx's presentation of the concept from the early 1860s onwards focuses primarily on the distinction between the 'formal' and 'real' modes of labour's subsumption, and the majority of interpretations limit themselves to following this lead. By contrast, without disregarding this distinction (indeed, it remains crucial) in what follows, it will be necessary to develop a far more wide-ranging and dynamic theory of capitalist subsumption, as *the* concept of capitalist domination as such and the key to thinking the structure and development of capitalist societies as well as the multiple modes of antagonism and resistance within them.

However, there are theoretical difficulties here which are, at least in part, textually grounded. Whilst Chris Arthur rightly notes that the concept of subsumption 'is important to the whole architectonic of the presentation of *Capital*', its place and function change with each successive set of working manuscripts in which Marx developed his 'mature' critique of political economy.[12] Most notably, and perhaps symptomatically, explicit discussion of subsumption is almost completely eradicated from the final published text of *Capital* volume one (although its presence can be registered throughout the entirety of the long sections on absolute and relative surplus-value production) indicating, as Gilbert Skillman has argued, 'a fundamental change in the structural

---

12   Arthur 2009, pp. 148–62. The manuscripts are those collected as the *Grundrisse* (1857–9), the 1861–3 manuscripts, the 1863–5 manuscripts, and finally the first volume of *Capital* (along with manuscripts that would be incorporated into Engel's editions of volumes 2 and 3). The extent to which these four sets of manuscripts can be viewed as versions of a single coherent 'work' is a matter of debate. Dussel follows the editors of the MEGAII in assuming they do constitute four 'drafts' of his critique of political economy, see Dussel 2001, pp. 10–26. A different view is offered by Heinrich 2009, pp. 71–98 (esp. the table on pp. 86–7). See also: Murray 2009, pp. 163–177; Roberts 2009, pp. 188–201; Skillman 2013, pp. 475–504.

logic of [Marx's] critique'.¹³ Marx was apparently uncertain about the status of the concept and, while there is no explicit textual evidence justifying his 'puzzling decision to obscure and downplay' the account of subsumption in the published version of *Capital*, what he presents in the latter is 'a highly abbreviated and elliptical account of [the subsumption of labour under capital] in which its core concepts are neither defined nor fully characterised'.¹⁴ In light of these ambivalences, any theory of capitalist subsumption will of necessity be a *reconstruction*. This is what I undertake in the following two chapters: firstly, I aim to consolidate and contextualise Marx's fragmented comments about capitalist subsumption at the level of exchange and production with particular reference to his 1861–3 manuscripts and the 'Results of the Immediate Production Process' from 1863–4 (in this chapter); secondly, I address the weaknesses and ambiguities in Marx's discussion, problematising a number of interpretive strategies; lastly, I propose a comprehensive account of capitalist subsumption as a transformative dynamic operative at the level of social reproduction and historical development in the chapter that follows. By drawing on the materialist framework developed in the previous section, it becomes possible to comprehend the valorisation process of capital, not as the unceasing logical movement of an 'abstract, self-moving other' in relation to which class antagonism would be a secondary effect but in terms of its contradictory *articulation* with the 'socio-natural' basis of human practice and the ongoing contestation and transformation of social reality that arises both spontaneously and contingently from this conflictual relation.¹⁵

## 1   The Conditions of Subsumption: So-Called Original Accumulation

The initial act and moment of labour's subsumption and the first form which its confrontation with capital takes is its commodification: the subsumption of labour (and wealth, more generally) under exchange-value that is the condition for its sale and purchase. Only once inscribed within the commodity-form can the formative capacities of labour, as the *labour-power* commodity or 'wage-labour', enter into relation with capital, be appropriated and put to work as one of its 'organs'. Capital's functioning, the existence of labour within capitalist societies, and the entire movement of social reproduction in this form,

---

13   Skillman 2013, p. 479.
14   Skillman 2015.
15   Postone 1993, p. 278.

is thus dependent upon the establishment and perpetual re-enactment of the exchange relation between capital and labour. For Marx, this is a relation of dialectical interpenetration in which 'Capital ... presupposes wage-labour; wage-labour presupposes capital. They condition each other; each brings the other into existence.'[16]

But this mutual presupposition, however valid it may be once capital has taken hold of the social process, is nonetheless tautologous from a historically critical perspective. The dependence of labour and capital on one another which attracts them in their commercial circulation, even their commensurability as values, is not a 'naturally' given condition or disposition of human social being. This is the ahistorical fantasy affirmed by bourgeois political economy, which, as Ellen Wood charges, adheres to a circular 'account of historical development in which the emergence and growth to maturity of capitalism are already prefigured in the earliest manifestation of human rationality'.[17] Instead, for Marx, the commodification of labour – along with the entire capitalist mode of production based upon it – is a peculiar state of affairs that must be produced and therefore has a specific historical origin, a causality irreducible to that generated immanently once capitalist social relations are established:

> This relation has no basis in natural history, nor does it have a social basis common to all periods of human history. It is clearly the result of a past historical development, the product of many economic revolutions, of the extinction of a whole series of older formations of social production.[18]

Marx refers ironically to this historical genesis, satirising a concept derived from Adam Smith, as 'so-called original accumulation' (*sogenannte ursprüngliche Akkumulation*): 'an accumulation which is not the result of the capitalist mode of production but its point of departure'.[19] It is through such an 'accu-

---

16   Marx 1981.
17   Wood has convincingly argued against this error, particularly insofar as it is reproduced unconsciously by Marxist historiography: 'Since historians first began explaining the emergence of capitalism, there has scarcely existed an explanation that did not begin by assuming the very thing that needed to be explained. Almost without exception, accounts of the origin of capitalism have been fundamentally circular: they have assumed the prior existence of capitalism in order to explain its coming into being. ... Capitalism always seems to *be* there, somewhere; and it only needs to be released from its chains' (Wood 2002, pp. 3–4).
18   Marx 1976, p. 273.
19   Ibid., p. 873; Marx 1993, p. 590.

mulation' of social wealth that the most immediate circumstances of labour's subsumption under capital first arise, namely:

> The confrontation of, and the contact between, two very different kinds of commodity owners; on the one hand, the *owners of money, means of production, means of subsistence*, who are eager to valorise the sum of values they have appropriated by buying the labour-power of others; on the other hand, *free workers, the sellers of their own labour-power*, and therefore the sellers of labour.[20]

What is at stake in 'so-called original' or 'primitive' accumulation is therefore a division of social classes based on a differential relationship to property, the monopolistic concentration of productive wealth in the hands of one class and the complete dispossession of the other. But whereas the ideological conception of 'previous accumulation' taken up from Smith by Torrens tells the story of a gradual process of diligent stockpiling by industrious individuals, Marx shows how such 'robinsonades' occlude the violent and conflictual character of this accumulation, which begins with 'the expropriation of producers', primarily peasants. The processes of 'original accumulation' from which the capital-labour relation arises follow a political rather than purely economic logic and consist in a restructuring of society that dissolves the old social bonds tying indivdiuals to one another to their means of survival (typically land) before recomposing them into social classes distinguished on the basis of property ownership: those 'two very different kinds of commodity owners'. As the basic constituents of production that 'really belong together', labour and the means of production through which it can be realised [*verwirklicht*] are torn apart from each other, have their immediate practical unity within the social reproduction process annulled, such that they end up standing opposed to each other in the guise of 'independent persons' and classes with antagonistic interests.[21] This does not only effect a separation of the 'social subject' from its 'practical object'. It equally entails a progressive liquidation of the social subject's collective unity and the introduction of a mediating form of impersonal, competitive sociality in the form of juridical property relations between 'free

---

20   Marx 1976, p, 874, emphasis added.
21   'The historic process was the divorce of elements which up until then were bound together; its result is therefore not that one of the elements disappears, but that each of them appears in a negative relation to the other – the (potentially) free worker on the one side, capital (potentially) on the other.' Marx 1993, p. 503.

and equal' persons.²² Communities and communal forms of property (such as common lands) are dissolved into atomised legal subjects and their private property, as in the famous case of the 'enclosure acts' which Marx takes as an exemplar of this form of accumulation by dispossession.

In the case of England at least, the expropriation of peasants from the lands that are their means of production and subsistence was for Marx a key condition of possibility for the transition to a capitalist mode of production and the subsumption of labour, 'the premiss on the basis of which the sale and purchase of labour-power can proceed and living labour can be absorbed into dead labour as a means of maintaining and increasing it, i.e., of enabling it to valorise itself'.²³ This 'law-making violence' inaugurated a whole new set of conditions under which society's reproduction could take place, based on 'the transformation of feudal exploitation into capitalist exploitation'.²⁴ On the one hand, there was an immense concentration of objective wealth in the hands of landowners and capitalists. On the other, there was a mass 'liberation' (i.e., expulsion) of labour from both its feudal obligations and its means of subsistence, leaving it apparently 'vogelfrei' ('free as a bird') – both free to buy and sell its property as it chooses, without obligations to a lord or master, but also free of anything to buy or sell other than its own subjective capacity to toil, 'that very labour-power which exists only in [its] living body'.²⁵

However, even as 'a mass of 'free' and unattached proletarians was hurled onto the labour-market by the dissolution of the bonds of feudal retainer', it was by no means an automatic result that capital found at its disposal a willing and able reserve of productive labourers, readily awaiting exploitation.²⁶ Marx instead suggests that at the dawn of capitalism, '[t]he propertyless are more inclined to become vagabonds and robbers and beggars than workers'.²⁷ What ensued after the decomposition of the peasantry was therefore a process of coercive subjectivation, of 'bloody legislation against the expropriated' in which the state deployed an apparatus of violence and repression, of 'grossly terroristic laws' intended to inure those newly 'denuded subjectivities' to a buyer's market. Marx lists some of the techniques of violent schematisation that arose in that moment – prosecution, torture, imprisonment, branding,

---

22 'The recognition of free and equal individuals, and their subsumption under an abstract social power, are two "sides' of the same coin" (Basso 2013, p. 2).
23 Marx 1976, p. 1017.
24 Marx 1976, p. 875.
25 Marx 1976, p, 272.
26 Marx 1976, p. 979.
27 Marx 1993, p. 736.

enslavement – all designed to elicit in the worker a willingness to give up sovereignty over their own life-activity at a price expedient to the 'rising bourgeoisie': 'Disgraceful proceedings of the state which employed police methods to accelerate the accumulation of capital by increasing the degree of exploitation of labour'.[28] Jairus Banaji highlights the importance of these coercive policies by pointing out that, whilst forms of waged labour existed in many different places and times throughout history, 'what was distinctive about agrarian, mining and industrial capital was not the existence of wage-labour markets *but their forcible creation*'.[29]

The ultimate effect of all of this 'immediate extra-economic violence' [*außerökonomische unmittelbare Gewalt*], was, historically speaking, to set in motion the economic cycle and 'logic' of capitalist accumulation ('accumulation by exploitation') whose conditions could then perpetuate themselves as if they were 'natural laws of production'. The historical function of the processes identified by Marx as 'so-called original accumulation' was to inscribe subjects of labour within a social configuration in which their subsumption to capital was underwritten both materially (in their separation from 'all the objects needed for the realisation of [their] labour-power' as well as through regulative mechanisms such as 'relative surplus populations') and ideologically (insofar as it 'develops a working class which by education, tradition and habit looks upon the requirement of that mode of production as self-evident natural laws').[30] By offering destitute proletarians no other means for their reproduction than to bring themselves to the market place, to present their subjective capacity in the form of objective wealth, a commodity to be exchanged (the use-value 'promise' of labour-power), their social being was systematically captured within the representational order of economic value proper to capitalist reproduction.[31] It is this formalisation and generalisation of labour as a commodity that first opened the possibility of its subsumptive internalisation to capital through exchange.

But just as it has no natural or eternal basis, there is no necessity or innate historical tendency towards this dispossession and commodification of labour. Rather, it is the outcome of a series of complex and diverse processes of social transformation shaped by multiple inter- and intra-class conflicts, demographic changes, geopolitical upheavals and commercial and technological

---

28   Marx 1976, p. 905.
29   Banaji 2009, emphasis added.
30   Marx 1976, pp. 272–3; p. 899.
31   See Haug 2006, pp. 18–24.

innovations (which, although concentrated in England, were not the endogenous outcome of a 'hermetically sealed' domestic or even exclusively European context).[32] It is also crucial to note, as Bonefeld and Tomba do, that both 'accumulation by dispossession' and state-arbitrated coercion against those who 'refuse to work' are permanent rather than 'exceptional' features of any society that reproduces itself on a capitalist basis, albeit to varying degrees of spread and density (this is something about which Marx was equivocal).[33] Rather than extra-economic violence simply subsiding into the 'mute compulsion of economic relations' with the generalisation of wage relations, we can detect a far more complex oscillation between the two, one that is modulated by the struggles between class actors and for the most part arbitrated by state institutions. Here, however, from a 'genetic' standpoint, it is sufficient merely to grasp the violence of separation in terms of its significance as a historical intervention in the social reproduction process (the *substance* of social being) that precipitates a mutation in its structure (its historic *form*). With this mutation, the process through which society reproduces itself begins to be recomposed according to a new politico-economic order based on capitalist relations of production and economic classes. This mutation is the condition of possibility for labour's subsumption under the commodity form of capital and gives rise to a whole new set of relations, conflicts and dynamics which are immanent to that subsumption.

## 2   Exchange: Subsumption under Value

The separation of social individuals and means of production effected by those processes gathered under the euphemism of 'original accumulation' thus forms the 'historic presupposition' of the capitalist social relation through which they are subsequently composed and reproduced. The point at which the

---

32   See Anievas and Nisancioglu 2015, ch. 6 and 7; Tomba 2013, pp. 167–8: 'The state's intervention in conflicts is an instrument that aims to monopolise violence and neutralise conflicts, not simply to look after the affairs of one class. Given the fact that, in some historical periods, there may be conflicts between different segments of the ruling classes, and between these and other non-proletarian and not fully synchronised sectors, like smallholders and declassed middleclass strata, what emerges is a conflict between political temporalities that may have different outcomes. The state-mechanism attempts to synchronise these temporalities, even by using asynchronous temporalities against each other.'

33   On the issue of 'permanent primitive accumulation', see Bonefeld 2002; Bonefeld 1988, pp. 54–66; Tomba 2013 (appendix).

extraordinary transition to this mode of production ceases is the point at which the separation of productive elements congeals into the determinate social forms proper to capital, those forms that, in their practical interconnection, are both the starting point and result of capitalist production – its *systematic* presuppositions: commodity, money, wages, abstract labour, credit, etc. Through these forms, Bonefeld argues, 'the historic form of primitive accumulation is raised to a new level where its original form and independent existence is eliminated (or cancelled) at the same time as its substance or essence [*Wesenhaftigkeit*] is maintained, putting it on to a new footing.'[34] Capital's 'historical' presuppositions are therefore 'suspended [*aufgehoben*] in its being', carried over into the 'systematic' presuppositions that are reproduced on an ever expanded scale once production on a capitalist basis is underway. (This separation of the historic and systematic is, to say the least, problematic, and we will complicate it further in what follows, but it here serves a useful heuristic function – to distinguish as Marx does between 'conditions of [capital's] becoming' and 'results of its presence'.)[35] The social forms of capital are then precisely those modes of objectivity under which labour and society (as a practical totality) are subsumed in the course of their realisation and reproduction on a capitalist basis. More specifically, they are abstract forms of wealth – the practical object through which society reproduces itself – registered economically as value and 'autonomised' as capital, a 'social relation existing as being-for-itself'.[36]

The most 'elementary' of these forms is the commodity, which Marx famously takes as the starting point of his exposition in *Capital*. It is as commodities that the separated elements of production are brought to market

---

34  Bonefeld 2002, p. 4.
35  Marx 1993, p. 460.
36  Ibid., p. 302. Echeverría highlights the objectivism guiding Marx's theoretical approach: 'to speak of the contradiction between value and use-value is to make a biased reference to society's reproduction process as such; it is to deal with society by way of the object through which it reproduces itself, which is to say, of its wealth, of the products/goods that it produces and consumes. When we speak of value and use-value we make reference to the reproduction of the produced and consumed object. The theory selects a determined element of that process in order to – in analysing it – discover or specify determinate characteristics of the global contradiction. This methodological procedure avoids for a moment the entirety of the reproduction process and adjusts itself exclusively to an object: to the object in so far as it is produced and consumed in order to give rise precisely to that process of reproduction' (Echeverría 1998a, pp. 10–11). Seen in this way Marx's method might be correlated methodologically with what Sartre referred to as 'totalising compression', see Sartre 1991, p. 49.

by their different owners and schematised in the act of exchange, and as a commodity that labour comes to be subsumed by capital. This schematisation is possible, firstly, because the commodity is 'the immediate unity of use-value and exchange-value'; its internal structure conjoins the transhistorical socio-practical objectivity of the product of labour with an abstract economic objectivity specific to capitalist society (the value that is expressed relationally as a quantitative equivalence between different commodities).[37] Rotta and Teixeira conceptualise the distinction between these two aspects of the commodity as one between concrete and abstract wealth, reminding us that, just as with concrete and abstract labour, these are 'not two types of wealth but the two co-existing determinations of the same wealth produced in capitalism':[38] Co-existing determinations which nevertheless, as Chris Arthur argues, correspond to 'two different regions of being in which what is present in the one region is absent in the other'.[39] It is this Janus-faced objectivity that leads Marx to describe the commodity as 'an immediate contradiction' and Hans-Jürgen Krahl to suggest that whilst its 'concept is real' (i.e., socially actual) 'it is a negative phenomenon', i.e., it cannot be grasped empirically or even in practical terms but only critically, dialectically, by 'the power of abstraction', as Marx says in his preface to the first volume of *Capital*.[40]

We have already seen in the analysis of the reproduction process what, in its most general (*historically underdetermined*) sense, the content of this wealth is in its concrete or 'natural form' of objectivity: '[C]onsidered as use-values, they are both material conditions of labour and products of labour', i.e., goods for consumption (be it productive or unproductive) whose practical significance is determined by their situation and effects within a process of social reproduction.[41] By contrast, the content of the commodity in its 'value form' is nothing more than an abstractly conceived quantum of society's total wealth into which 'not an atom of matter enters'.[42] It is devoid of any reference to the commodity's specific practicality, the concrete qualities of the labour that gave rise to it, or the technical structure of the society to which it belongs. Instead, the commodity's value is determined solely by the portion of total social labour *time* objectified in it (that is, labour that is socially necessary and abstractly general: 'abstract labour'). It is thus only *temporally* that value registers a con-

---

37   Marx cited in Reichelt 2005, p. 31.
38   Rotta and Teixeira 2015, p. 4.
39   Arthur 2001, p. 34.
40   Krahl 1978, p. 27; Marx 1976, p. 90.
41   Marx 1971.
42   Marx 1976, p. 138.

nection with the social process to which it belongs, although this is expressed concretely in the form of the relative magnitudes in which one commodity exchanges for another, its exchange-value.

The 'immediately contradictory' structure of the commodity bears the internal opposition of these two modes of social objectivity: a socio-natural form (use-value) and a socio-capitalist form (value).[43] It is important to clarify that what is at stake in this opposition is not reducible to the distinction between matter and form or the 'natural' and 'social' dimensions of the commodity.[44] In order to avoid this distortion, we must retain the distinction Marx makes in his *Theses On Feuerbach* between 'sensuousness' [*Sinnlichkeit*] and 'intuition' [*Anschauung*]. Sensuousness, for Marx, is not a passive modality of relation (as intuition is) but rather one of intentional interaction in the determinate context of a social process of production and consumption: 'sensuousness as practical activity'.[45] Conceptualising objectivity in sensuous terms already implies a constitutively social dimension that exceeds the merely empirical qualities and the 'single individual' characteristic of the object of intuition, hence the designation of practical objects as *socio-natural*, as constituted in the historical dialectic of the metabolism between nature and humanity. This practical objectivity is a quality basic to wealth in all forms of society, although it is only in its capitalist form that it takes on the form of use-value (i.e., of an internal aspect of the commodity) and becomes a theoretically salient category in contradistinction to exchange-value.[46] By contrast, insofar as the commodity is a value, it 'changes into a thing which transcends sensuousness', thus transcending its concrete practical objectivity and its uses.[47] The value-form of the commodity not only negates the immediate empirical qualities of the object as use-value does, but it also involves a second, historically unique negation of the practical significance the commodity carries as a use-value. The

---

43  See Echeverría 1998a.
44  This is an equivocation (in part present in Marx' own writings) that persists in much contemporary Marxist theory, e.g., Heinrich 2012, pp. 40–41: 'The "natural form" of the chair is simply its material composition (for example, whether it is made of wood or metal). "Social form", on the other hand, means that the chair is a "commodity"'.
45  Marcuse 2005, pp. 98–9. Marcuse's account is interesting but insufficiently developed. For a richer account see Echeverría 1986 ('El materialismo de Marx').
46  'The problem of the 'natural-ness' of social forms and of the definitions of 'use-value' appears emphatically in real life only when capitalist development shatters everywhere the millennial local equilibria between the system of needs for consumption and that of productive capacities; when, in the imperialist enterprise, European Man experienced the relativity of its humanity' (Echeverría 2014, pp. 23–4).
47  Marx 1976, p. 163.

'supersensuousness' of the value-form dissolves that qualitative character into a merely quantitative magnitude, a simple relation of equivalence with other goods. Thus whilst both use-value and value are social objectivities, one is practico-concrete (socio-natural) and the other is abstract-economic (socio-capitalist).

It's not clear, however, that we can already speak of a subsumption when dealing abstractly with the commodity. In fact, in terms of its formal structure the commodity presents only a contradiction ('sensuous-supersensuousness') without its resolution through the subsumption of one term under the other. The commodity also has a long history, its social existence stretching back several millennia at least, long before the preponderance of capitalist relations (Aristotle, for example, famously refers to the coexistence of use-value and exchange-value in things in the *Politics*).[48] But once the wealth of society *as such* takes the form of a vast collection of commodities, and individuals are instutionalised as their owners, that is, as 'free' legal subjects whose principal social relation is based on exchange, then already from a social standpoint an asymmetrical relation between the two poles of the commodity emerges.[49] This is because under conditions of generalised commodity circulation and the private division of social labour (within which useful things are 'produced for the purpose of being exchanged'), it is on the basis of the *economic* rather than practical content of the commodity that productive elements of society as a whole are schematised and brought into community; it is only as *value* and not as a practical object that the product of labour has an immediately 'social' existence (although this is not to suggest that the social aspect of use-value disappears altogether, only that it is subject to mediation, distortion and repression by value).[50] Once comprehended within the ambit of capitalist society as a totality, then, the commodity reveals a structural overdetermination of its inner form whereby 'use-value is universally mediated by exchange-value'.[51] And it is on this level that it must be grasped: For as William Clare Roberts points out,

---

48 Aristotle 1984, I.1257a.
49 'The reciprocal and all-sided dependence of individuals who are indifferent to one another forms their social connection. The social bond is expressed in *exchange value*', Marx 1993, p. 157. It is this socialising function of exchange that at the level of appearance gives rise to the commodity's 'fetish character'.
50 Marx 1976, p. 166; 'In the modern or capitalist epoch, the objects produced and consumed by society can exist only as socially effective objects – produced by some, consumed by all – that is to say, can only *circulate*, amongst the individuals that compose the social subject in so far they have a *value* and are thus exchanged for one another as commodities' (Echeverría 1986, p. 86).
51 Marx 1976, p. 951.

like the other social forms of capital, the commodity cannot 'without grave distortion, be broken down into or analysed in terms of individual agents performing individual actions for the sake of individual goals'.[52] Generalised commodity circulation is a situation that presupposes 'the whole system of bourgeois production ... before exchange-value appears as the simple point of departure on the surface'.[53] Marx's analysis of the commodity therefore refers not to some imagined historical phase or 'model' of pre-capitalist commodity production but dialectically to the process and relations through which the immediacy of its contradiction is suspended (in exchange, production and finally reproduction).[54] The social function and effects of the commodity as determined within a capitalist context, wherein it 'first becomes the *general* form ... that every product has to assume', are unique to this context.[55]

Capitalist social relations thus presuppose the commodity as the *elementary form of social wealth*, a form whose value aspect stands over and above the qualitative particularity of its use-value aspect and subsumes it as a result of its subjection to commercial circulation. At this first level of the contradiction between capital and labour, there is in fact a double subsumption at work. Firstly, the generalised subsumption of use-value to exchange-value: 'sale and purchase seize hold of not only surplus production but also subsistence itself', meaning that all goods are both in principle and in practice subject to exchange.[56] The predominance of exchange establishes a sphere of universal economic equivalence to which all goods belong, a sphere composed of value, as abstract labour in objectivised form, 'dead labour' as Marx often refers to it. Secondly and most importantly, commodification becomes the primary mode of socialisation, not only for goods in society, but also for the activity of the producers themselves, who, compelled by their lack of external property (along with the coercive techniques listed above), participate in exchange by offering their labour on the market in the commodity-form as labour-power. This has phenomenological as well as directly practical consequences insofar as it generates a historically new relation of the worker to his or her own activity: '[T]he totality of the free worker's labour capacity *appears to him* as his property, as one of his moments, over which he, as subject, exercises domination, and which he maintains by expending it.'[57] The peculiar representational prac-

---

52  Roberts 2009, p. 189.
53  Marx cited in Banaji 2015, p. 29.
54  See Campbell 2013, pp. 149–175.
55  Marx 1988, p. 313.
56  Ibid., p. 313.
57  Marx 1993, p. 465, emphasis added.

tice at work here schematises labour's *subjective* activity as an *objective* form, formalising its reality or 'presence' within an economic order of being (this is the core of Marx's early critique of private property and money as alienation).[58] The penetrating reach of this order of being and the dominant actuality of its abstractness is grounded in the political relations by which individuals are inscribed within demarcated class positions, forced to operate within the 'exclusive realm of Freedom, Equality, Property and Bentham'.[59] Thus we can see that 'what is reproduced and produced anew' as a result of the separation of labour and means of production 'is not only the *presence* of these objective conditions of living labour, *but also their presence as independent values*'.[60] Under capitalist social conditions, all things stand in relation to one another as values: Being a value is the condition for 'social' existence. This transpires in a process of 'reification' through which even that which is not inherently objective, an external object, namely 'that very labour-power which exists only in [the worker's] living body', is given a thing-like objectivity, is socially constituted as discretely alienable.[61] Thus not only does commodification involve the abstractive reduction of the qualitative to the quantitative, of use-value to exchange-value, it also depends on a specific act of temporal dissociation between alienation (*Entäusserung*) and manifestation (*Äusserung*) whereby, in Kant's formulation, 'I must be able to think that I am in possession of this object independently of being limited by temporal conditions, and so independently of empirical possession'.[62] The commodification of labour is nothing but this thought systematically actualised at the level of social objectivity and practice. 'Labour-power' synthesises these two reductions (qualitative to quantitative and future to present), giving future concrete activity the present form of an abstract quantum of objectified labour, such that what is purchased is the *promise* of a specific 'expenditure of vital forces' whilst what is paid for is the

---

58  The social actuality of this representational practice is key to grasping the way in which abstract labour is posited as the 'purely social' form of concrete labour, as Fausto notes: 'It is not the biological reality of the universality of labour ... that constitutes abstract labour, but rather the *positing* of this reality, and, in this sense, the *positing* is not biological any more.' Fausto cited in Robles-Baez 2004, p. 152.
59  Marx 1976, p. 280.
60  Marx 1993, p. 462.
61  Marx 1976, p. 272; 'The only thing distinct from *objectified* labour is *non-objectified* labour, labour which is still objectifying itself, *labour* as subjectivity. Or, *objectified* labour, i.e. labour which is *present in space*, can also be opposed, as *past labour*, to labour which is *present in time*. If it is to be present in time, alive, then it can be present only as the *living subject*, in which it exists as capacity, as possibility; hence as *worker*' (Marx 1993, p. 272).
62  Kant 1999b, § 4*b*.

past labour needed to produce those vital forces. Whilst the worker 'sells [themselves] as an effect. [They] are absorbed into the body of capital as a cause, as activity.'[63]

This representational formalisation of labour activity as the labour-power commodity is the single most important aspect of subsumption under commodity exchange as well as being the key to Marx's critique of classical political economy, as he himself stressed:

> Political Economy has indeed analysed, however incompletely, value and its magnitude, and has uncovered the content concealed within these forms. But it has never once asked the question *why labour is represented* [*dargestellt*] *by the value of its product* and *labour-time by the magnitude of that value*.[64]

This insight also forms the basis for Marx's account of capitalist exploitation, given that it is from the differential between what this labour-power is worth (the value of the subsistence goods needed to produce it) and what it is capable of (the value that it can generate during the time it is employed) that surplus-value arises.

Subsumption to commodity circulation subverts the 'traditional' (i.e., pre-modern) relationship between the practical object and the social subject (in both its synchronic and diachronic aspects): Rather than consumption needs and productive capacities directly underpinning the unity of the social process – however unevenly production and consumption may have been organised and distributed historically – they now become 'universally mediated' and unified by the abstractions of value. Exchange relations thus replace the violent schematisation underlying the 'code' of pre-capitalist societies with the abstract and dynamic schematisation of the market, which displaces and defers this violence in such a way as to make the power of individuals over one another reside in the power of their commodities. This effects a uniquely modern displacement of the political itself, sublimates direct political contestation into economic competition and transforms an immediately 'political' community into an economic community made up of abstractly free, self-interested individuals and their administrative-institutional regulation, subsuming them within what Hegel famously conceptualised as 'bourgeois civil society' [*bürgerliche Gesellschaft*].[65]

---

63   Marx 1993, p. 674.
64   Marx 1976, pp. 173–4. I am using Banaji's modified translation in Banaji 2015, p. 31.
65   Neocleous 1995, p. 396.

The reality of this inversion and displacement, as Marx had already argued in 1844, is most clearly expressed in the external objectivity and 'seemingly transcendental power' of money, through which 'the unfettered domination of the estranged thing *over* man becomes manifest'.[66] It is in the form of money that the abstraction of value overcomes its own negativity and achieves an independent, 'sensuous' existence beyond its relational, 'supersensuous' inherence in the body of the diverse use-values that bear it.[67] Money is a commodity among all others, yet it is also the one commodity whose 'natural specificity is extinguished' and that counts *directly* as a 'universal material representative' of value – it *is* value – 'not only a form, but at the same time the content itself. ... general wealth realised, *individualised* in a particular object', 'the true generality [*Allgemeinheit*] of exchange value in substance and in extension'.[68] As the commodity whose use-value *is* its exchangeability, money functions uniquely as a 'socially objective measure of value', which as Tony Smith points out 'is a necessary precondition for generalised commodity exchange'. This connection links the commodity and money together systematically at the core of Marx's value-theory.[69] Money is the crucial mediating form through which the order of value is actualised concretely and penetrates into the order of use-value in its 'self-sufficiency', which is why for the Marx of 1844 it signals the 'corporeal existence' of alienation. In practical terms, the social autonomisation of the value-abstraction in money is expressed in the fact that in the capitalist 'stage of production', it is money that mediates all commodity exchanges (in the metamorphoses C–M, M–C, etc.), acts as the nexus through which the essential elements of the reproduction process are brought into relation, 'forms the starting-point and the conclusion of every valorisation process' and, crucially, schematises *future* and *past* (or concrete and abstract, living and dead) labour in the exchange of labour-power for wages.[70]

---

66   Marx 1993, p. 146; Marx 1992, p. 270.
67   'The internal opposition between use-value and value, hidden within the commodity, is therefore represented on the surface by an external opposition, i.e. by a relation between two commodities such that the one commodity, whose own value is supposed to be expressed, counts directly only as a use-value, whereas the other commodity, in which that value is to be expressed, counts directly only as exchange-value' (Marx 1976, p. 153).
68   Marx 1993, p. 218; p. 165; p. 225. This peculiar quality leads Marx, in a striking passage from the first edition of *Capital*, to suggest that with money 'it is as if alongside and external to lions, tigers, rabbits, and all other actual animals ... there existed in addition *the animal*, the individual incarnation of the entire animal kingdom.' Cited in Nelson 1999, p. 147.
69   Smith 2003, p. 25.
70   Marx 1976, p. 255; See Marx 1993, p. 214: 'As medium of exchange, money appears in the role of necessary mediator between production and consumption. In the developed money

It is in this last function that money enables the initial moment of labour's subsumption under capital, its absorption and command under an abstract social power and its representational positing as *abstract labour* in the act of exchange.[71] This is central to Marx's value-theoretical account of capitalist power, as Diane Elson points out:

> The domination of the abstract aspect of labour, in the forms of value, is analysed, not in terms of the obliteration of other aspects of labour, but in terms of the subsumption of these other aspects to the abstract aspect. That subsumption is understood in terms of the mediation of the other aspects by the abstract aspect, the translation of the other aspects of labour into money form.[72]

As Marx narrates so compellingly in his chapter on 'The Sale and Purchase of Labour-Power' from the first volume of *Capital*, the owner of labour-power and the owner of money meet on the market as formal equals and exchange their respective goods (labour-power and money wages), which are schematised as equivalent sums of value. In doing so, the owner of money (the capitalist) is able to *buy* the right to command and direct a certain amount of the worker's labour time. From the perspective of circulation, Marx calls this 'a simple sale and purchase, a simple relation of circulation, like any other', in the sense that both parties are formally free, exchange commodities of equal value, and enter 'willingly' into the exchange (although this situation is conditioned for the labourer, as we have seen, by the *freedom from* owning any property). Nonetheless, even though 'the specific and distinctive character of the transaction is not apparent', this seemingly equal exchange is 'coloured' by its peculiar content, that of the use-value of labour-power: 'With his money, the money owner has ... bought disposition over labour capacity so that he can use up, consume, this labour capacity as such, i.e. *have it operate as actual labour*, in short, *so that he can have the worker really work*'.[73] This is crucial because what appears as a

---

system, one produces only in order to exchange, or, one produces only by exchanging. Strike out money, and one would thereby either be thrown back to a lower stage of production (corresponding to that of auxiliary barter), or one would proceed to a higher stage, in which exchange value would no longer be the principal aspect of the commodity, because social labour, whose representative it is, would no longer appear merely as socially mediated private labour.'

71   As Alan Freeman argues, 'value is neither reduced to money nor to abstract labour but subsumes a definite relation between the two' (Freeman 2004, p. 60).
72   Elson 2015, p. 174.
73   Marx 1988, p. 64, emphasis added.

merely formal metamorphosis in value terms – of money into commodity – in fact contains concealed within it a relation of subjugation:

> Through the mediation of its sale and purchase it disguises the real transaction, and the perpetual dependence which is constantly renewed, by presenting it as nothing more than a financial relationship. ... The constant renewal of the relationship of sale and purchase merely ensures the perpetuation of the specific relationship of dependency, endowing it with the deceptive illusion of a transaction, of a contract between equally free and equally matched commodity owners.[74]

The compulsion to wage labour, to submission to the command of the capitalist as a condition of possibility of the worker's survival, which is inherent in the class structure of capitalist society, i.e., in the juridical separation of labour from its objective means of realisation, is therefore concealed by the surface appearance of a purely voluntary exchange. As Pierre Macherey explains:

> [T]his exchange occurs within the framework of a power relation wherein one party, the seller, occupies the subordinate position and the other, the buyer, the dominant position, enabling the latter to impose their interests. ... the miracle that the system of wage-labor performs consists in separating power from its action by artificially creating conditions that allow a power to be considered independently from its action, as if a non-acting power, a power that would not be active, would still be a power. From the physical point of view, this is more than a mystery: it is an absurdity.[75]

This point is key, because it renders explicit the degree to which capitalist subsumption *in actu* is premised upon the organisation of individuals into structurally determined class positions, through which the majority section of the body politic is separated from the practical objects needed for its reproduction, thereby allowing relations of domination and alienation to traverse the laws of the market imperceptibly. Through exchange that separation is then – temporarily – suspended: '[Labour] is made into a real activity through contact with capital – it cannot do this by itself, since it is without object'.[76] This is what undergirds labour's mediation by and dependency on capital, which it requires

---

74   Marx 1976, pp. 1063–4.
75   Macherey 2015.
76   Marx 1993, p. 298.

in order to make the transition from capacity [*Vermögen*] or potency [*dynamis*] to an effectively actualised power [*Kraft*].[77]

Historically, this exchange of labour-power for wages is how the reabsorption of dispossessed workers into capitalist production processes paradigmatically (although not exclusively) took place (and indeed is how it continues to do so). Money therefore appears as a definitive factor in the dissolution of non-capitalist modes of reproduction and their incorporation into the circuits of capitalist accumulation, as Marx points out:

> Money wealth neither invented nor fabricated the spinning wheel and the loom. But, once unbound from their land and soil, spinner and weaver with their stools and wheels came under the command of money wealth. ... When the formation of capital had reached a certain level, monetary wealth could place itself as mediator between the objective conditions of life, thus liberated, and the liberated but also homeless and emptyhanded labour powers, and buy the latter with the former.[78]

Once established, however, it is also in a 'logical' sense that the wage is 'one of the essential mediating forms of capitalist relations of production, and one constantly reproduced by those relations themselves.'[79] It is what enables the transition from labour's subsumption under commodity-value to its subsumption under capital. The purchase of labour-power is the basis for its subsequent determination as activity that is productive for capital, that can be set to work in order to *valorise* and therefore *become* capital: '[T]hrough the exchange with the worker, capital has appropriated labour itself; labour has become one of its moments, which now acts as a fructifying vitality upon its merely existent and hence dead objectivity.'[80] It is the means by which the worker, qua living labour, qua labour-power commodity, is incorporated into capital, functionally determined as one of the elements – the essential element in fact – of its life-process: *variable capital*.

This functional determination, which Marx calls 'functional form' in the second volume of *Capital*, is in general what constitutes *belonging to* capital or *being as* capital.[81] It has a mode of operation distinct from representational

---

77  Dussel 2001, ch. 1.
78  Marx 1993, pp. 507–9.
79  Marx 1976, p. 1064.
80  Marx 1993, p. 298.
81  'What is at issue here is not a set of definitions under which things are to be subsumed. It is rather definite functions that are expressed in specific categories' (Marx 1978a, p. 303).

value-determination, which, although still practically constituted is simply an abstractly differential relation (an 'axiomatic of abstract quantities' in Deleuze and Guatarri's terms).[82] Marx is clear that, contra political economy, capital and its forms (e.g., fixed, circulating) cannot be defined empirically or typologically, cannot be reduced to some set of 'natural properties' possessed by things in themselves:

> The crude materialism of the economists who regard as the natural properties of things what are social relations of production between people, and qualities which things obtain because they are subsumed under these relations, is at the same time just as crude an idealism, even fetishism, since it imputes social relations to things as inherent characteristics, and thus mystifies them.[83]
>
> In themselves money and commodities are no more capital than means of production and subsistence are.[84]

Capital is constituted processually, through and as a 'social relation of production' within which its elements and forms are situated functionally; it is an internally structured totality that particularises itself in those things that it determines *subsumptively* as its own moments (conceptually, the model for such a totality is the subject, above all in its Hegelian conception, as authors such as Arthur and Dussel have argued).[85] A discrete social element therefore becomes capital only by virtue of being assigned a place in the total process of capitalist accumulation, what Marx refers to as capital's life-process [*Lebensprozess*]. This is how it can be the case 'that many things are subsumed under capital which do not seem to belong within it conceptually'.[86] The historically specific function given to productive and economic elements within capitalist reproduction transforms their social and practical character, as Patrick Murray has pointed out:

---

82  Deleuze and Guatarri 2004, p. 249.
83  Marx 1993, p. 687.
84  Marx 1976, p. 874.
85  'Money always remains the same form in the same substratum; and can thus be more easily conceived as a mere thing. But one and the same commodity, money etc., can represent capital or revenue etc. Thus it is clear even to the economists that money is not something tangible; but that one and the same thing can be subsumed sometimes under the title capital, sometimes under another and contrary one, and correspondingly is or is not capital. It is then evident that it is a relation, and can only be a relation of production.' Marx 1993, p. 514; See Schmidt 1981, p. 31.
86  Marx 1993, pp. 476–7.

Marx argues that commercial forms such as the commodity, value, money, capital, wages and wage-labor, interest, rent, merchants' capital, usurers' capital, and more are all ancient, but, in modern capitalism, all of these forms are co-determined in new ways which required reconceiving all these categories and how they belong together. That task lies at the heart of Marx's project in *Capital*, where, for example, the truth of the commodity in capitalism is shown to be that commodities are commodity capital. The recognition of different senses of all these commercial terms, and of capital in particular, opens the door to multiple equivocations.[87]

In this sense, subsumption under capital is fundamentally about (i) *incorporation within* and (ii) *subjection to* the internal hierarchy of capital's multiple determinations and the new objectivity given to the subsumed elements as a result (here, the moment of *incorporation* corresponds to the wage exchange described above, whilst it is in the phase of production that practical *subjection* to its inner hierarchy and *telos* takes place – firstly as a *formal* or *passive* and secondly as a *substantial* or *active* mode of integration and domination). As Murray mentions in the citation above, the 'truth' (i.e., the social actuality) of commodities is dialectically transformed once they are understood as elements in the circuit of capital. The same is true for money, means of production and labour-power; they all 'receive this specific social character only under certain particular conditions that have developed historically'.[88] So although the key to Marx's critique of political economy lies in *labour*'s subsumption to capital, the same process of functional determination affects all other elements of production incorporated into the capitalist production process through their monetary purchase: For example, productive capital (raw materials, technology, premises, etc.) comes into the capitalist's possession by exchange and is thus constituted as a moment in the process of capital accumulation (as *constant capital*).

As a social relation of production, capital thus acts as a unifying or synthetic force, it is the subject that 'composes' the production process, the universal to which the particular labourers as well as the objective elements of production belong as particular moments. Through the economic exchange relation, capital integrates the constituents of production whose original unity is fragmented by processes of primitive accumulation. It merely executes or

---

87  Patrick Murray, 'Capital at the Margins', paper given at the 10th Annual *Historical Materialism* Conference, 'Making the World Working Class', London, 7–10 November 2013.

88  Marx 1978a, p. 121.

concludes the (subsumptive) judgement whose premises have already been posited materially: 'Capital proper does nothing but bring together the mass of hands and instruments which it finds on hand. It agglomerates them under its command'.[89] But in doing so, an inversion is effected such that for the individual workers who are related to each other 'in a purely atomistic way', capital appears as 'a unity falling outside them': It is 'the concentration of many living labour capacities for one purpose' and thus posits 'itself as the independent and external unity of these many available existences'.[90] Capital is therefore the subject that unifies and directs this process, whilst the workers have become functionally determined as its moments and the means to its end: 'Individuals are subsumed under social production; social production exists outside them as their fate; but social production is not subsumed under individuals, manageable by them as their common wealth.'[91] This is the basic meaning of the alienation and inversion of the social productive powers of labour with which Marx constantly engaged and which drives the revolutionary problematic. At the level of exchange relations, however, this can only be grasped in formal terms through the metamorphoses of money into commodities and commodities into money. It is in the alternate phase of production, in the using up of the labour power commodity, its productive consumption – which Marx describes as 'a process qualitatively distinct from the exchange ... an essentially different category' – that this circulatory movement is shown to contain 'a real metabolism'.[92] Here the 'physiognomy' of the *dramatis personae* change as 'the buyer and the seller enter into a new relation with each other', giving rise to a whole new set of conflicts and determinations of capitalist subsumption.[93]

## 3    Subsumption in Production

If, as Marx argues, 'the relations of capital are essentially concerned with controlling production', we have nonetheless seen how this can only occur via the economic mediation of commodity exchange: the subsumption of labour, as well as wealth as such, under the commodity-form of value and exchange rela-

---

[89]    Marx 1993, p. 508.
[90]    Marx 1976, p. 187; Marx 1993, p. 590.
[91]    Marx 1993, p. 158.
[92]    Marx 1988, p. 54; Marx 1993, p. 217.
[93]    Marx 1988, p. 105.

tions.⁹⁴ The circulatory processes that take place on the visible surface of capitalist society, that is, 'socially', are the means which enable a very different logic and form of power to obtain 'privately', within the arena of production. Here, in a mode that is the direct result and expression of those conditions established through 'so-called original accumulation' and reproduced by capitalist social relations themselves, the basic constituents of production are brought together – their separation is 'superseded' – in the course of a labour process that is directed under the command of the capitalist and organised around a specifically capitalist end: the production and realisation of surplus-value. When we shift our focus to this sphere, that of production, we see that with their command over labour, the right to which has been bought with wages, the capitalist compels the worker to perform surplus labour, to produce an excess of economic value over and above what they receive in order to reproduce their own existence as living labour. The worker is productive in this situation, but for capital rather than for themselves. As such, both capitalist and worker cease to be merely different kinds of sellers and truly enact the real class roles determined for them socially:

> The capitalist, who exists only as a potential purchaser of labour becomes a real capitalist only when the worker, who can be turned into a wage-labourer only through the sale of his capacity for labour, *really does submit to the commands of capital*. The functions fulfilled by the capitalist are no more than the functions of capital – viz. the valorisation of value by absorbing living labour – executed consciously and willingly. *The capitalist functions only as personified capital, capital as a person, just as the worker is no more than labour personified*.⁹⁵

The command structure and power relation that operate internally to capitalist production therefore enact the second moment of labour's subsumption, its functional determination as a moment of capital – of value valorising itself – on the basis and in the course of its active realisation as a metabolic process of practical form-determination. In the same moment that human labour forms a concretely useful good, its subjection to the command of the capitalist ensures that it also forms abstract wealth – in excess of what it receives in order to do so. Human practice is here subjected to and stamped with the character of a historically specific form of domination and exploitation: '*The labour process*

---

94  Marx 1976, p. 1011.
95  Marx 1976, pp. 989–90, emphasis added.

*posited prior to value, as point of departure* – which, owing to its abstractness, its pure materiality, is common to all forms of production – here reappears *again within capital*, as a process which proceeds within its substance and forms its content.'⁹⁶

The capitalist production process therefore consists in an 'immediate unity of the labour process and the valorisation process': an articulation of *concrete* labour as a form-giving and socially reproductive activity with *abstract* labour as an activity that valorises capital and augments the social wealth of the capitalist class. These two elements of capitalist production, capital and labour, are repulsed in their contradictory objectives (as qualitative/quantitative totalisations) but at the same time attracted by their mutual dependence: The fact that 'the labour process is only the means whereby the valorisation process is implemented', whilst, as we have seen, 'labour itself is productive only if absorbed into capital, where capital forms the basis of production, and where the capitalist is therefore in command of production'.⁹⁷ Yet this mutual dependence does not imply equal standing but rather presupposes the dominance of capital over the worker:

> [T]he *means of production*, the material conditions of labour – material of labour, instruments of labour (and means of subsistence) – do not appear as subsumed to the labourer, but the labourer appears as subsumed to them. He does not make use of them, but they make use of him. And it is this that makes them capital. Capital *employs* labour. They are not means for him to produce products whether in the form of direct means of subsistence, or of means of exchange, commodities. But he is a means for them – partly to maintain their value, partly to create surplus-value, that is, to increase it, absorb surplus-labour.⁹⁸

Here, the 'immediate contradiction' of use-value and value internal to the commodity form is raised to a more concrete or deeper level within the total social process – from the static level of objective form to the active level of the processes whereby that form is constituted – with the contradiction finding its 'resolution', or at least neutralisation, in the subsumption of the former under the latter. In this case, however, subsumption effects not only a mode of abstract formalisation, a representational framework of equivalence that reg-

---

96   Marx 1993, p. 304.
97   Marx 1976, p. 991; Marx 1993, p. 308.
98   Marx 1971.

ulates exchanges, but rather an active, goal-directed mediation that regulates productive activity according to the logic and life-process of capital, so that 'the labour process is as it were incorporated in [the valorisation process], subsumed under it'.[99]

In order to grasp exactly how the subsumption of the labour process under capitalist command and the imperative to valorise affect its forms and functions, let us return to the concepts of labour and the labour process conceived from the standpoint of their general-abstract form, in their 'pure materiality' as the necessary metabolic basis of the social reproduction process. In a passage from his 1861–3 draft of *Capital*, Marx comprehensively describes the labour process as:

> [A] process in which the worker performs a particular purposive activity, a movement which is both the exertion of his labour capacity, his mental and physical powers, and their expenditure and using-up. Through it he gives the material of labour a new shape, in which the movement is materialised ... Whilst labour materialises itself in this manner in the object of labour, it forms it and uses up, consumes the means of labour as its organ. The labour goes over from the form of activity to the form of being, the form of the object. As alteration of the object it alters its own shape. The form-giving activity consumes the object and itself; it forms the object and materialises itself; it consumes itself in its subjective form as activity and consumes the objective character of the object, i.e., it abolishes the object's indifference towards the purpose of the labour. Finally, the labour consumes the means of labour, which likewise made the transition during the process from mere possibility to actuality, by becoming the real conductor of labour, but thereby also got used up, in the form in which it had been at rest, through the mechanical or chemical process it had entered.[100]

Marx here makes explicit the double, socio-natural character of the labour process, as at once a process with a 'purely natural' basis, as a physical/chemical process, and at the same time as a process that transcends that first order of being and is defined as an 'overcoming' of the merely natural form of the object, the latter's 'indifference towards the purpose of the labour'. That indifference is negated by the labour activity which gives a new form to the object, a 'pur-

---

99   Marx 1988, p. 67.
100  Marx 1988, p. 59.

posive' or practical form intended to satisfy some 'particular need' intelligible only from the standpoint of the social totality within which the worker and object co-exist. In the moment of labour (as well as in the moment of consumption), the relations that connect the two dimensions of social reproduction – the system of productive capacities and the system of consumption needs – are perpetually put into play, subject to affirmation, interpretation and contestation, and given concrete realisation.

What, then, occurs when this process takes place on the basis of the capitalist relation of production, that is, when the worker alienates their right to determine the realisation of their activity and it comes instead under the command of the capitalist?

What the worker has alienated to the capitalist for a specified duration is 'the expenditure of his life's energy, the realisation of his productive faculties'.[101] Even though the capacity to appropriate and give form to nature is inherent in and inseparable from the living body of the productive-subject – it is 'his movement and not the capitalists' – it nonetheless becomes the property of the capitalist that can be used up in order to valorise and thereby increase the mass of his or her capital: '[T]he capitalist supervises the worker, controls the functioning of labour capacity as an action belonging to him'.[102] The imposition of capitalist command upon the labour process is the imposition of a particular – capitalist – purpose upon the labour, which displaces and disrupts any 'organic' connection between the worker's conscious regulation of their metabolic relation with the materials and means of labour and the overall end toward which the labour is directed, between the constitution of the form of the object and the form itself, the object's 'instrumental operability' (or use) within the reproduction process. This connection is now mediated by capital, depends on capital for its unity. The worker's activity, which 'depends on his will and is simultaneously an expression of his will', must only satisfy the 'private' needs of its capitalist-owner, not the 'public' needs of society nor the individual needs of the labourer.[103] In the absence of this social or individual meaning, labour is performed only to secure the wages required by the worker to sustain their life:

> Labour is for [them] *just effort and torment*, whereas it belongs to the capitalist as a substance that creates and increases wealth, *and in fact it*

---

101   Marx 1976, p. 982.
102   Marx 1988, p. 93.
103   Ibid.

> *is an element of capital, incorporated into it in the production process as its living, variable component.*[104]

Labour as conscious regulation is thus recoded as an unconscious moment in an external – or at least *excessive* – system or life-process, that of capital; it is unconscious in the sense that its subsumption under the valorisation process enacts its transition to an order of functional intelligibility that is indifferent and alien to the concrete content of the labour itself, and where it counts only as *abstract labour*. Just as social production, therefore, recodes the natural processes underlying the human-nature metabolism as *practically* significant, so too in a similar sense does capitalist production recode the labour process as *economically* significant, as *value-producing* labour. This significance, as content and goal, is superimposed upon the process of the objectification of labour in use-values, or practical objects, a process that capital both represses and depends upon. We can thus see how through labour's subsumption 'a relation of domination and subordination enters the relation of production itself' and, equally, how 'this derives from capital's ownership of the labour it has incorporated *and* from the nature of the labour process itself'.[105]

## 4  Formal Subsumption under Capital

It would, however, be both theoretically insufficient and methodologically inconsistent to attempt to understand this subsumption as active within the labour process conceived in these ahistorical, general-abstract terms, 'in *no* specific economic determinateness ... divorced from all particular historical characteristics'.[106] In the discussion of the labour process in his 1861–63 manuscripts, Marx is clear that 'to what extent the character of the labour process is itself *changed* by its subsumption under capital is a question that has nothing to do with the general form of the labour process' (although, as we have seen, a conception of this general form is a precondition for understanding those changes).[107] The determination of labour process as capitalist does not emerge *ex nihilo*, 'nor drop from the sky', and neither is the concrete form of the labour which capital comes to dominate general and indeterminate, but rather

---

104   Marx 1976, pp. 989–90, emphasis added.
105   Marx 1994, p. 102.
106   Marx 1988, p. 63.
107   Marx 1988, p. 64.

belongs to 'production at a definite stage of social development', is concrete and historically specific. 'Capital did not begin the world from the beginning, but rather encountered production and products already present, before it subjugated them beneath its process'.[108] Thus what is subsumed under capital at the outset of this 'encounter' are non-capitalist production processes belonging to a pre-existing form of social reproduction (notably, in the case of Britain, feudalism):

> Historically, in fact, at the start of its formation, we see capital take under its control (subsume under itself) not only the labour process in general but the specific actual labour processes as it finds them available in the existing technology, and in the form in which they have developed on the basis of non-capitalist relations of production.[109]

How does capital take hold of and re-determine these labour processes as its own? In order to conceptualise this process, Marx makes use of the concept of subsumption in what has come to be its most explicit and widely recognised sense, in the distinction between the 'formal' and 'real' modes of labour's subsumption to capital, a distinction intended to clarify the manner in which the domination of capital is operative within the production process. Different forms of subsumption capture the diverse ways that capitalists exercise their power in order to accumulate – and transform society in the process.

Initially, Marx says, capital 'only subsumes [the labour process] *formally*, without making any changes in its specific technological character'.[110] In this phase, which Marx calls 'formal subsumption', production takes on a capitalist character purely at the level of *the social relationship* that constitutes it, that is, without any 'material' transformation of the (pre-existing) labour process.[111] The social basis upon which it takes place is nonetheless transformed into an economic relation between capitalist and wage-labourer, so that the compulsion and exploitation of the former by the latter can occur simply through the exchange of 'equivalents'. Roberts points out that, since capitalist production is defined by its adherence to the circulatory formula M–C–M', 'everything

---

108   Marx 1993, p. 675.
109   Marx 1988, p. 92.
110   Ibid.
111   The conceptual distinction between formal and real subsumption is first introduced by Marx in the *Grundrisse*, although not under this precise terminology, in Marx 1993, pp. 586–7. It is in the manuscripts written between 1861–3 that the distinction is termed formal/real and elaborated in detail.

required for production, including the workers' ability to work, must enter into production through sale and purchase'.[112] Thus unlike the relations of directly political domination that characterised for example feudal societies, where surplus labour was often extorted through violent means, in formal subsumption, the domination of capital over labour consists primarily in this 'money relationship', 'in the worker's subjection *as worker* to the supervision and therefore to the command of capital or the capitalist'.[113] As Marx explains:

> The subsumption is formal, in so far as the individual worker, instead of working as an independent commodity owner, now works as a labour capacity belonging to the capitalist, and therefore under his command and supervision; also works no longer for himself but for the capitalist; the means of labour, moreover, no longer appear as means to the realisation of his labour: his labour appears instead as the means of valorisation – i.e. absorption of labour – for the means of labour. This distinction is formal in so far as it can exist without causing the slightest alteration of any kind in the mode of production or the social relations within which production takes place.[114]

Marx is somewhat misleading here when he writes that the social relations of production are unchanged by formal subsumption. In fact, insofar as it marks a new form of domination occurring within the production process, it is *only* at the level of social relations that the effects of formal subsumption can be registered. The political and social significance of this domination can be grasped in terms of the peculiarity of the supervision relation, a form of command and compulsion legitimated by the juridical relation between the seller of labour power and the one who consumes it – the 'legal fiction' that underwrites the 'forced' labour of 'free' subjects.[115] The capitalist *buys* the right to exert their command over labour's activity in the production process, and then – crucially – uses this right to ensure that the work is carried out with sufficient productivity to generate surplus-value, to ensure that their M will return to them as M'.

In this sense, the power exercised in the formally subsumed labour process, whilst directly interpersonal (between capitalist and worker) must nonetheless

---

112   Roberts 2009, p. 192.
113   Marx 1988, p. 93, emphasis added.
114   Marx 1988, p. 262.
115   Bellofiore 2009, p. 180.

be understood as directed toward the satisfaction of external and abstract pressures, namely those of competitive exchange. The capitalist does not dominate the worker in order to directly satisfy their own consumption needs but precisely in order to maximise the value objectified in the commodities they have commanded their workers to produce, a value that is determined by socially established standards of productivity. Hence, the capitalist exerts their authority over the worker in order to ensure that these competitive standards of productivity are met (or beaten): '[T]he capitalist will make sure that the worker really works, works the whole time required, and expends necessary labour time only, i.e., does the normal quantity of work over a given time'.[116] In this sense, through the juridical command relation, the capitalist really acts as capital personified, executes the judgement in which labour is particularised as capital, as productive of and for capital. The formally subsumed labour process thus acts as 'the general foundation of the capitalist system' by establishing an exploitative economic relation between capital and labour founded on a developed and widespread network of competitive commodity exchange.

Understanding the temporal aspect of this command relation, which is itself directly linked to the temporal aspect of value, is essential to grasping what is at stake both in capitalist exploitation as such, as well as the different modes of subsumption employed by capital as strategies for intensifying this exploitation.

Underlying the capitalist production process understood as a process of valorisation is the demand that the worker objectify *more* social labour in the commodities they produce than is returned to them in the form of wages; it is this 'surplus' that capitalist command must coerce form the workers. To this end, for capital (and thus for the capitalist) 'labour does not count as productive activity with a specific utility, but simply as value-creating substance, as social labour in general which is in the act of objectifying itself and whose sole feature of interest is its *quantity*'.[117] (It is in this sense that the subsumption of the labour process under the valorisation process is a logical extension of the subsumption of use-value under value; it is the penetrastion of abstract value-logic into the active level of production.) Because the value at stake here represents the quantity of labour objectified in commodities in *temporal* terms, that is, as 'definite masses of crystallised labour-time', the only means by which capitalists can realise their aim of extracting surplus-value from the labour force lies in establishing, maintaining and increasing a part of the working

---

116  Marx 1988, p. 93.
117  Marx 1976, p. 1012.

day in which workers are forced to perform surplus labour, that is, 'beyond the point at which the worker would have produced an exact equivalent for the value of his labour-power'.[118] Formal subsumption – understood not only as a specific mode but as the 'general foundation' of every capitalist production process – can thus be grasped, conceptually, as *the introduction of a time relation in the production process*, as the division of the working day into two parts: that in which necessary labour (for the reproduction of the labourer) is performed and that in which surplus labour (for the benefit of the capitalist) is performed. As Marx notes, '[t]he *productivity* of capital consists in the first instance – even if one only considers the *formal* subsumption of labour under capital – in the *compulsion to perform surplus-labour*, labour beyond the immediate need; a compulsion which the capitalist mode of production shares with earlier modes of production, but which it exercises and carries into effect in a manner more favourable to production'.[119] The distinctiveness of the mode of exploitation introduced with formal capitalist subsumption lies in the way in which this division between necessary and surplus labour is concealed by the 'free' exchange between the buyer and seller of labour power that is its precondition. At the surface-level of the social process, in circulation, the working day appears as one single block of time, because the wage-form represents it as such, with the worker selling their labour to the capitalist for a complete working day that does not distinguish between its necessary and surplus portions. It is for this reason that the wage relation appears to be (in the sense of *erscheinen*, necessarily taking the form of) an exchange of equivalents, even though it is on the basis of this temporal division that the possibility of capitalist exploitation and its increase arises:

> The fact that half a day's labour is necessary to keep the worker alive during 24 hours does not in any way prevent him from working a whole day. Therefore the value of labour-power, and the value which that labour-power valorises [*verwertet*] in the labour-process, are two entirely different magnitudes; and this difference was what the capitalist had in mind when he was purchasing the labour-power.[120]

Marx contrasts this mode of exploitation with for example, the direct forms of extracting surplus labour used under feudalism, where, under the threat of

---

[118] Marx 1976, p. 297; p. 645.
[119] Marx 1971.
[120] Marx 1976, p. 300.

violence, a certain amount of surplus product or money could be demanded as tribute or a specified number of working days directly requisitioned from peasants as *corvée*. Once the labour process is subsumed to capital, however, and initiated under the guise of commodity exchange, the exploitation of surplus labour is 'not directly visible' but remains submerged in the 'antinomy, of right against right'.[121]

Because the productivity (for capital) of a formally subsumed labour process depends solely on the length of the working day for which labour-power is bought, it is bound to the production of *absolute surplus-value*, which Marx describes as the 'material expression' of formal subsumption. Capitalists, both individually and as a class, strive to force the duration of surplus labour to its maximum in order to increase the quantity of value produced by their capital in *absolute* terms, i.e., as simply an addition to the total quantity of value in society. Yet conversely, the workers constitute themselves as an opposite force, striving to reduce the hours for which they must toil in order to reproduce themselves. In the section from *Capital* on '*the production of absolute surplus-value*', Marx charts the struggles over the length of the working day and the legislation introduced by the British state to mitigate capital's 'insatiable appetite for surplus labour', which, at the dawn of the industrial revolution in Britain, threatened to drive the working class to complete exhaustion.[122] Formal subsumption thus introduces a dynamic of integration/transcendence which takes the immediately political form of a struggle over time, the time of the worker's life captured by the capitalist in order to valorise their capital.

Without altering the actual process of labour in any way, there are two other factors aside from the duration of labour individual capitals can manipulate in order to potentially increase their production of absolute surplus value. Firstly, the capitalist may enlarge the scale of production by introducing increases 'in the volume of the means of production invested, and in the number of workers under the command of a single employer'.[123] Secondly, there are techniques for increasing the intensity of labour by simply forcing the workers to exert a greater effort via supervision and coercion. What is key to formal subsumption, however, is that despite these modifications, the specific material-practical content of the activity undertaken by the worker remains unchanged from its pre-capitalist form and any potential increases in the production of surplus value remain strictly within the ambit of the interpersonal relations between

---

121  Marx 1976, p. 344.
122  Marx 1976, p. 375.
123  Marx 1976, p. 1022.

worker and employer, underpinned by wage-dependency. As we shall see, once capital goes beyond this and begins to alter the objective material content of the labour process, it brings about an epoch-making change in society's form of reproduction.

Departing from the account of formal subsumption provided by Raju J. Das, we can characterise it through the following ensemble of conditions taken on by the labour process when brought under the formal economic command of the capitalist:

1. There is no extra-economic obligation or coercion directly underpinning relations of production; that is, labourers, who do not own means of production, are generally 'free' to choose their employers.
2. No more labour time is used in production than is socially necessary; there is competition to reduce the cost of production of commodities for sale, suggesting that the law of value is operating.
3. An *economic* relation of supremacy and subordination exists at the point of production, as the worker is supervised by the capitalist.
4. The means of production and consumption are bought on the market (by the capitalist) and confront the worker as capital.[124]

To these conditions outlined by Das, we can also add that:

5. The actual labour processes themselves are unchanged by capital's ownership of the labour process. The scale and intensity of labour may be increased, but the specific technical-metabolic character of the activity remains as it was prior to capitalist control.
6. Labour-power is exchanged for wages. (There are also important non-waged forms of exploitation by capital, but they fall under the rubric of 'hybrid forms' as we shall see below.)

## 5    Hybrid Forms

In his various discussions of formal and real subsumption, Marx also mentions briefly the existence of various 'hybrid forms' [*Zwitterformen*] through which surplus-value is 'extorted' by capitalists without the production process being even formally subsumed to their command.[125] As in formal subsump-

---

124   Das 2012, pp. 180–1.
125   Marx 1976, p. 645. Banaji notes that Marx also refers to them in the *Grundrisse* as '*Mittelgattungen*' and '*Zwittergattungen*', see Banaji, *2011*, p. 63. Gilbert Skillman has contested the interpretation of these 'hybrid forms' as forms of subsumption – claiming that they are 'from Marx's standpoint more accurately understood as involving *no* subsumption of

tion, a financial rather than political relationship characterises such forms and is the basis for the exploitation of labour by capital, but this exploitation takes place without the mediation of a direct wage and without instituting specific relations of production between the producers and the capitalist.[126] 'Instead', Marx says, 'the capitalist merely steps between these independent workers and the definitive purchaser of their commodities as middleman, as merchant', or alternatively, as a usurer, and 'feeds on them like a parasite'.[127] In this sense, the exploiter acts as at best a kind of proto-capitalist, bearing the 'antediluvean' forms of usurer's or merchant's capital, whilst the workers utilise what are at least 'nominally' their own means of labour and carry out production independently. Marx gives the example of the usurer's capital in the Indian Ryot system, which

> advances raw materials or tools or even both to the immediate producer in the form of money. The exorbitant interest which it attracts, the interest which, irrespective of its magnitude, it extorts from the primary producer, is just another name for surplus-value. It transforms its money into capital by extorting unpaid labour, surplus labour, from the immediate producer.[128]

This type of exploitation presupposes, if not the complete dispossession that characterises the double freedom of wage-labour, then nonetheless a degree of immiseration sufficient for producers to be willing to enter into exploitative relationships – even in the absence of 'political restraints' obliging them to do so – in order to gain access to the money or means of production needed

---

labor at all' – and argues instead that they be more adequately thought of as 'hybrid forms of social production', see Skillman 2015. I am convinced by Patrick Murray's response: that ultimately it is of negligible theoretical significance whether Marx is referring to hybrid forms of subsumption or hybrid forms of production here, the discussion fits entirely within the problematic of capitalist subsumption in its multiple and developing forms, see Murray, 'Capital at the Margins' (conference paper). Furthermore, hybrid forms *do* involve subsumption of labour as the labour is incorporated into, exploited by, and thus functionally form-determined within capital's life process, however indirectly. See also Tomba 2009 and Das 2012 for further discussion of hybrid forms. Murray also argues that Marx theorises a fourth form of subsumption: 'ideal subsumption', which involves 'treating labour that is not *actually* subsumed under capital (whether formally or in a hybrid manner) as if it were.' Murray 2004, p. 265. I will not discuss 'ideal subsumption' here, as it does not directly refer to a mode of capitalist domination.

126   Marx 1976, p. 645.
127   Marx 1988, p. 270; Marx 1976, p. 645.
128   Marx 1976, p. 1023.

for their subsistence. The economic dependency conditioning this exploitation and the maintenance of producers at a subsistence level (or in many cases even worse) is why Banaji has described the relationship as effectively constituting a 'concealed wage'.[129] The idea that capitalist exploitation can proceed even without contractual wage relations is not only borne out as a prevalent phenomenon by extensive historical research but also supported by Marx himself in various texts, for example in *The Class Struggles in France* where, referring to the French peasantry, he states that: '[U]nder the pretence of being a private proprietor ... their exploitation differs only in *form* from the industrial proletariat. The exploiter is the same: *capital*'.[130] Marx also emphasises this in the case of the Ryot, who

> does not work under alien direction, for another and under another, and thus he is not subsumed as a wage labourer to the owner of the conditions of production. These therefore do not confront him as capital. Thus even the *formal capital-relation* does not take place, still less the specifically capitalist mode of production. And yet the usurer appropriates not only the whole of the surplus value created by the Ryot, i.e., all the surplus produce over and above the means of subsistence necessary for his reproduction, but he also takes away from him part of the latter, so that he merely vegetates in the most miserable manner. The usurer functions as a capitalist in so far as the valorisation of his capital occurs *directly* through the appropriation of alien labour, but in a form which makes the actual producer into his debtor, instead of making him a seller of his labour to the capitalist.[131]

The existence of 'hybrid forms' must therefore be associated with, on the one hand, processes of 'accumulation by dispossession' and the concentration of wealth and means of production by a capitalist class and, on the other hand, with the propagation of money-mediated market relations. As such, hybrid forms of subsumption must be figured within a broad constellation of capitalist social relations and circulatory agglomerations.

As Murray has argued, there are two primary senses in which Marx refers to hybrid subsumption. The first is as 'transitional forms' [*Übergangsformen*],

---

129  Banaji 2011, p. 98.
130  Marx 1969; For a discussion of this passage in relation to the problem of waged/unwaged exploitation, see Wallerstein 2001, p. 153 ff.
131  Marx 1994, pp. 118–9.

which act as the basis for the historical emergence of formal subsumption, and appear in a variety of guises where capitalist production is incipient. In addition to this, they also endure as 'accompanying forms' [*Nebenformen*] alongside properly capitalist (i.e., industrial) production relations and are even produced anew, either directly or indirectly, by both formal and real subsumption.[132] Industrial capital can interact with hybrid forms and incorporate them within its circuits, it can also enhance its grasp of labour by its contrast with such forms or take advantage of such forms as outsourcing mechanisms when state intervention, class struggle, economic crises or simply competition with other capitals deter its direct contraction of labour, as Das has highlighted with reference to agricultural production in India.[133] In this sense, hybrid forms must be grasped not simply as residual forms of exploitation but as a permanently present strategy of exclusion and outsourcing that is functional for capital as a response to both cost-cutting imperatives and class resistance.

Even where 'pre-capitalist' forms of production are maintained or reabsorbed into capital's accumulation process, Marx argues that their 'physiognomy is completely changed' as they 'acquire a new and specific historical character under the impact of capitalist production'.[134] The use of organicist language here is not incidental. As we have seen, the actuality of social forms derives from their functional determination within the reproductive life-process of a social subject. It therefore makes reference to the adaptation or, perhaps more appropriately, *mutilation* of social forms by their incorporation within a social reproduction process that proceeds on a capitalist basis. Such an incorporation, Marx stresses, 'heightens the exploitation of the producer, drives it to its uttermost limits, without in any way ... introducing the resulting heightened productivity of labour and the transition to the specifically capitalist mode of production'.[135] Indeed, it is precisely their exclusion from the 'normal' conditions of capitalist exploitation and their associated production costs that characterises the subsumption of the labour of 'surplus populations' under hybrid forms, allowing the capitalist 'to speculate directly upon the misery of the workers'.[136] In this way, hybrid subsumption is not simply residual but rather 'is itself the EXTRANEOUS PRODUCE of the capitalist mode of production'.[137] What occurs

---

132  Murray 2004, p. 264.
133  Das 2012.
134  Marx 1976, p. 645; p. 950.
135  Marx 1994, p. 119.
136  Marx 1994, p. 120.
137  Ibid.

under such forms 'is exploitation by capital without the mode of production of capital', which simply worsens the conditions under which the worker works:[138]

> [It] makes labour sterile, places it under the most unfavourable economic conditions ... Here in fact the means of production have ceased to belong to the producer, but they are *nominally* subsumed to him, and the mode of production remains in the same relations of small independent enterprise, only the relations are *in ruins*.[139]

There are many examples, both historical and current, of such forms and their importance is far from negligible to the reproduction of capitalist societies. As 'transitional' forms, Banaji argues that they 'were never of purely limited scope or passing significance' even though, as Murray notes, 'the concept is marginal to *Capital*'s systematic dialectic'.[140] In the form of exploitative credit 'accompanying' circuits of industrial capital, hybrid subsumption today pervades the life of the rural poor on a mass scale in 'developing' countries such as Mexico and India (where Skillman points out 'moneylending at usurious rates has seen a dramatic resurgence').[141] It should be clear, then, that the diverse forms of 'hybrid' subsumption constitute an integral element of the overall dynamic of capitalist domination and surplus-value extraction, even if they are characterised by the indirect *form* taken by the relations of exploitation.

## 6     Real Subsumption: The Objective Positing of Capitalist Command

Whilst the formal subsumption of the labour process is significant in introducing capitalist relations into production, it does not yet for Marx signal a properly capitalist 'mode of production' because the technical organisation and objective means by which labour is carried out remain unchanged; what capital commands is a labour process structured around the requirements of an 'archaic' mode of production. As such, and in spite of the potential increases in the scale and intensity of labour that subsumption under the command

---

138   Marx 1993, p. 853.
139   Marx 1994, p. 119.
140   Banaji 2011, p. 63; Murray 2004, p. 264. See also Marx's discussion of the historical significance of usurer's capital in Marx 1991a, pp. 732–3.
141   Skillman 2015; for the case of Mexico, see Bartra 2006. They also relate in important ways to the 'unproductive' forms of credit exploitation pervasive even in the most 'developed' capitalist societies, such as short-term 'payday loans'.

of a single capitalist affords, these labour processes come into contradiction with capital's unceasing drive to increase the production of surplus-value. Most obviously, this contradiction takes the form of the social and natural limits to the working day which place constraints on the amount of surplus labour capitalists can effectively demand from a formally subsumed workforce. Following the establishment of capitalist social relations of production and once the capitalist has command of the labour process, however, a second strategy of increasing surplus-value becomes available: the transformation of the material content and technical structure of the labour process in order to increase productivity – what Marx calls the 'real subsumption' of labour under capital. Real subsumption involves the development of the social productive power of labour through the technical re-organisation of the labour process, through the implementation of co-operation, divisions of labour, machinery and industrial technology, etc., in such a way that capital can overcome the barriers to accumulation present when it has only formally subsumed the labour process.

The dynamic driving real subsumption must be understood as simultaneously operative across two levels of the social process: individual capitals and total social capital. The technical transformations brought about with real subsumption are directly motivated by competition between individual capitals vying to accumulate surplus-value. By introducing productivity-raising innovations which competitors do not possess and thereby lowering their production costs, an individual capitalist can, as Marx points out, benefit by either selling their commodities above their 'real' value and reaping extra-ordinary profits or simply reducing prices and outselling competitors (reducing the rate of turnover etc.). Nonetheless, although not centrally or socially planned, these innovations have a crucial aggregate effect once generalised amongst the majority of producers throughout society: They lower the value of the commodities needed for the reproduction of the workforce and as a result reduce wages.[142] In this way, the value-component of the working day dedicated to necessary labour shrinks. Rather than increasing the amount of surplus labour extorted from the worker by simply making the working day longer – as in formal subsumption – capitalists are here able to take advantage of productiv-

---

142   It must be remembered that for Marx value is produced only by the socially useful expenditure of human energy, nerves, muscles, brain, etc., and that no extra value is created if the material productivity of labour increases within a fixed time period. Instead, the same quantity of objectified labour will be distributed amongst a greater number of products, thus making each individual commodity the bearer of less value, 'cheapening' their relative cost.

ity increases to appropriate a greater portion of the value produced in the same duration of labour. This is why the real subsumption of the labour process brings about the possibility of *relative* surplus-value production, i.e., increases in surplus-value only relative to total value-production rather than in absolute terms.

In the face of natural and social limits, therefore, capitalists find another technique for ensuring constantly increasing accumulation: altering the material content of the labour process and the technical means and methods of working in a manner adequate to the demands of valorisation. In doing so, 'the entire real form of production is altered and a specifically capitalist form of production comes into being (at the technological level too)'.[143] Real subsumption and the production of relative surplus-value that accompanies it consummate the dominance of capitalist relations within society's reproduction process. In consequence, not only does production take the *form* of a process actively directed towards the augmentation of value but this goal comes to be inscribed in the concrete *reality* of its diverse particular moments and determines its means, methods and development; the entire production process comes to be progressively determined *by*, *as* and *for* capital.

Marx conceptualises three primary forms in which the transformations associated with real subsumption occur: (i) cooperation, (ii) division of labour and manufacture and (iii) machinery and large-scale industry.

### 6.1    *Cooperation*

Marx defines cooperation generally as 'the direct *collective labour* – unmediated by exchange – of many workers' aimed at a shared goal, the production of the same use-value.[144] It is the 'basic form' of real subsumption and the 'general form upon which all social arrangements for increasing the productivity of labour are based'.[145] Where the division of labour and machinery are introduced as successive forms, it is always as 'specifications' of cooperation that rely on and presuppose it as their principle (just as all three of them presuppose the exchange relations brought about by formal subsumption). But cooperation is also treated by Marx as a specific form, existing alongside manufacture and industry and conceptually distinct from them. Taken in this sense, Marx calls it the 'most rooted in nature, the crudest and the most abstract of its own varieties', presumably because versions of it can be found in almost every historical

---

143   Marx 1976, p. 1024.
144   Marx 1988, p. 255.
145   Ibid.

form of human society.¹⁴⁶ However, as a specific aspect of real subsumption, it has a more precise meaning.

Although the concentration of many workers under one capital was already in place when the subsumption of the labour process was merely formal, those workers may in many cases have continued to undertake their labour individually and in separate locations, and therefore consumed the same quantity of materials and means of labour as they would have done previously. This changes with capitalist cooperation, where many individual workers are brought together in the same location by a capital and undertake their work simultaneously. This still in no way alters the technical structure and organisation of the labour process itself, meaning that the difference is primarily 'purely quantitative', but it nonetheless offers the possibility of some subtle qualitative increases in productivity over and above a bare multiplication of the individual labour-powers, in addition to opening the way to further modifications of the labour process. Most obviously, many workers labouring in the same space will require a smaller outlay on constant capital than if they were working in separate locations, as they share resources like buildings, tools and materials. As more labourers are employed to work cooperatively, individual differences in skill and strength tend to even out, meaning that the labour employed attains an average level of intensity. There are also potentially greater capacities unleashed by the many workers acting in unison – Marx uses the example of lifting a heavy weight – which 'the isolated worker is completely incapable of developing'.¹⁴⁷ Marx describes this as the initiation of 'a new productive power, which is intrinsically a collective one'.¹⁴⁸

This collective power signals a heightened realisation of human social being in the sense that, 'when the worker co-operates in a planned way with others, he strips off the fetters of his individuality and develops the capability of his species'.¹⁴⁹ Such a heightened socialisation of labour and its productive powers is something which, for Marx, is consistently developed by capitalist production, as its most significant progressive consequence. But as something brought about under capitalist conditions, these capacities are confiscated from the workers and transposed into a productive power of capital; they are 'gifted' to capital for nothing (as with the discoveries of science), given that the capitalist pays only for individual labour-powers, not their potential collective productivity. This gives rise to a phenomenological inversion that constitutes the

---

146   Ibid.
147   Marx 1988, p.259.
148   Marx 1976, p. 443.
149   Marx 1976, p. 447.

most important effect of co-operation as a form of real subsumption, as Marx describes in his notebooks from 1861–3:

> The capitalist buys not one but many individual labour capacities at the same time, but he buys them all as isolated commodities, belonging to isolated, mutually independent commodity owners. Once they enter into the labour process, they are already incorporated into capital, and their own cooperation is therefore not a relation into which they put themselves; it is the capitalist who puts them into it. Nor is it a relation which belongs to them; instead, they now belong to it, and the relation itself appears as a relation of capital to them. It is not their reciprocal association, but rather a unity which rules over them, and of which the vehicle and director is capital itself. Their own association in labour – cooperation – is in fact a power alien to them; it is the power of capital which confronts the isolated workers. In so far as they have a relation to the capitalist as independent persons, as sellers, it is the relation of isolated, mutually independent workers, who stand in a relation to the capitalist but not to each other. ... They find that they are agglomerated. The cooperation which arises from this agglomeration is for them just as much an effect of capital as the agglomeration itself. Their *interconnection and their unity* lies not in themselves but in capital, or, the social productive power of their labour arising therefrom is a productive power of capital. just as the power of individual labour capacity not only to replace but to increase itself – surplus labour – appears as a capacity of capital, so does the social character of labour and the productive power which arises from that character.[150]

With formal subsumption, capitalist control of production was superimposed upon the labour process via ownership of its elements, making the presence of capital as an externally enforced mediation explicitly manifest: The capitalist purchased the inputs and received the final product bearing the unpaid labour of the workers. But once capital begins to act as the unifying force and subject of the composition of the labour process, its mediation of production becomes essential and indispensable to the internal aspect of that production. With real subsumption, capital is the relation that brings all of the elements of production together in a *material* as well as economic sense, brings about the concentration and articulation of many individual productive acts into a single

---

150   Marx 1988, pp. 261–2.

coordinated process, and gives rise to augmented social productive powers. Because the social form of the cooperative labour process is formed 'quite independently of the individual labourers', it confronts them as a property of capital, and in this way it really is, in a sense, capital that *produces*, whilst workers merely act as its organs. 'Not merely at the level of ideas, but also in reality, the social character of his labour confronts the worker as something not merely alien, but hostile and antagonistic, when it appears before him objectified and personified in capital.'[151] As such, labour is not only functionally determined by capital as part of its circulatory life-process, that is, *formally*, but is now also subsumed in material terms, in its concrete realisation, that is, *really*.

Marx argues that the 'twisting and inversion' [*Verdrehung und Verkehrung*] realised here on a material level 'takes on a form that is all the more real the more on the one hand their labour-power itself becomes so modified by these forms that it is powerless as an independent force, that is to say, *outside* this capitalist relationship, and that its independent capacity to produce is destroyed'.[152] This modification, as we will see, is the essential tendency of real subsumption and acts 'as a band with which capital fetters the individual workers' in the sense that, thanks to the innovations it introduces, 'capital gains a monopoly on productivity', as Roberts points out, and becomes 'hegemonic', meaning that non-subsumed labour cannot be realised competitively, is unable to carry on independently, and will therefore perish unless it is incorporated into the capitalist production process.[153] Whilst the form of cooperation introduced by capitalists is merely 'simple', however, this hegemony and the concreteness of the inversion and dependency it introduces into production remains subtle. It is only once capital begins to truly recompose the labour process that its revolutionising effects on production and in the subsumption of workers are truly felt.

### 6.2    *Division of Labour and Manufacture*
It is the development of simple into distributive cooperation within a single production process that marks the transition to the division of labour in the system of manufacture for Marx. The division of labour in production 'develops the differentiation of social labour' by dissecting the labour process into its constituent elements or 'partial operations' that are then recombined within a single productive totality: the workshop unified under the command of the capitalist. This involves on the one hand a 'subdivision of the operations and

---

151    Marx 1976, pp. 1024–5.
152    Marx 1971.
153    Marx 1988, p. 262; Roberts 2009, p. 197.

subsumption under them of definite multiple numbers of workers' and on the other 'their *combination* in one mechanism'. In this way, manufacture 'seizes labour-power by its roots': Instead of distinct tasks being carried out in succession by the same individual worker, as was the case even with simple cooperation, they are here distributed amongst a large group of workers, each of whom specialises in the realisation of one particular function and therefore refines its efficiency.[154] This differentiation and integration of distinct activities is in turn reflected in the social division of labour in that it can precipitate the aggregation of multiple distinct handicrafts previously separated in the same workshop producing a single commodity, in such a manner that the realisation of each particular craft and its tools are altered in light of the specific production process it forms part of. Alternatively, partial operations previously forming an organic unity with other actions within a particular craft can become isolated as the unique product of discrete capitals. 'Here division and combination condition each other', Marx argues, as traditional processes are broken down and subsequently recomposed in forms more adequate to the end of valorisation; what therefore took place on a political and economic level with 'so-called primitive accumulation' has its parallel within the practical structure of the labour process itself.[155]

The system of manufacture characterised by such a division of labour brings about a transformation in the 'temporal structure' of the labour process. With its subdivision into partial operations, the activity of each labourer is materially decoupled from the production process of a commodity in its entirety, becoming instead an isolated moment of its realisation. 'The complementarity of the different processes is here transferred from the future to the present', as the various operations are completed side by side rather than serially.[156] This synchronicity of different specialised functions increases the efficiency of the labour process hugely, and has the effect of further breaking down natural and practical limits to unceasing production, thus raising the productive power of the 'collective working organism' to a far greater degree that simple cooperation was capable of. It is this heightened productivity that drives capitalists to implement and refine the division of labour in their workshops. Specialised workers, subsumed under their specific functions, develop in accordance with this system and perform their assigned operations with 'virtuosity'. But for the workers themselves, this comes at the cost of monotony and dissociation from

---

154   Marx 1988, p. 271.
155   Marx 1988, p. 277.
156   Marx 1988, pp. 277–80.

the final product of their labour, as the rhythm of their activity is no longer correlated with the full production process of a single product in its various stages and techniques but is instead marked by the incessant repetition of particular minute tasks. (This same tendency to specialisation is expressed objectively in the means of labour, for example in specialised tools designed for particular rather than general applications.) Whereas previously an individual worker would have possessed the knowledge, skills and resources to see this process through to the completion of the final product, in the system of manufacture, individuals produce only a partial, one-sided, aspect of the product and are thus reduced to personifications of each isolated stage, which they perform monotonously:

> This independence becomes solidified, personified, when each simple and monosyllabic process of this kind becomes the exclusive function of a particular worker or a definite number of workers. They are subsumed under these isolated functions. This work is not divided among them; they are divided among the various processes, each of which becomes the exclusive life-process of one of them – in so far as they function as productive labour capacity. The heightened productivity and complexity of the production process as a whole, its enrichment, is therefore purchased at the cost of the reduction of labour capacity in each of its specific functions to nothing but a dry abstraction – a simple quality, which appears in the eternal uniformity of an identical function, and for which the whole of the worker's productive capacity, the multiplicity of his capabilities, has been confiscated.[157]

The actuality of capital's abstraction reaches a new degree here, as the individual worker's life-activity and identity as producer no longer even corresponds to a particular product – a product to whose objectivity they become increasingly indifferent – but simply to the repetitive completion of a single, uncreative 'abstract' function. Marx suggests that this 'constant labour of one uniform kind disturbs the intensity and flow of a man's vital forces, which find recreation and delight in the change of activity itself' and that it 'converts the worker into a crippled monstrosity by furthering his particular skill … through the suppression of a whole world of productive drives and inclinations'.[158] With the division of labour in capitalist production the reality of human practice

---

157   Marx, 1988, p. 277.
158   Marx 1976, p. 460; p. 481.

thus takes on an increasingly abstract, simple and generic quality: '[I]n every craft it seizes, manufacture creates a class of so-called unskilled labourers'.[159] Both the organic unity and anticipatory organisation of the series of actions that constitute the entire process of producing a single discrete commodity fall increasingly to the side of capital, 'knowledge, judgement and will ... are faculties now required only for the workshop as a whole'.[160]

> [F]or the worker himself no combination of activities takes place. The combination is rather a combination of the one-sided functions under which every worker or number of workers is subsumed, group by group. His function is one-sided, abstract, partial. The totality which is formed from this is based precisely on his *merely partial existence* and isolation in his separate function. It is therefore a combination of which he forms a part, but it depends on the fact that his labour is not combined.[161]

This has the effect of strengthening and intensifying the real subsumption of labour initiated with simple cooperation, where capitalist relations of production constituted a merely 'temporary connection' between the elements of production, 'a contiguity, which by the nature of things may easily be dissolved'. In that case, the domination of capital had not yet cemented itself as an indispensable *technical* mediation but rather emanated from the will and economic authority of the capitalist; with the system of manufacture it begins to do so because of the way in which workers are individually subsumed in their functions and connected to other workers only as 'appendages' to the workshop, as fragments of the whole that cease to function outside of it. This intensifies the conditions under which the worker is isolated and dependent on their subsumption under capital:

---

159   Marx 1976, p. 470. As Arthur argues, 'labour considered in itself is concretely universal, being able to expend itself in a wide variety of concrete specifications on demand. Moreover ideally the labour process would proceed in the manner outlined in *Capital*, in which the worker is said to be like an architect in conceptualising the product before producing it. But, with the real subsumption of the labour process under capital, the adaptability of labour is taken advantage of to redraw labour so as to make the workers more like bees, supplying their efforts to the collectivity of production but without attaining any meaningful individual relation to the enterprise as a whole, which is beyond their ken, being put together by the representatives of capital on the basis of the technical specification of labour, machinery and materials' (Arthur 2004, p. 47).
160   Marx 1976, p. 460.
161   Marx 1988, pp. 278–9.

Originally he had to sell to the capitalist, instead of the commodity, the labour that produced the commodity, because he was not in possession of the objective conditions for the realisation of his labour capacity. Now he has to sell it *because his labour capacity only continues to be labour capacity in so far as it is sold to capital*. Thus he is now subsumed under capitalist production, has now fallen under the control of capital, no longer just because he lacks the means of labour, *but because of his very labour capacity, the nature and manner of his labour*; now capital has in its hands no longer just the objective conditions, but *the social conditions of subjective labour, the conditions under which his labour continues to be labour at all*.[162]

Thus even though 'the workers form the building blocks' of the combined workshop, it is not 'subsumed under them as a united group'.[163] Capital has been autonomised as the unifying principle of the overall production process which 'confronts the workers as an external power, dominating and enveloping them, in fact as the power of capital itself and a form of its existence, under which they are individually subsumed, and to which their social relation of production belongs'.[164] This inversion intensifies the degree to which real subsumption 'strips off the form of production for subsistence, and becomes production for trade', the only barrier to which, given its indifference to individual needs, is 'the magnitude of the capital itself'.[165] Here, the minimum level of capital needed to form a competitive enterprise begins to rise as the technical complexity of the single productive entity increases, further dwarfing the productive significance of the individual worker.[166] In this way, manufacture 'is the first system to provide the materials and the impetus for industrial pathology', although this pathology is only realised once the despotism of capitalist command begins to develop the objective means peculiar and adequate to the accumulation process of capital: *machinery*.[167]

---

162  Marx 1988, pp. 279–80, emphasis added.
163  Marx 1988, p. 279.
164  Marx 1988, p. 278.
165  Marx 1994, p. 106.
166  'Hence it is a law, springing from the technical character of manufacture, that the minimum amount of capital which the capitalist must possess has to go on increasing. In other words, the transformation of the social means of production and subsistence into capital must keep extending' (Marx 1976, p. 480).
167  Marx 1976, p. 484.

## 6.3    Machinery and Large-Scale Industry

The material inversion, separation and integration characteristic of real subsumption, which proceeds on the basis of the social relations introduced with labour's formal subsumption and develops through the stages of cooperation and manufacture, achieve their apotheosis in large-scale industry based on machinery, the technical from of production most adequate to the valorisation of capital:

> The increase of the productive force of labour and the greatest possible negation of necessary labour is the necessary tendency of capital, as we have seen. The transformation of the means of labour into machinery is the realisation of this tendency.[168]

What distinguishes the stage of large-scale industry is the complete revolution it brings about in the instrument of labour, in the 'practical object' that mediates the metabolic transformation of nature, from tools (which are shared by both simple cooperation and manufacture, undergoing only minor modifications in the latter) to machinery: '[O]nce adopted into the production process of capital, the means of labour passes through different metamorphoses, whose culmination is the machine, or rather, an automatic system of machinery'.[169] Machinery is not simply a larger or more complex tool, which would still require its operation to originate in a human source, but a self-moving mechanism which can perform its functions free of the limits of 'the human frame' (for example, the maximum number of implements operable or the maximum speed of working); 'it is the machine which possesses skill and strength in place of the worker, is itself the virtuoso'.[170] The entire technical paradigm of human civilisation accrued over millennia and culminating in the system of manufacture (the human as a 'tool making animal') is thereby superseded with machine production, which no longer seeks to refine a labour process based on human physical capacities but rather harnesses vast forces of nature in order to function with a degree of power and scale inaccessible even through the coordinated cooperation of huge numbers of human labourers.

In machinery, this is achieved by developing the principle of a 'rational' division of labour designed to maximise the efficiency of the production process – that same principle underlying manufacture – but in a manner that surpasses the barriers set by its foundation in coordinated manual labour:

---

168   Marx 1993, p. 693.
169   Marx 1993, p. 692.
170   Marx 1993, p. 693.

# CAPITALIST SUBSUMPTION: ABSTRACTION IN ACTION 161

> Here we have again the co-operation by division of labour which is peculiar to manufacture, but now it appears as a combination of machines with specific functions. ... In manufacture, it is the workers who, either singly or in groups, must carry on each particular process with their manual implements. The worker has been appropriated by the process; but the process had previously to be adapted to the worker. This subjective principle of the division of labour no longer exists in production by machinery. Here the total process is examined objectively, viewed in and for itself, and analysed into its constitutive phases.[171]

The scientific analysis of the labour process that accompanies industrial production is thereby liberated from an 'anthropological schema' of labour, objectifying in the means of production an entirely new rhythm and motion founded on the life process of capital rather than the worker.[172] It transforms the workshop into the factory, 'an automaton consisting of numerous mechanical and intellectual organs', an 'articulated system' of processes and machines whose 'regulating principle' is an ever perfected continuity of production, a drive to eliminate all interruptions to the labour process.[173] Yet this refinement of productivity is not done for intrinsically technical ends or to maximise the production of use-values for the sake of their consumption but only to intensify the objectification and appropriation of labour and nature by capital:

> Like every other instrument for increasing the productivity of labour, machinery is intended to cheapen commodities and, by shortening the part of the working day in which the worker works for himself, to lengthen the other part, the part he gives to the capitalist for nothing. The machine is a means for producing surplus-value.[174]

Whilst reducing necessary labour-time to an absolute minimum, machinery at the same time creates new means and incentives to extend the working day as far as possible, pushing absolute surplus-value production 'to its uttermost limit'. Large-scale industry drives production away from natural or human rhythms and toward the unceasing, homogenous continuum of the time of

---

171  Marx 1976, p. 501.
172  See Read 2003, p. 115 ff.
173  Marx 1993, p. 692.
174  Marx 1976, p. 492.

accumulation. With its introduction at the end of the eighteenth century, Marx notes, 'every boundary set by morality and nature, age and sex, day and night, was broken down'.[175]

This occurs primarily by a further intensification of the abstraction and simplification of human labour introduced with manufacture. However, in this case this does not proceed by way of technical specialisation, as it does in manufacture, but rather by its opposite, a generic 'specialisation in passivity' based on 'completely simple labour' characterised by 'uniformity, emptiness and subordination to the machine'.[176] Large-scale industry 'robs the labour of its singularity', reducing it to its most average, undifferentiated and replaceable quality, to the extent that it precipitates the mass employment of women and children through its abolition of skill and dexterity from the labour process.[177] 'Here the last remnant of the worker's satisfaction in his own labour disappears, to be replaced by absolute indifference, which is itself conditioned by the labour's lack of real content.'[178] Because machinery does not require direct operation but functions automatically, requiring only 'supplementary assistance', the activity of the workforce becomes 'determined and regulated on all sides by the movement of the machinery, and not the opposite'.[179] The worker is displaced from the centre of the labour process to its margins by the system of machinery, 'cast merely as its conscious linkages', overseeing its operation as 'watchman and regulator' rather than 'chief actor'.[180] By the same token, the principle of capitalist command, which seeks to 'pump out' the maximum quantity of effort from labour-power in every moment of its use, not only emanates from the subjective relations between capitalist and worker but becomes objectively imprinted into the technical structure of the means of production, as Kliman and McGlone argue:

> With machinery, it is no longer just competition in the market, the threat of unemployment, and the watchful eye of the foreman that force workers to produce according to [socially necessary labour time]; rather, the production process is designed such that the workers' activity must keep pace with the unyielding pace of the machine.[181]

---

175   Marx 1976, p. 390.
176   Marx 1991b, p. 488.
177   Marx 1994, p. 112.
178   Marx 1991b, p. 488.
179   Marx 1993, p. 693.
180   Marx 1993, p. 692.
181   McGlone and Kliman 2004, p. 147.

Even without extending the working day, machinery can increase the productivity of labour by dictating the pace of work, resulting in a '*condensation of labour time*, in which every part of the time increases its labour content' and through which 'the pores of time are so to speak shrunk through the compression of labour.'[182]

All this occurs not simply in the neutral drive to increase material productivity, but bearing all the contradictions that the exploitation of labour by capital generates and raising them to their highest degree. Whereas with formal subsumption, the conditions of labour produce for the workers 'an *alien circumstance*', with the full realisation of real subsumption under the factory system, this 'antithesis or alienation develops further, into an *antagonistic contradiction*'.[183] The means of production themselves stand over living labour as an oppressive force, 'animated by the drive to reduce to a minimum the resistance offered by man, that obstinate yet elastic barrier'.[184] All of the productive powers embodied by machinery, as well as the system of scientific knowledge that is its basis, whilst serving to reduce necessary labour to a minimum suffer a 'dialectical inversion' with real subsumption, such that both in practice and in their forms of appearance they confront the worker as 'weapons' serving only to raise their exploitation and domination to the highest possible degree:

> Here too past labour – in the automaton and the machinery moved by it – steps forth as acting apparently in independence of [living] labour, it subordinates labour instead of being subordinate to it, it is the iron man confronting the man of flesh and blood. The subsumption of his labour under capital – the absorption of his labour by capital – which lies in the nature of capitalist production, appears here as a technological fact. The *keystone of the arch is* complete. Dead labour has been endowed with movement, and living labour only continues to be present as one of dead labour's conscious organs. The *living connection* of the whole workshop no longer lies here in cooperation; instead, the system of machinery forms a unity, set in motion by the prime motor and comprising the whole workshop, to which the living workshop is subordinated, in so far as it consists of workers. Their *unity* has thus taken on a form which is tangibly autonomous and independent of them.[185]

---

182   Marx 1988, p. 335.
183   Marx 1991b, p. 480.
184   Marx 1976, p. 527.
185   Marx 1994, pp. 29–30.

Large-scale industry thus represents the culminating form of capital's social autonomisation and domination. It is no longer the individual producer-subjects who consciously regulate their metabolism with nature but the machine, whose scientific conception already guarantees the carrying out of labour on a capitalistic basis. The human is no longer the subject of production – the one who consciously gives form to the product – but has become the implement of capital's own anticipatory conceptualisation.[186] This conceptualisation becomes a specific area within the social division of labour, as science, design and technological innovation; where it does persist within a single enterprise, it is nonetheless separated off from the direct labour involved in the production of concrete commodities, as the distinct activity of 'research and development'.[187] Through the 'enormous development of scientific powers' underlying industrial production, workers become increasingly dispensable and replaceable (although of course industry also produces a hierarchy of workers and creates a class of technically skilled workers), as their capacity to labour and to resist is increasingly delimited by the preset modes of operation built into the system of machinery. It was in this sense that Marx suggested that 'it would be possible to write a whole history of the inventions made since 1830 for the sole purpose of providing capital with weapons against working class revolt'.[188] Castillo Mendoza emphasises this, arguing that with machinery, 'technique operates as an artefact of power subsumed as a mediation of the political in the factory, constituted in the structure most suitable to impose vigilance and discipline, and to neutralise the control of workers over work. In it, the workers now have "a social relation of production" amongst themselves, and with the capitalist, in the organic interior of capital'.[189]

---

[186] 'The combination of this labour appears just as subservient to and led by an alien will and an alien intelligence – having its *animating unity* elsewhere – as its material unity appears subordinate to the objective unity of the *machinery*, of fixed capital, which, as *animated monster*, objectifies the scientific idea, and is in fact the coordinator, does not in any way relate to the individual worker as his instrument; but rather he himself exists as an animated individual punctuation mark; as its living isolated accessory' (Marx 1993, p. 470).

[187] 'The full development of capital only takes place – or capital has only posited the mode of production corresponding to it – when the means of labour is not merely formally determined as *fixed capital* but is superseded in its immediate form, and *fixed capital* confronts labour within the production process as machinery. The entire production process then appears no longer as subsumed under the immediate skill of the worker, but as technological application of science. Capital thus tends to impart a scientific character to production, and immediate labour is reduced to a mere moment of this process' (Marx 1993, p. 699).

[188] Marx 1976, p. 563.

[189] Castillo Mendoza 2002, p. 7.

## 7 Conclusion

Through its subsumption of labour, capital 'radically remoulds all its social and technological conditions', dissolving and recomposing relations, practices and instruments in order to meet the demands of competitive valorisation and, ultimately, expanded reproduction.[190] The exposition of the formal, hybrid and real modes of this subsumption charts the various strategies through which the capital relation and the class domination that it sustains attain a more concrete existence, a more effective subordination of labour and a deeper penetration into the material structure of the social reproduction process as a whole. First appearing as an external and arbitrary mediation imposed upon producers from outside, at the level of exchange, capitalist power subsequently develops into a 'technological fact' built into the labour process as its material presupposition, thereby displacing and diversifying the sources of class antagonism beyond the surface level of intersubjective (albeit 'impersonal', i.e., economic) social relations. However, the distinction between these forms of subsumption is neither an empirical typology nor a historical periodisation of different forms of capitalist production but rather a conceptual differentiation of the modes in which the exploitation and domination of labour's productive activity by capital can be structured and developed, as well as the material and social effects that result from these modes.[191]

We have seen how, from its most subtle, 'formal' incarnation right up to its most developed, 'real' form, capitalist subsumption functions through a dual figuration or form-determination. Firstly, there is the specific conjunction of accumulated historical acts, monetary and commodity forms, and the permanence of an entire legal-economic apparatus governing the circulatory patterns in which wealth moves across society in the course of its reproduction. Together, these factors constitute the system of economic representation within which discrete social elements are inscribed as alienable and commensurable property through their commodification and subsumption under the forms of value. Secondly, there is a specific form-determination of production, both in terms of the social relations which govern it (capitalist command and direction of co-ordinated labour) and the objective-technical structure of

---

190   Marx 1994, p. 30.
191   This is missed by Ernest Mandel in his introduction to Marx's 'Results of the Immediate Production Process' and Etienne Balibar, both of whom mistakenly historicise the distinction by associating manufacture with formal subsumption and large-scale industry alone with real subsumption. See Mandel, 'Introduction' to 'Results' in Marx 1976, p. 945; Balibar, 'Elements for a Theory of Transition' in Althusser and Balibar 1997, pp. 302–3.

labour process itself (from cooperation to machinery). These two latter factors combined institute a dimension of direct *subordination* in the 'hidden abode' of production through which the realisation of labour is consciously regulated and refined as a means to valorise capital.

The relation of capitalist subsumption is therefore constituted through the combination of two series of form-determining mechanisms that establish the presence and action of human labour on two distinct but interconnected levels of social actuality – that of value (being) and that of capital (process). The two moments of figuration, occurring in exchange and production, mutually presuppose each other as the basic conditions of this subsumption and, crucially, whilst both are necessary, *neither is sufficient for subsumption without the other* (hybrid forms in which capitalist control of production is *indirect* and supported by contextual socio-economic factors notwithstanding). This is something Diane Elson has argued with reference to Marx's value theory:

> The process of exploitation is actually a unity; and the money relations and labour process relations which are experienced as two discretely distinct kinds of relation, are in fact one-sided reflections of particular aspects of this unity. Neither money relations nor labour process relations in themselves constitute capitalist exploitation; and neither one can be changed very much without accompanying changes in the other.[192]

The unity of the two sets of relations binds together the 'logical' discourse of value's formal metamorphoses in circulation (M–C–M') with the 'materialist' discourse of metabolic synthesis in production to constitute the realisation and expansion of capitalist exploitation.[193] In the first instance, commodification

---

[192] Elson 2015, p. 172.
[193] As Kant argued, the possibility of a subsumptive relation between two heterogeneous elements or orders depends on their schematic adaptation, their mediation through a third thing common to them both. The dialectical character of this process exceeds mere inclusion or the nominal exteriority of what is simply 'not-yet' subsumed. This is what the 'secret' of schematic synthesis proved in Kant's thought: that inclusion, or representation under a concept, only grasps the completed subsumptive procedure from the standpoint of its conceptualised result, but that this alone is tautological. The very thing to be explained is the *possibility* of a logical identity between heterogeneous elements, hence the need for a theory of mediation and synthesis, that is, the *formation* of the manifold according to the concept. Marx too grasps this, and his account of the subsumption of labour in production is precisely a dialectical account of subsumption *and* synthesis – the valorisation process *and* the labour process – in which the *formation* of labour (in the sense of 'activity') by capital determines the fact and degree of its value productiv-

and wage relations are necessary for labour's formal alienation as *labour-power* (the act which forms the basis for the transformation of money into capital and the possibility of surplus-value) and incorporation into capital as *variable capital*, property of the capitalist. As Marx states, 'without the *exchange* of variable capital for labour-power, the total capital could not valorise itself and so the formation of capital and the transformation of the means of production and means of subsistence could not take place'.[194] This first (circulatory) form-determination, in the unity of its moments, 'is an inescapable condition for capital, a condition posited by its own nature, since circulation is the passing of capital through the various conceptually determined moments of its necessary metamorphosis – its life process'.[195]

The production process is however equally necessary for purchased labour-power to valorise capital by objectifying itself in a commodity product: Once under the command of the capitalist, variable capital is used up in order to generate the surplus which can then be accumulated. It is only through this process that variable capital (*labour*) acts *as* capital, which is to say, is functionally determined as a moment of its valorisation process, subsumed under it. Because of the privileged function assigned to the exploitation of labour within the capitalist economy (as the sole source of surplus-value), the productive capacity of the labour process is of paramount concern for individual capitals in their competitive development. Therefore, even though, from the standpoint of circulation, 'the production process appears simply as an unavoidable middle term, a necessary evil for the purpose of money-making', the material configuration of the production process becomes one of the most intensive sites in which the effects of capitalist domination manifest themselves.[196] It is precisely here that we find the second moment of (material) form-determination.

These two phases of figuration are therefore intertwined as the constitutive poles of capitalist production as a whole – i.e., the total process [*Gesamtprozeß*] of expanded reproduction implicit in the capitalist social relation – each one acting as the necessary mediation of the other. In addition (or rather, as a result), they constitute the two levels of form-determination which are bound

---

ity. Crucially, Marx recognises that this process of synthetic formation is not unilateral and that capitalist command is required to negate the independent subjectivity of a commodity with 'variable' effects (labour-power). This struggle is exactly what gives rise to the dynamic of subsumption.

194  Marx 1976, p. 1017.
195  Marx 1993, p. 658.
196  Marx 1978a, p. 137.

together and reproduced as the basis of capitalist power: commodification and alienation in circulation, and subjection and exploitation in production. These are the two basic aspects of capitalist domination and the two modalities of form-determination, both equally essential to its functioning. Capitalist subsumption must therefore be grasped comprehensively as a process that unfolds across both the sphere of economic objectivity (market relations) and the sphere of practical objectivity (production relations) tied together by a single unified relation of reproduction. The internal correlation of the two series which structures and regulates the social process as it unfolds in practice is the basis for the ongoing division and composition of the social totality, the distribution of resources and labour-power across various branches of production and, with the increasing socialisation of labour, of the integration of (re)productive practices within a single world market.

It is vital to note, however, that there is no inherent unity between commodity exchange and labour outside of their historically specific capitalist articulation.[197] For Marx, 'the labour process as such has nothing to do with the act of purchasing the labour capacity on the part of the capitalist', whilst at the same time, 'the concept of the commodity in and for itself excludes labour as process'.[198] Yet the two moments presuppose one another insofar as, taken together, they form the 'life-process' of capital, which involves the constant movement of values between production and circulation, between the 'positing' of surplus-value in the former and its realisation in the latter. They are not simply bound together in mutual indifference but 'constantly run into one another and interpenetrate, and in this way their distinguishing features are continuously blurred'.[199] The unity of these two moments of subsumption – corresponding to exchange and production: subsumption of labour to the commodity and value, and subsumption of labour to capital and the valorisation process – therefore constitutes *the distinctive synthesis of the capitalist social relation*, and the articulation through which the labour process is determined practically as 'for capital', as a moment of capital's own being 'which proceeds within its substance and forms its content'.[200] Crucially, the tendency of capitalist subsumption instituted materially with labour's real subsumption

---

197  As Banaji argues, 'by late antiquity, both wage-labour and capital (the basic *elements* of the capitalist mode of production) were fully formed but ... their conjunction was much less obvious. It took another five centuries before something like a capitalist system began to emerge in the Mediterranean.' Banaji 2011, p. 130.
198  Marx 1988, pp. 65–6; Marx 1994 p. 71.
199  Marx 1991a, p. 135, translation modified.
200  Marx 1993, p. 304.

is to guarantee the reciprocity of exchange and production through a progressive adequation and adaptation of the two moments, such that each becomes increasingly inherent and integral to the other's functioning, reinforcing their overall unity. Capitalist production intensifies commodification, and capitalist circulation drives the development of subsumption in production. The initial indifference of commodity exchange and the labour process is thus progressively negated as their unity within the capitalist social relation becomes a social and material fact imprinted in their inner structure.

But even within the terms of the articulation specified by this distinctive synthesis, the correlation of the two spheres is not fixed but in a perpetual process of contestation and transformation. This transformative dynamic is immanent to the logic of subsumption itself, which, even with its culmination in real subsumption, does not mark the 'completion' of a transition but rather installs a program of 'complete (and constantly repeated) revolution' in the social and material conditions of the reproduction process. In this sense, the relation between the forms of subsumption cannot be contained within the reductive framework of an evolutionary, 'internalist' conception of necessary stages experienced by each and every individual capital (a framework which gives rise to an impoverished schema of more or less 'developed' capitals, national economies and regions). Rather, the way in which the process of subsumption unfolds across the spheres of production and circulation constitutes a fluid dynamic (within which the distinct forms can be contemporaneous moments) capable of realising itself on a social scale with radically diverse local results. Whilst Marx's analysis of the forms of subsumption is limited to the terms of a single production process (in spite of the constitutive character of exchange relations), it is clear that the conditions of subsumption in production and, indeed, of their unity with capital's circulatory conditions, presuppose the unity-in-indifference of multiple competing capitals. This presents the necessity of thinking subsumption on a social scale, that is, at the level of these multiple and diverse processes of production and circulation, all of which have their unity within the reproductive framework of society as a total 'structure-in-process'. This throws up new problems regarding the conceptualisation of capitalist subsumption, new forms and contradictions emerging from the conflict between capital and labour conceived 'globally' and inscribes the theory of subsumption within the critical context of an open process of historical development.

CHAPTER 4

# The Dynamic of Subsumption on a Social Scale

If production has a capitalist form, so too will reproduction.[1]

∵

The account of capitalist subsumption found in Marx's writings outlines a theory of the synthetic structure, conflictual character and developmental tendency immanent to the production process of capital. Through the subsumption of living labour under the commodity-form and the labour process under the command and logic of the valorisation process, capital appropriates and directs – first 'socially' and then 'materially' – the form-determining capacity of human praxis in its metabolism with nature. In doing so, capital shapes this metabolism according to its own interests both quantitatively (in the duration and intensity of labour) and qualitatively (in the technical organisation and objective *telos* of the metabolism). With its culmination in 'real subsumption', this synthesis establishes a transformative dynamic that not only modifies the technical basis of the labour process but also, as its mediated result, sets in motion a revolutionary recomposition of the social reproduction process that affects its historical development in a decisive manner. It is to this that Marx and Engels refer when they famously declare in their *Manifesto* that 'the bourgeoisie *cannot exist* without constantly revolutionising the instruments of production, and thereby the relations of production, and with them the whole relations of society'.[2] At the core of Marx's theory of subsumption, then, a fundamental connection is posited between the immanent tendency of capitalist production (its synthetic 'logic' of form-determination) and the reproduction and development of capitalist society (its 'history' or 'real movement'). This corresponds directly to the second problematic associated with the critical concept of subsumption: the constitutive relation between the discrete acts of subsumptive form-determination and the compositional totality within which those acts occur. It is at the level of this relation that Marx's

---

[1] Marx 1976, p. 711.
[2] Marx and Engels 1976, p. 487.

profound theoretical breakthrough occurs in relation to the thought of subsumption, allowing him to grasp the effects and actuality of capitalist social forms without overdetermining them with reference to a closed structure of composition (be it 'reciprocal' as in Kant or speculatively totalised as in Hegel). However, insofar as Marx presents the forms of subsumption in the linear mode of an abstract-logical progression (from 'formal' to 'real'), a number of fundamental ambiguities arise concerning how this tendency is actualised concretely and integrated into the historical unfolding of the social process (in terms of the double movement *reproduction-development* established at the close of chapter 2). The Brighton Labour Process Group highlighted this in 1977, noting that on the one hand 'the relation between capital and labour, at a general social level, cannot be derived from, or reduced to, the capital-labour relation within production', whilst on the other, 'the actual structure of the [labour] process is not historically determined by the abstract logic of capital accumulation, since capitalist production relations can only be reproduced as a totality of social relations'.[3] If the dynamic of subsumption in production cannot be mapped onto a historical or systematic account of the total social process in any direct or schematic way, then further mediations are required to render its effects intelligible at a social scale. But if this is, as in Marx's presentation of wages, a case of 'holding them fast at the beginning' in order to make their 'development possible without confounding everything' and later correcting 'the idealist manner of the presentation, which makes it seem as if it were merely a matter of conceptual determinations and of the dialectic of these concepts', then that further development and correction is conspicuously absent in Marx's own writings, blocking the way to a richer conceptualisation of the process of capitalist domination and social recomposition in its 'fluid' motion.[4]

The insufficiency of Marx's account has two principal aspects, each of which generates a distinct although related set of problems which have shaped subsequent attempts to think subsumption socially and historically. Firstly, subsumption is considered by Marx only 'generically' in relation to an individual production process, that is, in terms of the antagonistic command relation between capital and labour in production. Thus, although competition and the reproduction of labour-power are invoked functionally by Marx in order to explain the mechanisms driving the dynamic of subsumption, the impact of these (and other) factors in determining how the dynamic actualises itself

---

3   Brighton Labour Process Group 1977, pp. 23–4.
4   Marx 1993, p. 817; p. 151.

on a social scale, where multiple capitals and modes of exploitation are combined, as well as how that actualisation in turn shapes those factors, all remain external to the theory.[5] It thus leaves room for uncertainty regarding the relation between the abstract dynamic of the forms of subsumption and their spatial and historical distribution and interaction, resulting in a number of readings which crudely project Marx's 'logical' exposition of the forms onto linear schemas of historical development.

Secondly, Marx's comments on subsumption bear the mark of a wider discursive *tension* present in *Capital*, in that they are developed from the internal standpoint of capital's accumulation process. Thus whilst subsumption marks the crucial moment of integration/resistance through which not only production but society as a whole is recomposed, if this is grasped from just one pole of the capital-labour contradiction in an idealist fashion, solely as a moment of capital's 'systematic dialectic', the complex mediating role of the subsumptive moment is reduced to a logical residue, a passive artefact of capital's 'automatic' progress. This lends itself to functionalist reductions of class struggle and social reproduction, as well as to economistic, capital-centric accounts of historical development, all of which attenuate the critical core of Marx's wider theoretical-revolutionary project. At the outset of the previous chapter, I noted Marx's seeming ambivalence towards the concept of subsumption and the instability of its role within his critique of political economy. In this context, Marx's vacillation and ultimate repression of the concept can be seen as symptomatic of the tension in which the discourse of subsumption sits with respect to the dialectical structure of *Capital*, given that the shift of perspective on capitalist power and exploitation this discourse introduces disrupts the 'organic unity' of *Capital*'s categorial system.[6]

Taken together, these two spaces of ambiguity produced by the abstractness of Marx's linear form-exposition constitute a significant theoretical problem and not merely one to be resolved empirically. In what follows, I will attempt to extend and develop Marx's insights into the subsumption of labour by capital (reconstructed in the previous chapter) in a non-linear and non-economistic manner open to the highly complex dynamic of antagonism that grounds the concrete development and effects of the process of subsumption

---

5   On Marx's abstract treatment of competition, see Heinrich 2009, p. 82; for an account of Marx's incomplete treatment of the reproduction of labour-power, see Lebowitz 2003.
6   In this sense, the discourse of subsumption runs asymmetrically to the systematic exposition of economic categories. As Patrick Murray notes, the 'Results of the Immediate Production Process', in which Marx expounds one of his richest accounts of capitalist subsumption, 'does not advance the dialectical train of reasoning in Capital' (Murray, 2009, p. 173).

at a 'social scale' (i.e., at the level of society's 'reproduction-development'). This involves re-orienting the perspective on subsumption found in Marx in such a way that the contradictory articulation and ongoing conflict over the form-determination of social being takes theoretical precedence over the dialectic of capitalist accumulation in its systematic totality, thereby undoing the 'tendential' or 'provisional' closure effected in *Capital* (a closure in which social reproduction, understood in the broadest sense, is only registered as a moment of capital's accumulation process, owing to Marx's treatment of capital as an 'organic system').[7] In order to do so, I first problematise a number of strategies for conceptualising the dynamic of subsumption in a socially comprehensive manner which have been proposed within Marxist theory. These positions, I argue, reinstate or consolidate such a closure, dissolving the critical-deconstructive character of the theory by collapsing reproduction into production, either diachronically (via historical totalisation) or synchronic (via systematic totalisation). Overcoming the conceptual, empirical and interpretive weaknesses underlying these perspectives requires treating the relation between process of subsumption in production/circulation and the other spheres of social reproduction in an experimental fashion that resists any predetermined closure or finality. This is key, not only because those other spheres react back upon production as its determining conditions but also because they constitute further, necessary sites in which capitalist subsumption unfolds, as Castillo Mendoza has argued:

> [S]ubsumption appears as an expression of a global process that cannot be reduced to the incorporation of labour, science, technology, etc., but rather many other dimensions – cultural, political, etc. – will be estab-

---

[7] The problem of closure is broadly to do with the analytic relation between 'system' or 'logic' and 'history' or 'totality', as I will explore further below. As Albritton summarizes: 'The issue of levels of analysis continually comes up in Capital itself, but Marx never actually formulates such a conception, and hence leaves completely open the question of how to relate the theory of capital's inner logic to the history of capitalism. Often Marx moves from one level to another ... without signalling the reader. Marx's use of many expressions in his struggle to differentiate the theory of capital's inner logic from more concrete levels of analysis, indicates that he never came to grips with this problem. Some of the contrasts that are to be found in the three volumes of Capital are: "the inner nature of capital versus competition", "the ideal average versus actual movement of competition", "basic forms versus special study of competition", "general character versus detailed forms", "general analysis of capital versus competition", and "general structure of capital versus concrete detail". ... the theory of capital's inner logic is the mere tip of the iceberg so to speak with respect to a complete study of capitalism' (Albritton 2003, p. 97).

lished as conditions for the reproduction of capitalist society or come to form an active part of the composition itself of capital in order to assist its movement in the expansive articulation 'production/reproduction' of surplus value. All this brings with it both the complex subsumption of individuals in the social division of labour, with its deepening as subsumption in the class structure and in dominant ideas, and its necessary and strategic articulation with the system of private property, the structuring of the state, the development of productive forces, the generalisation of exchange and the consolidation of large-scale industry. Furthermore, this weave of articulations serves, not only to enhance each one of the mechanisms, alluded to in their specificity, but, above all, to reinforce the socio-structuring implication of the subsumption of individuals under the logic of a social organisation regulated by the indispensable and permanent valorisation of capital.[8]

Such a 'weave of articulations' is the horizon of a comprehensive theory of capitalist subsumption, understood as the regulatory and transformative action of capital upon the reproduction of society in its totality. Orienting the theory adequately toward this horizon poses the necessity of going both *extensively* beyond the analysis of subsumption in exchange/production, as well as *intensively* into the interconnection and development of the forms of subsumption at ever more concrete levels of the reproductive process, implying an ongoing engagement with a vast range of empirical, historical and theoretical materials.[9] The aim of this chapter is far narrower than that demanded by such an endeavour and proceeds critically, aiming to undermine closed, schematic readings of the dynamic of subsumption and arguing that it should instead function as a critical *framework* for conducting further research. In this latter sense, subsumption has a unique role due its crucial mediating function within capitalist society, in that it marks the point of antagonism at which divergent logics of form compete to determine the course of social reproduction. Finally, I sketch out two basic coordinates through which subsumption may be fruitfully explored in relation to the production/reproduction relationship, focusing firstly on the formation of subjectivity and secondly on the political form of reproduction and the question of state power.

---

[8] Castillo Mendoza, 2002, p. 9.
[9] For a recent exchange that adopts this orientation, see Das 2012 and Skillman 2015.

## 1    Historicity and Closure

It is necessary to consider the dynamic of labour's subsumption by capital *beyond* the immediate production process, and conceive of it instead as a process that traverses and interpenetrates the movement of social reproduction on multiple levels and in diverse ways. Although in the course of twentieth-century Marxism, the problematic of how to think this extension was posed, it was in almost every case done so in a manner entirely absorbed into and overdetermined by a secondary problematic, that of *historical transition* or *the historicity of 'capitalism'*, with the effect of seriously distorting the reception of the concept of capitalist subsumption and undermining its critical force. Whilst these two problematics must indeed be thought together if an adequate response to either is to be constructed, the weakness of such approaches is that they thought both together in the mode of an unmediated logical identity, rather than a complex – and, crucially, *underdetermined* – interrelation. In this way, the dynamic of subsumption and, more specifically, the transition from 'formal' to 'real' subsumption was and indeed continues to be deployed as the basis for constructing a periodisation of 'capitalism' and its political landscape. In its most general and 'benign' form, this simply lapses into a crude empiricism of social forms concerned with where the historical line between the 'formal' and 'real' phases of subsumption are to be drawn: 1848, 1914, 1968? Or concerned with which criterion to single out as the marker of this monumental transition: The end of the gold standard, the rise of communication technologies, 'post-fordism', etc. These are largely inconclusive yet nevertheless interminable debates. In its more extreme and better known variant, however, this thesis has generated the theoretically problematic and empirically dubious (if nonetheless provocative) diagnosis that asserts the historical completion or totalisation of capitalist subsumption, not just in the sphere of the traditionally conceived workplace but across the full compass of human life, penetrating the realms of culture, leisure, education, affect and sociality as such. I take Theodor W. Adorno's model of 'total administration' and Antonio Negri's account of the 'real and total subsumption of labour' as the exemplars and historical precedents of this tendency.[10] In both, the concept of subsumption is deployed in order to characterise the particular mode of capitalist domination in the present period as *total* in its colonisation of the social world or life of humanity: a vision of complete integration, in which any exteriority of (living) labour

---

10    Adorno 1997, p. 17; Negri 1988, p. 95. Another early, although less influential, example of this tendency is Camatte 1988.

to capitalist command has been dissolved. This is a tendency that continues to hold currency in Marxist literature, as evidenced in a passage from Frederic Jameson's recent book on volume one of *Capital*, which re-articulates his earlier conception of postmodernity within the conceptual terminology of subsumption. He refers to the present as:

> a stage of 'subsumption' in which the extra-economic or social no longer lies outside capital and economics but has been absorbed into it ... Where everything has been subsumed under capitalism, there is no longer anything outside it.[11]

Jameson's words are a symptomatic of the degree to which this thought has become an unconscious cultural orthodoxy in leftist theory.[12] As Stewart Martin suggests, if the vision of life's subsumption is not always adopted unequivocally, it is at least 'plausible to consider it as the regulative idea of a number of theories of late capitalism'.[13]

### 1.1   *Negri: 'Total Subsumption'*

Antonio Negri is responsible for having produced perhaps the most notorious and controversial variant of this 'totalised' account of capitalist subsumption, which went on to become established as a central tenet of the post-*Operaista* paradigm that would be continued in his own influential work with Michael Hardt and developed by Paulo Virno and Maurizio Lazzarato in conjunction with the concept of 'immaterial labour'. The emergence and development of Negri's reading must be interpreted with a sensitivity to the conjunctural significance of the revolutionary experiences of 1960s and 70s Italy.[14] Two

---

11   Jameson 2011, p. 71.
12   So much so that Harry Harootunian lambasts it as a 'a familiar story in cultural studies, a staple of current accounts among Marxists and non-Marxists alike that has become a classic cultural cliché', whilst simultaneously reproducing its premise that the concept of real subsumption corresponds to 'capitalism as a completed totality' (Harootunian 2015, introduction).
13   Martin 2008, p. 38. Whether formulated in the framework of subsumption, postmodernity or otherwise, such pronouncements tend to gravitate around iconic moments of defeat for the left in its historic forms, particularly '68 and '89, e.g., for Negri: 'May '68 is not simply an important date in terms of the student revolt or the emergence of new intellectual or moral desires within the intermediate classes of society; it is also a moment of extraordinary significance, above all in terms of the realisation of capitalist domination of society; in other words, in terms of real subsumption' (Negri 2003, p. 105). This chronology has been reproduced recently by Jason Read 2003, p. 137.
14   For a contextualisation of those struggles and their impact upon the formation of worker-

lines of thought derived from *Operaismo*, which developed immanently to that experience, are crucial to Negri's account of subsumption. The first of these is the so-called 'Copernican turn' which, in the face of 'extreme left-wing militancy and rapid industrial expansion', inverted capital's traditional theoretical privilege as the active force driving historical change.[15] For the *operaisti*, it was the intransigence of the working class that propelled the movement of society, forcing capital to continually develop social and technical strategies in order to retain its grip over labour's productive but resistant energies. This is what *grounds* the dynamic of progression from formal to real to total subsumption for Negri. The second line of thought is that of the transition from the concepts of 'mass worker' and 'social capital' to the 'social factory' and 'social worker'. The political engagement of Tronti, Negri and others in the early 60s had led to the identification of the mass worker as the 'class-protagonist' emerging at the nexus of Taylorism, Fordism, Keynesianism and 'the planner state'.[16] But following the intense economic and political turmoil of the following two decades, the conditions of struggle were perceived to have changed to the extent that a new form of political subjectivity was operative: one based not solely on conflicts played out on the factory floor but whose antagonism with capital 'covers all the time of life, and invests all of its regions'.[17] Negri's account carries Marx's prognosis of the progressive socialisation of both capital and the worker to the point at which their antagonistic relation, classically thought of as limited to the point of production, is 'totalised' with 'the real subsumption of *world* society under capital'.[18]

For Negri, then, the period of 'real subsumption' marks a new phase of intensity in capitalist class relations, one in which 'capital constitutes society' directly, in the sense that 'the mechanism of the production and reproduction of labour power is wholly internal to capital'.[19] As he describes it, real subsumption

> is a hegemony of capital without limits. Here the form of capitalist production has intervened in and occupied every space in society. Society itself has been converted into a factory. The walls of the central factory have come down, so to speak, and the whole of society has been invaded

---

ist and post-workerist thought, see Wright 2002; Bowring 2004, pp. 101–132; Toscano 2009, pp. 76–91; Tronti 2012.
15  Bowring 2004, p. 104.
16  Negri 1988, pp. 102–114.
17  Negri 2005, p. 28.
18  Negri 1991, p. 121, emphasis added.
19  Negri 1991, p. 114; Negri 1988, p. 126.

by the factory regime and, consequently, by a generalised disciplinary regime. This subsumption is, precisely, a real subsumption of society by capital; society is configured in a disciplinary way through the development of the capitalist system. This is the situation in which we have found ourselves since the middle of the twentieth century.[20]

This position, developed most comprehensively in two texts written whilst Negri was imprisoned in the early 80s, 'The Constitution of Time' and 'Archaeology and Project', is theoretically premised on 'the breakdown of the regulatory principles of capitalist development', the fundamental mediations of the capital-labour relation as conceived of by Marx: 'the market; value; the division between production and reproduction, etc.'[21] More specifically, the possibility of a direct confrontation staged between 'social capital' and the 'social worker' arises from the 'dialectical resolution' or 'complete realisation' of the law of value, which in Marx's account (whose validity Negri consigns to a historical past) integrates the two essential moments of capitalist domination – exchange and production – by regulating the multitude of individual transactions and productive activities carried out across the social body. Most significantly, in Negri's account, the consequence of excising the value-theoretical core of Marx's theory of capital is that time as measure no longer mediates the exploitation of labour. This principle, which for Marx not only regulates the economy but motivates every transformation in the structure of capitalist production (extension of the working day, introduction of machinery, replacement of fixed capital, etc.) dissolves because the distinction upon which it is based, that between value and use-value, no longer holds: '[T]here is no longer an external vantage point upon which use value', i.e., the sphere of concrete needs and capacities 'can depend'.[22] Through 'the complete socialisation and abstraction of all the productive and reproductive segments of labour', labour is rendered 'materially homogenous' and thus 'immeasurable', eliminating the quality/quantity opposition through which it is commodified and thus related to capital. But although their classical ground is thereby abolished, capitalist command and exploitation do not disappear for Negri, they are rather transposed onto a level of social immanence such that the whole of society now

---

20   Negri 2003, p. 105.
21   Negri 1988, p. 114.
22   Negri 2005, p. 25. This is a well-worn trope of post-modern theory, but variations of this trope circulate equally within Marxism, e.g., in Tomba 2013: 'Value has supplanted use-value, such that the individual no longer experiences use-value, but rather value and the status that value confers.' pp. 61–2.

functions as a productive totality internal to capital, without any exogenous source of antagonism:

> The capitalist supersession of the law of value – what Marx calls the process of real subsumption – dislocates the relations of exploitation as a whole. It transforms exploitation into a global social relation. ... What does it mean to struggle against capital when capital has subjugated all of lived time, not only that of the working day, but all, all of it. Reproduction is like production, life is like work.[23]

The divergences from Marx's own views on real subsumption are vast here, but it is the collapse of production and reproduction into one another, such that they are 'now in parallel and on equal terms', that poses the greatest problem in Negri's account.[24] By projecting the dynamic of subsumption, which in Marx is restricted to the analytical level of the immediate production process of an individual capital, *directly* onto the social totality in its historical development and simultaneously announcing its completion (a paradox which we will come to shortly), the determining presence of the value-form and its circulatory mechanisms are repudiated as an anachronistic artefact of a bygone cycle of struggle. Consequently, Negri lapses into a theoretical 'productivism' in which the moment of economic mediation central to Marx's thought is jettisoned and a logic of domination specific to the production process is applied wholesale to the social totality: '[T]he real subsumption of labour can't but be (in the same moment) real subsumption of society', which is also to say that it has 'become the production of that same society.'[25] But how, then, is 'the exploitation of society under the control of capital' structured, if not according to the commodification and temporal measure of labour?[26] Negri may well assign this breakdown to historical conditions rather than his own theoretical decision and rhetorically ask: 'When the entire time of life has become the time of production, who measures whom?' But as Dauvé and Nesic wryly point out, actually existing capitalist practices do not conform to this picture: 'Managers know their Marx better than Toni Negri – they keep tracing and measuring productive places and moments to try and rationalise them more and more'.[27]

---

23  Negri 1991, xvi.
24  Negri 1988, p. 114.
25  Negri 1991, p. 124.
26  Negri 1988, p. 113.
27  Negri 2005, p. 29; Dauvé and Nesic 2008, p. 135. Negri, however, remains unperturbed by such objections: 'While it is evident that this kind of discourse [of real subsumption]

As I argued in the previous chapter, it is only through the inner unity of production and exchange that labour's subsumption under capital functions, that is, both formally and durationally. It is in light of this that the contradictions of Negri's historicist interpretation of real subsumption become manifest, revealing the limitations of his productivist ontology. Negri leapfrogs over the necessity of this relation by simultaneously holding two seemingly incompatible positions on real subsumption: that it is both 'real *and* total'.[28] In doing so, he places its status as subsumption in doubt. Logically speaking, as Hegel established and Marx recognised, a relation of subsumption is a dialectically unresolved relation that remains stuck in an abstract opposition of universal and particular without passing over into a higher unity (this is precisely what makes subsumption inadequate in Hegel's dialectical development of the concept and perfectly adequate in Marx's description of the capital-labour relation).[29] Negri seems to grasp the paradox of an accomplished subsumption, if only in a single passage, written in 1972:

> Marx made certain predictions regarding advanced capitalist development; he described lucidly the moment in which the law of value would come to be extinguished and labour would be *no longer subsumed but formally suppressed* within capitalist command. All this is now present reality.[30]

For Negri, the paradoxical apotheosis and completion of labour's subsumption reveals itself to in fact mark the transition *out of* subsumption to capital and into suppression within 'command' as the form of domination characterising contemporary capitalist power. Because value – more precisely competition over surplus-value – is no longer the organisational logic guiding production, Negri resorts to an ontologically grounded theory of exploitation that takes place 'outside any economic measure' and whose 'economic reality is fixed exclusively in political terms'.[31] The dull compulsion of economic relations and

---

entails excessively sweeping generalisations in terms of the examples or ideas put forward as models, and any number of objections can be raised with respect to these, it is nevertheless the case that we are dealing with objections that serve to enrich the framework without invalidating it as a whole' (Negri 2003, pp. 105–6).

28  Stewart Martin also highlighted this paradox in paper entitled 'What is the subsumption of life by capital?', delivered at the 10th Annual *Historical Materialism* Conference, 'Making the World Working Class', held in London, 7–10 November 2013.

29  Hegel 1999, 'The Judgement' and 'The Syllogism'; Marx 1985, p. 332.

30  Negri 1988, p. 48, emphasis added.

31  Negri cited in Wright 2005.

the accumulation process are thus displaced by a unifying form of power Negri simply identifies as 'command': '[O]nce within real subsumption, we pass from the aporia [of use-value's relation to value] on to a pure and simple tautology'.[32] Whereas for Marx, value in capitalist societies was an end in itself (expressed succinctly in the general formula M–C–M') and command over production a means to realise that end, Negri sees 'command' as the end in itself of capital in the phase of real subsumption: 'Command becomes even more fascistic in form, ever more anchored in the simple reproduction of itself, ever more emptied of any rationale other than the reproduction of its own effectiveness.'[33]

Because this command must 'be exercised in a way that is intrinsic to the totality of social relations', traversing the entire reproduction process and 'forming a homogeneous tissue of exploitation', it totalises all social conflict within the ambit of a singular, ontological opposition.[34] This point is crucial because it demonstrates the loss of Marx's complex conception of power, as composed of a multiplicity of interacting but heterogeneous forms that orbit around a central contradiction, and marks its replacement with an ahistorical Spinozist ontology of power, internally differentiated as *potentia* and *potestas*. In Negri's conception, the contradiction between capital and labour is recoded as a differentiation within time itself, of its 'proletarian' pole on the one hand and its 'capitalist' pole on the other, where the former is the 'multiplicitous' time of productive, constituent activity and the latter is the 'empty', constituted time of 'analytical command'. What is pernicious about capitalist command under real subsumption, on this account, is not social division (which was contested by the mass worker's 'refusal of work') but the *displacement* of the productive multiplicity of collective time into the form of an abstract totality:

> [Real subsumption] is a unity which is founded on the overcoming of the capitalist capacity to impose the *asymmetry of power* along *vertical axis* that traverse life; it is a unity that imposes itself at the level of the horizontality of the collective: so, not the division of the class in itself, but separation of *the time of social composition* from the time of the totality of exploitation.[35]

Because of Capital's dependency on the 'omniversal' time which it at the same time denies, this separation has the Sisyphean quality of an 'activity of neg-

---

32   Negri 2005, p. 25.
33   Negri 1988, p. 95.
34   Negri 1988 p. 95; p. 126.
35   Negri 2005, p. 75.

ation of an irrepressible antagonism'.[36] As the form of capitalist domination shifts from measure to 'command' under conditions of real subsumption, it is for Negri the state that enforces command, both undertaking exploitation and absorbing the resistance of living labour (the two moments having become indiscernible). In the absence of the coercive function of time-as-measure, the continued 'institutional' management of this separation becomes the state's project, in its role as the 'active non-being' that actualises command. The conflict of capital and labour thus plays itself out as an opposition between the 'internal time' of composing subjects (good) and the 'external time' of the composition itself (bad) underwritten by the state. Capitalist power is no longer understood by Negri in terms of the extraction of surplus value by individual, competing enterprises but as social capital's capacity to systematise and mould collective time, in order to produce 'a *surplus of* command'.[37]

This gives rise to a double conflation: on the one hand, of exploitation and political repression, on the other, of productive practices and political resistance. It is the state whose activity subtracts the 'ontological plenitude' from productive time of living labour: 'The state operates under the necessity of removing the collective dimension and the productive autonomy of time, of temporal being, because their emergence means antagonism.'[38] Correspondingly, capital has produced an immediately social worker, directly capable of communism without a party or any other form of collective institutional mediation. At the level of political subjectivity, the labouring activity which gives content to the capitalist composition is not distinguished in kind from political acts which might challenge the system as a whole.[39] This is because the productive time of creative labouring *is already* the time of liberation – 'the matter that weaves together the productivity of being is the collective time of liberation, which is the same as production' – which lacks only the adequate social form of collectivity within which this content can flourish unhindered.[40] Negri thus claims 'communism is a constituting praxis'. Yet if it is the 'real movement' that abolishes the contemporary form of society, what then distinguishes

---

36   Negri 2005, p. 84.
37   Negri 2005, p. 66.
38   Negri 2005, p. 80.
39   This is a problem recognised by Virno, but only insofar as it is treated as a historically actual condition: 'political action now seems, in a disastrous way, like some superfluous duplication of the experience of labor, since the latter experience, even if in a deformed and despotic manner, has subsumed into itself certain structural characteristics of political action' (Virno 2004, p. 51).
40   Negri 2005, p. 109.

it as a specific, politically charged (i.e., revolutionary) form of praxis from praxis as such (i.e., human activity, labour)? A properly revolutionary theory would have to situate itself critically in relation to those practices that actively constitute and contribute to the reproduction of capitalist power, distinguishing these from others which carry the potential to disrupt it and introduce alternative logics of reproduction. This demands a more developed account of the complex and changing relation between the 'basic politicity' of everyday social practices and the 'specific politicity' of revolutionary and counter-revolutionary practices. Such a relation, and therefore the possibility of this critical perspective, is only obscured by the ontological reductionism of 'good' and 'bad' forces of composition, a tendency taken to its extreme by Hardt and Negri when they melt these opposed poles down into the essential figures of 'empire' and 'multitude' in a manner that erases the internally structured terrain and diverse forms of capitalist power. As Noys points out:

> [T]hey extrapolate the tendency to an achieved state of capitalism's own fantasy of itself, and so overwrite this realised fantasy back onto its existent forms. In doing so, they neglect the contradictory tendencies of subsumption, in which formal and real subsumption do not simply form discrete historical stages, but also heterogeneous ensembles and strategies.[41]

The aporetic double status of real subsumption – as at once totalised and by the same token suspended – is thus only an expression of a deeper contradiction in Negri's thought, that between its ontological and historical commitments. Negri's is an unmistakably theological take on real subsumption, which takes it to be both a specific historical stage and also the consummate unveiling of an ontological conflict underlying all of history. As such, the schema of antagonism outlined above tends toward a fundamental opposition of essential forces indifferent to concrete historical determinations, so that the agency of diverse individuals, capitals and states is eclipsed by an ubiquitous antagonism given at the level of being itself. In light of this, we must ask how the Manichean opposition unveiled by the realisation of the dynamic of subsumption relates to the ongoing process of reproduction-development, that is, to real history.[42] It is clear that Negri's account of real subsumption cannot adequately

---

41   Noys 2010, p. 127.
42   As Alberto Toscano points out: 'The mere positing of a duality, say between Empire and multitude, without the conflictual composition that can provide this duality with a certain degree of determinateness, can arguably be seen to generate a seemingly heroic, but

resolve this question without enacting a closure through the ontological overdetermination of struggle. As such, subsumption for Negri is best thought of as what Haug, referring to 'immaterial labour', has labelled a 'non-concept', a marker drawing together a constellation of different positions and relations on a totalised plane of political conflict. But this plane cannot be grasped in any conceptually determinate sense that would open itself to the concrete specificity of struggles because, as Negri himself observes in keeping with the Spinozist notion that *'determinatio negatio est'*: '[W]hat do resistance, revolt, and revolution signify within subsumption? They signify everything and nothing.'[43]

### 1.2  Adorno: Subsumption as 'Total Administration'

A similar emphasis on the historical totalisation of capitalist domination circumscribes Adorno's attempts to think capitalist subsumption in its widest social implications. Adorno and Horkheimer describe in *Dialectic of Enlightenment* a stage of 'totalitarian capitalism' in which the reduction of 'the overwhelming mass of the population ... to mere objects of administration, which preforms every department of modern life right down to language and perception, conjures up an illusion of objective necessity before which they believe themselves powerless'.[44] The subsumption of individuals under capitalist relations of production has, for Adorno, 'integrated all internal human characteristics' such that 'people are now totally controlled'.[45]

Retaining the more general philosophical sense of the concept, specifically that given to it the context of Kantian epistemology, Adorno's use of subsumption is not explicitly grounded in the technical distinction Marx makes between its formal and real modes, or even limited to the labour process. As such it is not deployed to denote a specific social content, but rather refers to a generic conceptual operation ('identifying judgment') which, when applied to the context of 'late' capitalist society, becomes synonymous and interchangeable with other related – and in fact for Adorno more socially substantive – concepts such as 'integration' and 'administration'. For Adorno and Horkheimer, this generality of subsumption is key, however, because it manifests the connection, incipiently present in Marx, between conceptual and social abstraction, seeing them both as expressions of the same underlying tendency proper to

---

ultimately ineffectual horizon for theoretical analysis and political militancy' (Toscano 2009, p. 89).
43    Negri 2003, p. 106.
44    Horkheimer and Adorno 2002, p. 30.
45    Horkheimer and Adorno 2002, p. 187; Adorno 2003, p. 117.

enlightenment reason, namely, of adequating the particular to the universal in a manner that liquefies any excessive individuality.[46] In this way, conceptual equivalence is read as an expression of the broad historical tendency to 'the systematic domination over nature' which lies at the root of all forms of domination, from class, as 'the social subsumption of atoms to a general concept that expresses their constitutive as well as heterogeneous relations', to the annihilating racism of Nazi Germany, which was founded on 'the complete abstraction of subsuming human beings under arbitrary concepts and treating them accordingly'.[47]

For Adorno, the primacy of the problem of subsumption establishes an inner unity between methodological and political concerns. In the theoretical register, Horkheimer had already counted subsumption under universal concepts amongst the procedures of 'traditional theory', which he and Adorno contrasted to dialectics as a 'critical theory'.[48] More fundamentally still, at the level of the social practice which determines theoretical consciousness, conceptual equivalence formed 'the prevailing principle of reality' of an 'administered world' in the form of subsumption to the value-form and commodity exchange.[49] It was Alfred Sohn-Rethel who had first suggested this connection to Adorno in the 1930s with his conception of exchange as a process of conceptual abstraction established not in thought but in 'the action alone' and therefore a 'real abstraction'.[50] For Sohn-Rethel, it was because exchange

---

46 Kant is taken as an avatar of instrumental rationality in its enlightened form, insofar as for him 'reason is the agency of calculating thought, which arranges the world for the purposes of self-preservation and recognises no function other than that of working on the object as mere sense material in order to make it the material of subjugation. The true nature of the schematism which externally coordinates the universal and the particular, the concept and the individual, case, finally turns out, in current science, to be the interest of industrial society. Being is apprehended in terms of manipulation and administration. Everything – including the individual human being, not to mention the animal – becomes a repeatable, replaceable process, a mere example of the conceptual models of the system' (Horkheimer and Adorno 2002, p. 65).

47 Adorno 1997, p. 255; Adorno 1973, p. 236.

48 Horkheimer 1972, pp. 188–243; 'The central nerve of the dialectic as a method is determinate negation. It is based on the experience of the impotence of a criticism that keeps to the general and polishes off the object being criticised by subsuming it from above under a concept as its representative. Only the critical idea that unleashes the force stored up in its own object is fruitful; fruitful both for the object, by helping it to come into its own, and against it, reminding it that it is not yet itself' (Adorno 1993, p. 80).

49 Adorno 1997, p. 83; Osborne 2007.

50 Sohn-Rethel 1978, p. 20 ff. This conception of 'real abstraction' remains rather limited however insofar as it conceives of the reality of the abstraction simply by virtue of the fact that it is *an action* rather than more comprehensively in terms of its effects 'in action', i.e.,

established equivalence in practice, by wiping out the 'entire empirical reality of facts, events and description' differentiating use-values, that equivalence in thought became possible, the 'social synthesis' of diverse commodities effected by money thus forming the material basis for the conceptual synthesis of disparate representations.[51] Adorno, influenced by Sohn-Rethel's idea of the unconscious but real conceptuality of exchange, highlighted this point in a seminar on Marx delivered in 1962:[52]

> Exchange itself is a process of abstraction. Whether human beings know or not, by entering into a relationship of exchange and reducing different use values to labour values they actualise a conceptual operation socially. This is the objectivity of the concept in practice.[53]

Because capitalist society is founded on the universalisation of exchange, this subsumption of qualitative individuality under the value-form becomes 'the objective abstraction to which the social process of life is subject' (the Kantian equation of universal validity with objectivity is important here insofar as it

---

as shaping and guiding concrete social reality and its conflicts (see ch. 3 of this thesis). That it is merely the actualisation of an ideality does not establish the full 'reality' of value, given that diverse forms of ideality and abstraction coexist and interact with value throughout the social process, all of which possess different functions, effects and potentialities, which is to say, different social actualities. As Alberto Toscano and Brenna Bhandar argue in relation to race: '[W]e cannot treat the question of the practical reality of abstraction as one which is simply adjudicated at the (very abstract) level of the formal analysis of capital. What we would seem to require is a way of thinking the *articulation* between distinct and sometimes independent modalities of abstraction. We would need to be able to think the articulation between *events* and *processes* of abstraction/dissolution (the moments of primitive accumulation or accumulation by dispossession); the 'unconscious' abstracting social *practices* (as grasped, for instance, in Sohn-Rethel's account of the exchange-abstraction); the high-level *logic* of abstraction intrinsic to value as a social form of capitalism; and the relatively autonomous and deliberate *practices* and *devices* of abstraction (scientific, mathematical, linguistic, but also political and *juridical*) that are either articulated with real abstraction or posed by it as its "presuppositions"' (Bhandar and Toscano 2015, p. 11).

51  Sohn-Rethel 1978, pp. 48–9.
52  Adorno refers to Sohn-Rethel as 'the first to point out that hidden in this principle [the transcendental], in the general and necessary activity of the mind, lies work of an inalienably social nature.' Adorno 1973, P. 177; however, other members of the Frankfurt school (Horkheimer in particular) were far less approving of Sohn-Rethel's thesis. See Abromeit 2011, pp. 384–5.
53  Adorno 2018, p. 155; Bellofiore notes a similar argument made by Colletti, which is also limited by its basis in a theory of generalised exchange, see Bellofiore 2009, p. 180.

establishes exchange as both the principle of social totality and, correspondingly, the basis for a theory of fetishism).[54] Generalised exchange thus brings about 'a conceptuality which holds sway in reality itself', acting upon the vast mass of exchangers 'behind their backs' as a law of survival (or not, as the case may be), binding them together and delimiting their activity through a monetary rather than directly practical nexus.[55] As Bellofiore and Riva point out, for Adorno, 'exchange is the synthetic principle that immanently determines the connection of every social fact' and 'the principle of mediation that guarantees the reproduction of society through a process of abstraction'.[56]

It is this objective validity of the exchange abstraction that, on Adorno's account, becomes socially totalising in 'late capitalism', governing not only the noisy sphere of circulation, but penetrating all those hitherto 'independent' realms of life (independent from exchange relations, at least) and subjecting them to 'total administration'. The best known and enduring illustration of this diffusion of economic logic is the industrialisation of culture, famously depicted in *Dialectic of Enlightenment*, that produces 'art's total subsumption under usefulness' and 'the process of identifying, cataloging, and classifying' that is fully realised in that which has been 'rigorously subsumed'.[57] Tracing back the isomorphism between mental and practical abstraction, Adorno and Horkheimer argue that the culture industry's 'prime service to the customer is to do his schematising for him', following the trend of mass production to replace 'a real act of synthesis' with 'blind subsumption' (it is in this sense, an extension of the social function of money).[58] The individual, as object, becomes a site of colonisation by the exchange relations they effect as subject. In a fascinating fragment from *Minima Moralia* entitled 'Novissimum Organum', Adorno suggests that

---

54  The key link is Marx's description of the commodity as the 'universally necessary social form of the product' (Marx 1976, p. 949), mirroring Kant's account of the transcendental object as the universally necessary form of all objective experience. 'The crucial difference between the dialectical and the positivistic view of totality is that the dialectical concept of totality is intended 'objectively', namely, for the understanding of every social individual observation, whilst positivistic systems theories wish, in an uncontradictory manner, to incorporate observations in a logical continuum, simply through the selection of categories as general as possible. In so doing, they do not recognise the highest structural concepts as the precondition for the states of affairs subsumed under them.' 'Introduction' to Adorno 1976, p. 14; Adorno 2003, p. 120; see also Lotz 2013, pp. 110–123.
55  Adorno 1976, p. 80.
56  Bellofiore and Riva 2015, p. 25.
57  Horkheimer and Adorno 2002, p. 128; p. 104.
58  Horkheimer and Adorno 2002, p. 98, translation modified; pp. 166–7.

the 'alteration of the technical composition of capital' is prolonged *within those* encompassed, and indeed constituted by, the technological demands of the production process. *The organic composition of man is growing.*[59]

These phenomena all express the extension of objective abstraction and correspondent industrial methods to every sphere of the social process. Such descriptions of the integrative effects of industrial logic resonate strongly with Marx's account of capitalist subsumption, for example his portrayal of industrial labour as a 'specialisation in passivity'. One can indeed find occasional remarks which intimate a deeper reflection on the dynamic of capitalist subsumption on Adorno's part, for example his assertion that 'the forces of production are mediated more than ever by the relations of production', the 'Novissimum' fragment referred to above, or when he describes 'a shift in the inner economic composition of cultural commodities'.[60] But in substance, a developed theory of subsumption is absent from Adorno's conception of modern domination. Instead, it is primarily through the frame of exchange relations and their reifying power that the regime of 'total administration' is conceived. If Adorno speaks of capitalist subsumption, then, it is subsumption under the commodity-form rather than capital that is at stake. The influence of Lukács, who treated the commodity as 'the central, structural problem of capitalist society in all its aspects' looms large here.[61] Ingo Elbe summarises the limits of Lukács' approach:

> Although the first to understand the character of capitalist rule the way Marx did – anonymous, objectively mediated, and having a life of its own – the 'founding document' of Western Marxism, Lukács' *History and Class Consciousness*, avoids a reconstruction of Marx's theory of capitalism. Instead of an analysis of Marx's dialectic of the form of value up to the form of capital, which in the theory of real subsumption offers an explanation of the connection – so decisive for Lukács – between commodification and the alienated structure of the labor process, one finds merely an analogising combination of a value theory reduced to the 'quantifying' value-form (due to an orientation towards Simmel's cultural critique

---

59  Adorno 2005, p. 229, emphasis added. I am grateful to Stewart Martin for first drawing my attention to this passage in his 2013 paper 'What is the subsumption of life by capital?'
60  Adorno 2003, p. 121.
61  Lukács 1971, p. 83.

of money) and a diagnosis, oriented towards Max Weber, of the formal-rational tendency of the objectification of the labor process and modern law.[62]

Whilst Adorno was sceptical of Lukács's romantic critique of reification as false consciousness (rather than it being the 'reflexive form' of what is 'objectively untrue'), these criticisms are broadly valid for his own understanding of the mechanisms of capitalist domination insofar as he fails to theorise them beyond the level of exchange relations and equivalence in any comprehensive manner. Adorno's philosophically sophisticated account of the 'socialisation' effected by fetishism alludes to that 'decisive connection' between exchange and production, in that 'historical materialism is the anamnesis of the genesis' that critically deconstructs fetishised forms (whereas political economy succumbs to ideology by taking them at face value).[63] But as his student Helmut Reichelt would later note, the full dialectical deconstruction of these forms 'remains in embryo in Adorno's writings' and is limited to 'the terrain of asseveration' because the genesis of the commodity-form is not constructed at the level of the social reproduction process *in toto* or even followed through into an analysis of the production process.[64] Restricting it instead to the exchange principle, Adorno establishes the horizon of his theory of domination as the totalisation of the fetish-character of the commodity in an integrative apparatus of 'mass deception' through which 'illusion dominates reality'.[65]

If, then, for Negri the completion of subsumption is dependent on the abolition of economic equivalence, raising production to the status of an ontological absolute, the inverse is true for Adorno, who puts forward a 'circulationist' theory of subsumption in which commodity exchange 'provides the objectively valid model for all essential social events' and is the 'law which determines how the fatality of mankind unfolds'.[66] As such he too, like Negri, misses the crucial inner connection between exchange and production, commodification and valorisation, in which the subsumptive dynamic of capitalist power is grounded.[67] This is especially clear in the way that Adorno theorises the eco-

---

62  Elbe 2013.
63  Sohn-Rethel cited in Bellofiore and Riva 2015, p. 26.
64  The so-called 'The *Neue Marx-Lektüre*' instigated by Adorno's students arose in response to these issues as 'a project to deepen and even to ground Adorno's critical theory of society' in Marx's critique of political economy, see Bellofiore and Riva, 2015, p. 26.
65  Adorno 1976, p. 80.
66  Ibid.
67  As Lotz argues: 'Adorno, in other words, does not see that the commodity *form* cannot be reduced to exchange and, instead, needs to be put in relation to all other economic

nomic structure of domination in a world of 'total administration'. For Adorno, 'human beings continue to be subject to domination by the economic process' in the face of which 'the individual is entirely nullified'. At the same time, he notes 'the absence of a theory of surplus value' or an 'objective theory of value' adequate to 'late' capitalism.[68] Whereas in the late 1940s he described individuals as 'the mere agents of the law of value', it's not clear that for the later Adorno the market continues to regulate capitalist domination in its 'totalitarian' form. Horkheimer likewise wrote in 1943 of 'the now vanishing sphere of circulation' and 'the gradual abolishment of the market as a regulator of production', such that the social process was no longer determined by 'anonymous processes' but rather 'decided or convened upon by elites'.[69] In this they were both influenced by Friedrich Pollock's idea of 'state capitalism', which asserted that liberal market capitalism had been replaced by a mixed or command economy ruled over by monopolistic conglomerates and bureaucratic structures and that, as a result, the profit motive had been replaced by the power motive. The extent to which Adorno and Horkheimer adopted Pollock's theory is debated – Deborah Cook, for example, argues that Adorno's concept of 'administration' referred to the manipulations of the welfare state rather than Pollock's all-encompassing 'state capitalism' – and they certainly rejected his optimistic conclusions (the 'undialectical position that in an antagonistic society a non-antagonistic economy was possible') but nevertheless they clearly affirmed the notion of a new era of capitalism in which domination did not take place solely, or even primarily, on the basis of anonymous economic mediations.[70]

'Administration' thus signals a purer and more integral form of class domination than the free play of market forces. Ironically, and in spite of his exaggerated emphasis on the formal moment of exchange, this leads Adorno to a conclusion similar to that of Negri, namely that in the absence (or at least qualitative diminution) of an autonomous mechanism of economic regulation (value), capitalist command ('the steering of economic forces') increasingly becomes a function of political power. The totalisation of capitalist subsumption brings about an indiscernibility – if in essence rather than appearance – of

---

categories that Marx unfolds. Put differently, Capitalist schematisation does not simply consist of the exchange principle that takes away the uniqueness of things and turns them into something universal (as Adorno often seems to suggest); rather, the whole distinction of use and exchange is itself the *result* of capitalist reproduction. Accordingly the schema that we are in search of cannot be identical with the exchange principle' (Lotz 2013, p. 119).

68  Adorno 2003, pp. 115–6; Horkheimer and Adorno 2002, xvvii.
69  Horkheimer 2016.
70  Cook 1998, pp. 16–26; Adorno cited in Wiggershaus 1995, p. 282.

the economic and political moments, as relations of production 'have ceased to be just property relations; they now also include relations ranging from those of administration on up to those of the state, which functions now as an all-inclusive capitalist organisation'.[71] This view, however, scrambles the structural relations that distinguish and relate the different moments of the social reproduction process as well as the different sources of social power in Marx's thought, unifying them under the rubric of a singular controlling logic that reduces individuals to 'simple objects of administration':

> [M]aterial production, distribution, and consumption are administered jointly. Their boundaries flow into one another, even though earlier within the overall social process they were at once different from one another and related, and for that reason they respected what was qualitatively different. Everything is now one.[72]

There is a degree of equivocation in Adorno's writings about the completeness and character of this totalisation, with different texts both across and within periods conveying different impressions. An illuminating comment from its 1969 preface asserts that 'the development toward total integration identified' in *Dialectic of Enlightenment* had 'been interrupted but not terminated'.[73] That Adorno and Horkheimer reserved terms such as 'total integration' and the 'integral state' to their discussions of Nazi Germany and the USSR gives us grounds to think that they distinguished between 'administered' and 'dictatorial' forms of subsumption (echoing Marcuse's 'repressive desublimation' thesis distinguishing the cultural forms of oppression in 'East' and 'West') although the distinction was not made programmatically, with the aforementioned cases considered expressions of the same underlying tendency. At a more methodological level, this ambiguity is qualified by an important difference between totality and totalisation, connected to the fact that the unity of society is thought dialectically by Adorno as both true and untrue: true because 'there is no social fact which is not determined by society as whole', untrue because it projects a systematic coherence and completeness onto an incomplete and incoherent reality, one that is 'not in itself rationally continuous' nor 'at one with its subjects'.[74] Noting that the systematisation in social

---

71  Adorno 2003, p. 119.
72  Adorno 2003, p. 124.
73  Horkheimer and Adorno 2002, xii.
74  Adorno 1969–70, pp. 145–6.

sciences ('traditional theory') merely mimics the real systematisation of an administered world, the principle of Adorno's negative dialectics is to demonstrate the falseness of this whole. This is based on the non-identical opposition of society's character as both subject and object (that is, the product of human praxis but also a structure existing independently, 'over and against' it): 'Society as subject and society as object are the same and yet not the same.'[75]

Nonetheless, at a less abstract level, the exclusive dependency of Adorno's theory of capitalist domination on the exchange relation and its 'real abstraction' raises the problem of closure on a different front, insofar as it elevates the principle of equivalence to a social absolute encompassing all mediating – that is, practically constitutive and transformative – activity: 'the totality of the process of mediation'.[76] The closure of other categories of social mediation that this presupposes, specifically those of production (not to mention those external but essential to capital's accumulation process), theoretically extinguishes the dynamic of socio-technical transformation constituted between the relations and forces of production that is decisive in modern society. The dynamic of subsumption, which grounds the reproductive unfolding of the social process under the condition of capital, is therefore occluded by Adorno in favour of the 'irresistible progress' of a vague but all-encompassing administrative apparatus. However, failing to grasp the internal logic of capitalist constitution as a process in motion leaves Adorno open to his own charge of immobilising history 'in the unhistorical realm, heedless of the historical conditions that govern the inner composition and constellation of subject and object'.[77] As Krahl forcefully argued, 'Adorno's negation of late capitalist society has remained abstract, closing itself to the need for the determinacy of determinate negation'.[78] This is partly due to Adorno and Horkheimer's view that the logic of technical rationalisation deployed in real subsumption is simply a manifestation of 'instrumental reason', submerging capital's historically specific forms and structure in their meta-narrative of natural heteronomy, and partly to do with Adorno's methodological orientation toward negative critique elaborated above. The two tendencies converge in *Negative Dialectics*, where, Krahl remarked, 'the concept of praxis is no longer questioned in terms of social change in its specific historical forms'.[79]

---

75    Adorno 1976, p. 34.
76    Adorno 2003, p. 124.
77    Adorno 1973, p. 129.
78    Krahl 1974, p. 166, translation modified.
79    Ibid.

In this way, Adorno's theory not only enacts a closure to the comprehension of actual social conditions but also to the possibility of their revolutionary transformation. For Krahl, 'Adorno deciphered origin and identity as the dominant category of the sphere of circulation ... but the same theoretical tools which allowed Adorno this insight into the social totality, also prevented him from seeing the historical possibilities of a liberating praxis'.[80] Instead, Adorno's thought suffers from an 'objective inadequacy', in that it theoretically asserts the primacy of praxis whilst being simultaneously unable to register that praxis at the level of conjuncturally specific 'organisational categories'.[81] This more fundamental form of closure blocks the connection of social critique to a revolutionary horizon in Adorno's thought, which – despite remaining programmatically committed to a theoretical negation of subsumption – nonetheless lapses into an abstract defence of the non-identical that is at the same time bound to its foreclosure.[82] By focusing solely on undoing the 'anamnesis of the genesis', the critical deconstruction of objective illusion *supplants* practice rather than clearing the way for it or forming an organic moment in the construction of a new genesis. As a result, Adorno's critique cannot but be mobilised as a radical defence of the individual (both the social individual and the individual work of art) which for him is the political other to the all-encompassing command of the identitarian capital-state. This outcome both vindicates Krahl's charge that Adorno 'remained transfixed' by bourgeois individuality and also explains his retreat into the aesthetic as the privileged site of critique in an unfree society ('the question posed by every artwork is how, under the domination of the universal, a particular is in any way possible').[83] If however a theory of subsumption is to supersede such closure and retain critical force, it must open itself to the determinate comprehension of the *incomplete* and therefore *contestable* processes of domination as well as the forms of collective identity and action that would be the conditions for transcending those processes.

---

80   Ibid.
81   Krahl 1974, p. 165.
82   'The objective rationality of society, namely that of exchange, continues to distance itself through its dynamics, from the model of logical reason. Consequently, society – what has been made independent – is, in turn, no longer intelligible; only the law of becoming independent is intelligible' (Adorno 1976, p. 15).
83   Krahl 1974, p. 166; Adorno 1993, p. 351.

## 2  Rejecting Periodisation

Whilst the theoretical positions presented in the work of Negri and Adorno are products of highly specific theoretical and political trajectories, they nonetheless serve to exemplify the contradictions and limits of an interpretation of subsumption that (i) deploys it in an unmediated way to construct a periodisation of capitalist society and (ii) asserts its completion in a phase of 'total subsumption' marked by the breakdown of the core structural distinctions – particularly of the economic and the political – through which the social process is organised on a capitalist basis (i.e., those that give rise to the dynamic of subsumption in the first place). In following its latter form, we have seen how this reading of subsumption enacts a theoretical closure and overdetermination of the social process through its diachronic totalisation of capitalist subsumption, foreclosing the possibility of further qualitative development based on capital's inner dynamic as well as the possibility of a transcending praxis that is indissolubly bound up with that dynamic. In this context, Stewart Martin has noted 'the intense ambivalence that the contention of capital's subsumption of life has produced within neo- and post-Marxist thought'.[84] There is a stark contrast here between the pessimism of first-generation Frankfurt school thinkers, along with others like Baudrillard, for whom it marks 'the exhaustion of anti-capitalist politics, even its imagination' (the management of desires and 'growing organic composition of the human') and the quasi-theological optimism of Negri and other post-*Operaists* for whom it 'demonstrates the very creativity and growing autonomy of living labour, which capital only subsumes as an increasingly thin membrane of control, predisposed to disintegrate' ('the communism of capital').[85] Yet despite their divergent evaluations of its political repercussions, for both poles of this tendency, the historical completion of subsumption dissolves the possibility of an ongoing social struggle structured by the law of value, the distinction between living labour and labour-power and the distinct but interlocking mechanisms of capitalist and state power. By doing this, these theories lose precisely what is critically forceful in the theory of subsumption: its specification of the structure and forms of capitalist domination and the points of antagonism at which the dialectic of integration/transcendence unfolds. The terrain of conflict instead becomes vague and generalised as a single form of command regulating the social process, whether ontologically or natural-historically conceived. As Martin argues, 'the

---

84   Martin 2008.
85   Ibid.

consequences for the struggle against capitalism are self-evidently profound: the dissipation, if not outright negation, of the basic antagonism between living labour and capital.'[86]

These contradictions can be traced back to a number of basic theoretical inconsistencies and misconstruals of Marx's description of capitalist subsumption.

Firstly, the distinction between formal, real and hybrid subsumption made by Marx only applies directly to an individual production process, they are not concepts of social totality. This means that different capitals, branches and forms of production can and will, in the same historical moment, operate at different levels of capitalist development and, furthermore, in uneven interaction with each other (indeed, Marx says that as the process of subsumption matures in one branch of industry, it can act as a condition for the incipience of subsumption in another). It is not, therefore, plausible to totalise all production processes in society as being at the same conceptual stage of development. Even the same industries are subject to radical asymmetries in the structure of production, such that highly technical methods might be employed in some parts of the globe or aspects of the labour process while extremely rudimentary methods still dominate elsewhere. The identification of forms of subsumption with phases of a social totality's development misconstrues the theoretical function of the distinction between them, which is to register *change* and *difference* in the relations between capital and labour at the level of a given production process, that is, to grasp conceptually the diverse and changing modes of social and material command employed by a capital in the course of its expanded reproduction. The complexity of concrete configurations of subsumption forms and their dynamics of change is not only a theoretical postulate, it is documented in a vast number of empirical studies.[87]

Secondly, the forms of subsumption may be presented by Marx as 'logically' successive, but this tells us very little about the actual chronology of their appearance or the necessity of their development in the context of a specific production processes. Given that real subsumption is effective in even the most rudimentary rationalisations of the labour process – for example, in the implementation of cooperation – the historical gap separating formal from real subsumption is in many cases negligible, if present at all; the wage relation is established and the labour process is immediately subject to re-organisation. By contrast, it is also the case that capitalists may maintain the labour pro-

---

86   Ibid.
87   E.g., Banaji 2011; Das 2012; Anievas and Nisancioglu 2015; van der Linden 2008.

cess in conditions of formal or hybrid subsumption indefinitely or even 'revert' back to formal or hybrid methods, provided that it remains profitable to do so. Capital has no inherent imperative to technological progress for its own sake, only to accumulation: If there is a potential to increase profits then capitals will introduce technical innovations, but if, for example, factors such as low wages and poor environmental and safety regulations keep the cost of production 'competitive' then there may be little incentive to do so (both agriculture and extractive industries offer clear examples of this).[88] There is thus no necessary linearity to the transition between forms, only a competitive drive to maximise accumulation by whichever means possible.

Lastly, if it is implausible to posit a homogenous stage of subsumption across all labour processes, then the claim that all of 'life' or 'the social' has been subsumed is even more questionable. The developments brought about by real subsumption do of course have impacts that radically re-shape the reproductive process as a whole, and theorising these impacts demands going beyond Marx's account, but for them to be the effects of subsumption under capital they must nonetheless be mediated through the distinct phases of exchange and production (the latter being the only meaningful site in which we can speak of 'real subsumption') rather than derived from one or the other alone. Much more fundamentally, however, to assume that a direct subsumption of 'life' is possible is to collapse one of the central distinctions through which capitalist social relations are structured – that between living labour and the labour-power commodity – and thereby jettison the theory of commodification. The thesis of a 'total subsumption' conflates production and reproduction into one all-encompassing process, with no exteriority, meaning that capital not only consumes labour-power, but also directly produces it.

---

88  See Das 2012: 'Less developed societies such as India have a vast reserve army of labor, a part of which has been created under colonialism, including through primitive accumulation and deindustrialization through cheap imports. These processes continue now under new imperialism. Much of this reserve army is in the form of what I will call "vulnerable labourers": they are generally subjected to various forms of non-class oppression (e.g., gender and ethnicity), they tend to be not politically organised, and they work for less than the average wage and for long hours. Vulnerable labourers include migrants, tribals, women, and children. Capital is able to appropriate absolute surplus value from labourers through lower wages and through overwork. ... Real subsumption is less likely to emerge as long as there is ample scope for the appropriation of absolute surplus value through formal subsumption (and hybrid subsumption), as long as there is no strong imperative on the part of property owners to resort to methods of relative surplus value' (Das 2012, pp. 183–4).

Whether taken to its extreme as a completion or deployed more naively as an instrument of periodisation pertaining to an ongoing process of capitalist development, it is clear that to historicise the forms of subsumption in *any* way is to suffuse the concept with an evolutionism by transposing a developmental logic immanent to the individual onto the whole without a sensitivity to the qualitatively distinct mediations operative at this higher level of totalisation. The effect of this is to reinstate a dogmatic stageist conception of history internally to 'capitalism' and thus to situate the concept of subsumption within what Jairus Banaji has referred to critically as 'the whole tradition of abstract historical formalism'.[89] It is clear that the theory of subsumption forms must be decoupled from any such attempts at crude and all-encompassing periodisation. Equally, it is questionable whether anything other than the most heuristic and qualified periodisations can play a part in our understanding of the core dynamics of capitalist power. As Simon Clarke points out: '[P]eriodisation does not solve the problem which gave rise to it, that of getting beyond the static fetishism of simple "essentialist" structuralism, because it merely proliferates structures which remain, each in their turn, equally static and fetishistic.'[90] At any one time, capital's domination of the total social process must be understood as mediated and dispersed across a multiplicity of sites, each with their own determinations and results, as well as modulated by 'innumerable different empirical circumstances, natural conditions, racial relations, historical influences acting from outside, etc.' whose effects cannot be prescribed in advance by a 'supra-historical' theory but demand close concrete analysis.[91] A robust theory of subsumption would have to be open to all these sites and factors rather than homogenising and overdetermining them, allowing the specific configurations of the reproduction process to come into view. As Sayer points out, rather than focussing on carving up history into abstract chunks, 'it is more important to establish the actual combinations of forces and relations of production that exist and work out how they cohere and function.'[92]

## 3   Systematic and Reproductive Totality

If we reject the assumption that the dynamic of subsumption can be used to meaningfully distinguish between different epochs or phases of capital-

---

89   Banaji 2011, xiv.
90   Clarke 1992, p. 149.
91   See Brighton Labour Process Group 1977, p. 23; Marx 1991, pp. 927–8.
92   Sayer 1998, pp. 126–7.

ist world-history, how then can we conceptualise the relation between that dynamic (of form-determination) and the process of society's reproduction-development (composition)? How could we go about constructing a more mediated conception of capital's 'becoming' that opens itself to further levels of complexity both in terms of the real relations and conditions structuring the social process and the points of potential rupture and resistance to its rule by capital? In the first place, this would seem to require relinquishing the problem of chronology – that of when or in what sequence the forms can be ordered – and instead posing a different one – that of the distribution, interaction and development of subsumption forms. This would also suggest, much more broadly, a turn away from a directly 'historical' reading of Marxist categories (encompassing a spectrum of positions, from 'stageist' orthodoxy right up the 'heterodox' Marxisms that nonetheless deal with present conditions under the unifying and reductive rubric of 'real subsumption') and toward a 'systematic' reading capable of comprehending the combination of categories and relations within an internally differentiated conceptual totality.

The concept of 'mode of production' [*Produktionsweise*] is the obvious referent here, as the totality with which Marx is generally understood to have thought the unity of social forms and relations, with each mode possessing its own historically unique 'laws of motion'. Situating the forms of subsumption within such a totality and its 'laws' would thus seem to hold the key to their comprehension on a social scale.

The initial problem with such an approach, raised in chapter 2, is the instability and inconsistency of meaning Marx gives to the concept of mode of production in his writings, as numerous commentators have pointed out and extensive debates demonstrate. These meaning range from narrow descriptions of relations and methods of the immediate production process to an all-encompassing concept of social reality. In his discussions of subsumption, Marx tends toward the former, for example when he describes real subsumption as giving 'the very mode of production a new shape' and thereby creating 'the mode of production peculiar to [capital]'.[93] In this context, the concept of a 'specifically capitalist mode of production' is associated exclusively with real subsumption, denoting a labour process that has been formed by capital in the course of its subsumption under the valorisation process. This would suggest that Marx accords causal priority to the relation of subsumption, such that the mode of production is an *effect* of this relation. Elsewhere, Marx con-

---

93   Marx 1988, p. 92.

firms this, according a far broader effectivity to subsumptive relations than the mode of production, when he states that with real subsumption 'a complete (and constantly repeated) revolution takes place in the mode of production, in the productivity of the workers and in the relations between workers and capitalists'.[94] At other points, however, Marx inverts this picture, and it becomes the mode of production that acts upon the labour process and 'radically remoulds all its social and technological conditions'.[95] Despite these slippages, the mode of production is clearly not simply acted upon by the relations that form it, but also generates its own social effects. With the introduction of large-scale industry, 'the capitalist mode of production has already seized upon the substance of labour and transformed it'.[96] In addition, the creation of a class with nothing to sell but their own labour-power 'is due not only to the nature of the contract between capital and labour but also to the mode of production itself'.[97] The reciprocity at work here recalls the infamous passage from *Capital* in which Marx declares that

> [t]he specific economic form, in which unpaid surplus labour is pumped out of direct producers, *determines* the relationship of rulers and ruled, as it grows directly out of production itself and in turn, reacts upon it as a *determining* element.[98]

Taken in the narrower sense that Marx employs in these passages, the mode of production cannot itself be the conceptual totality within which subsumption occurs, but forms only a partial moment or site of a broader totality incorporating subsumption relations *and* modes of production.

In an important intervention into the 1970s debate around modes of production, Jairus Banaji sought to resolve this difficulty by distinguishing sharply between two senses of the term in Marx's writings: a narrow conception limited to the labour process, as in the above citations, and a second far broader conception of a 'historical organisation of production' or 'social form of production' (Marx's own terms).[99] According conceptual priority to the latter, Banaji criticised the identification of a mode of production with a single mode of exploitation (or subsumption) and instead proposed a much more expans-

---

94  Marx 1976, p. 1035.
95  Marx 1994, p. 30.
96  Marx 1988, p. 279.
97  Marx 1988, p. 291.
98  Marx 1991, p. 927.
99  Banaji 2011, pp. 349 ff.

ive conception internally differentiated by diverse forms and configurations of exploitation:

> To take modes of production first, these, for Marx, comprised the 'relations of production *in their totality*' (as he says in *Wage Labour and Capital*), a nuance completely missed by Marxists who simply reduce them to historically dominant forms of exploitation or forms of labour, for example, positing a slave mode of production wherever slave-labour is used or ruling out capitalism if 'free' labour is absent. The underlying assumption here is that Marx means by relations of production the relations of the immediate process of production, or what, in a perfectly nebulous expression, some Marxists call the 'method of surplus-appropriation'. But the immediate process of production can be structured in all sorts of ways, even under capitalism.[100]

By distinguishing between a totality of 'relations of production' and the multiple 'forms of exploitation' found within and across various production processes, Banaji conceives of modes of production as 'objects of much greater complexity', 'impenetrable at the level of simple [i.e., 'general'] abstractions' (e.g., formal and real subsumption).[101] This makes room for a much more nuanced understanding of capitalist totality that acknowledges the flexibility of combinations and diversity of forms – both economic and material – that its exploitation of labour takes:

> Relations of production are simply not reducible to forms of exploitation, *both* because modes of production embrace a wider range of relationships than those in their immediate process of production *and* because the deployment of labour, the organisation and control of the labour-process, 'correlates' with historical relations of production in complex ways.

The historiographic work undertaken by Banaji not only offers illuminating illustrations of the complexities of this correlation but also prompts fundamental theoretical questions that tarry with the problem of subsumption at its root. Acknowledging the diversity and complexity of forms of capitalist exploitation displaces the conceptual totality within which those forms are thought from the analytical level of mode of production (narrowly conceived) to an

---

100   Banaji 2011, p. 4.
101   Banaji 2011, p. 6; p. 59.

expanded notion of 'social relations of production': the ensemble of forms, roles, interactions and interdependencies through which capital's accumulation process functions, i.e., 'capital' itself in what Marx called its *Gesamtprozeß* (total process). However, the fundamental issue of mediation and reciprocal constitution between capital and its other – labour and nature – is not resolved through such a displacement, which only gives us a new 'definite totality of historical laws of motion'.[102] The subsumption of labour forms an integral moment of this totality and must be analysed as such – as undertaken in the previous chapter – but this still only leaves us with the abstract dynamic of subsumption as an effect of these historical laws (albeit one liberated from a narrative of linear historical evolution). Is even an *expanded* conception of social totality (be it as 'mode of production' or 'social relations of production') adequate to the task of critically grasping the relation between the dynamic of subsumption in the labour process and the historical process of social reproduction-development?

Since the 1990s, a number of Hegelian Marxist scholars associated with the 'systematic dialectic' perspective, most notably Christopher Arthur, have touched on this issue in seeking to develop a critical conception of capitalist totality.[103] Arthur's approach aims at a theoretical reconstruction of the capitalist mode of production's inner *logic*, drawing on a supposed homology between Hegel's *Logic* and Marx's *Capital* in order to develop a 'systematic dialectic of capital'. What is key in terms of the connection with Hegel here is the understanding of capital as an 'organic system', something which Marx himself asserted frequently, referring to 'the physiology of the bourgeois system ... its internal organic coherence and its life-process'.[104] For Arthur, capital's life-process forms a logical totality in the mode of Hegel's idea, 'a self-moving system of abstract forms' which 'reproduces all the relevant conditions of its existence in its own movement'.[105] This reproductive movement follows the logic of the value-form given by Marx in the general formula M–C–M', but, Arthur notes, in order to reproduce itself in this way, such that 'all presuppositions of the system are also posited by the system', capital has to take hold of production and reform it to match this end, which drives the dynamic of subsumption:

---

102  Banaji 2011, p. 60.
103  See the introduction to Arthur 2001 for an overview of some of the different positions within the systematic dialectics framework.
104  Marx 1989, p. 391.
105  Arthur 2009, p. 155.

> Because the material reality of production is *given* to capital, rather than created by it, capital has to shape this material into a 'content' more or less adequate to it; this I call the 'form determination' of the 'content'. It cannot be achieved through 'formal' subsumption alone; it requires real changes to the production process so as to make possible capital's fluidity in its other.[106]

Arthur's account is not entirely dissimilar to Marx's here, despite its hyper-idealised presentation (in which conceptual developments are constantly driven by a logical necessity or the 'inadequacy' of certain forms and relations to the existent totality in which they are situated). The problem with such an approach, however, is that a systematically totalised conception of capitalist relations of production (appearing, in Marx's words, as 'an *a priori* construction') is taken to be a closed logical totality within which relations of subsumption play out and can be explained, instead of an open totality existing in perpetual tension with the external other that it struggles to absorb. That is to say, because Arthur comprehends the subsumption of labour from the standpoint of what is logically necessary for accumulation to take place, subsumption is treated as a mediation already internal to capital rather than a substantive mediation *between* capital and what lies outside of it, labour and nature. Theoretically, this turns subsumption into the *explanans* rather than the *explanandum*, as the process of subsumption is characterised as a spontaneous function of capital, grasped as a self-moving, ideal structure, an 'abstract totality' that imposes itself upon the socio-historical process unilaterally and automatically. This is symptomatic of a return to a pre-critical understanding of subsumption, whose logical validity (and the identity between particular and universal this implies) requires no deeper analysis or further explanation.

Where Arthur does acknowledge that 'the system is prey to antinomies' and is 'rooted in real differences ... opposites incapable of reconciliation', these antinomies and differences are only comprehended in the mode of their functional overcoming – in terms of what capital 'must do' to meet its goal of self-expansion. Yet Arthur perceptively admits that subsumption 'marks an aporia in this ambition' and accordingly treats the forms of subsumption as 'mixed' rather than 'pure' categories, for reasons of their material content. However, this qualification fails to generate new conceptual determinations regarding the process of capitalist domination. Thus whilst 'the deconstruction of capital's repression of what is truly other is in order', this deconstruction is offered

---

106  Arthur 2005, p. 200.

only in the most abstract terms in Arthur's account, with labour's subjective potential for resistance and rupture appearing as nothing more than a postulate of contradiction. It is not clear in which way, if at all, this postulate could be further concretised via his closed functionalist model. As Werner Bonefeld notes, Arthur 'rightly argues that the dialectical method deals with 'a given whole', and he wrongly treats this whole as a closed logical system. ... The peculiar character of capitalist social relations cannot be found in some logic of immanent abstractness'.[107]

The attempt made by authors such as Arthur to integrate subsumption into a 'systematic dialectic' of capital is significant because it threatens to impose a *synchronic* form of theoretical closure on the necessarily open relationship between subsumption and the reproduction-development of the social formation. Arthur posits the radical separation of capital's dialectical and historical development, and in doing so concedes too much to Hegel and heeds Marx's critique of idealism too little. Capital may be an organic system, but it is not one with a truly independent, self-moving and ahistorical existence. Whereas Marx criticised Hegel for considering the 'real as the product of thought concentrating itself, probing its own depths, and unfolding itself out of itself', capital is understood by Arthur to be structured in homology with Hegel's idea, leading to the reinstatement of this autonomous and one-sided developmental movement as capital's reality.[108] Crucially, Arthur's interpretation is grounded in the assumption that 'right from its first sentence the object of Marx's *Capital* is indeed *capitalism*', meaning that capital's accumulation process, understood as a systematic totality, is identical in essence with a socially reproductive totality and thus only has to 'posit itself' through subsuming labour in order to secure its own actuality.[109] Arthur's view thus collapses the reproduction of society into the expanded reproduction of capital and correspondingly reduces the question of the relation between subsumption and social reproduction-development to the question of the relation between subsumption and the essential relations of capitalist accumulation (i.e., back to our starting point).

Arthur is correct to assert, contra Negri and Adorno, that 'what is ontologically constitutive of capital is the *process* (not an originally *given*, or finally *accomplished*, state) of reification', but his conception of processual openness is entirely devoid of material and historical determinations.[110] Capitalist subsumption is a *mediating* synthetic category with practical-historical conditions

---

107   Bonefeld 2014, pp. 88 ff.
108   Marx 1993, p. 101.
109   Arthur 2004, p. 18.
110   Arthur 2005, p. 214.

and effects that are more complex than those functionally presented at the level of capital's expanded reproduction process *in abstracto*. It is precisely this 'excess' of material effectivity that gives capital, through the real subsumption of productive forces, its unique and epoch-making power. Ignoring these – or at least, relegating them to yet to be explored levels of concretion beyond the 'ontological ground of capitalism' – misses the decisive role played by the dynamic of subsumption in the reproduction-development of capitalist societies, reducing this couplet to just one of its poles: an empty, functionalist notion of reproduction derived from capital's logic of accumulation. In this way, Arthur's pure dialectic of capital represses the theoretical comprehension of concrete development and is incapable of grasping systemic change, positing itself in opposition to a naïve conception of empirical history. In this regard, Alfred Schmidt's comments regarding the relation between systematic and historical elements in materialist thought are strikingly pertinent:

> The categorial expression of the relations of production investigated by Marx rested, in a mediated and/or unmediated sense, on their history. To the extent to which the thinking process is autonomous in relation to its subject matter and does not slavishly copy it, it leads to theoretical construction. Further, to the extent to which this process remains objectively related to the material of history (*and continuously subjects itself to control so as not to ossify into an empty 'system'*), it approaches the level of a critical historiography. *Both aspects*, relative independence and dependence of the thinking process vis-à-vis the historical basis, *belong together*. ... Whoever has established clarity concerning the objectively contradictory relationship between history and 'system' in *Capital* will not fuse, identify or *separate* the historical and logical but rather will seek to determine the weight and place of these moments in accordance with the level attained by the cognitive process.[111]

## 4   Mediating Reproduction and Development

In light of these criticisms, adequately theorising the impact of capitalist subsumption on the social process demands avoiding two forms of closure: a *diachronic* form that would totalise that impact historically and a *synchronic* form that would totalise it systemically. Instead, if conceived openly, the dynamic of

---

111   Schmidt 1981, p. 66, emphasis added.

subsumption will be seen to not only affect but also mediate the historical and systematic aspects of social reproduction, bringing them into relation in the way that it implants a unique logic of social development *within* the structure of reproduction itself, making real change a basic systemic presupposition rather than a contingency or nominal tendency. This is what generates the specific historical logic of 'uninterrupted disturbance' proper to capitalist production, at the core of which is a complexity surrounding the relation of its *being* and *becoming*. Marx grapples with this complexity in a crucial passage from the *Grundrisse* upon which the entire problem of closure can be seen to turn:

> It must be kept in mind that the new forces of production and relations of production do not develop out of nothing, nor drop from the sky, nor from the womb of the self-positing Idea; but from within and in antithesis to the existing development of production and the inherited, traditional relations of property. While in the completed bourgeois system every economic relation presupposes every other in its bourgeois economic form, and everything posited is thus also a presupposition, this is the case with every organic system. This organic system itself, as a totality, has its presuppositions, and *its development to its totality consists precisely in subordinating all elements of society to itself*, or in creating out of it the organs which it still lacks. This is historically how it becomes a totality. The process of becoming this totality forms a moment of its process, of its development.[112]

It is important to analytically distinguish the two levels of 'being' and 'becoming' operative here, in order to grasp how their articulation exceeds Marx's own conscious presentation. At the level of 'being', the mutual presupposition of relations and the positing of presuppositions are, Marx says, characteristic of 'every organic system' or *reproductive totality* (that is, a systematic totality of relations that exists in and through the process of reproducing its subjective and objective conditions). It is in this way that the capitalist mode of production is, for Marx, a reproductive totality: Reproduction is the mode of its existence or 'composition'. At the level of the system's 'becoming', capital is dependent on a mode of development that is also a negation or absorption of extant social forms, wealth and practices and the 'subordination' of these to itself. Capital's becoming is based on *subsuming* social elements and re-

---

112   Marx 1993, p. 278.

'organising' them through its own logic of reproduction. The difficulty with this organic model, however, lies in the idea of completion. The 'completed' bourgeois system that Marx refers to is capital at the point at which it can reproduce itself *and* its conditions:

> The capitalist process of production, therefore, seen as a total, connected process, i.e. a process of reproduction, produces not only commodities, not only surplus-value, but it also produces and reproduces the capital-relation itself; on the one hand the capitalist, on the other the wage-labourer.[113]

Yet at the same time capital can never reach a 'completed' state of being because its own reproductive logic is based on unceasing accumulation of *new* wealth. There is no 'simple' capitalist reproduction: Without self-expansion capital is not capital. Capital's circulatory movement is, echoing Hegel's description of dialectical development, 'a spiral, an expanding curve, not a simple circle'.[114] The capitalist system always demands more and – as the most characteristically 'modern' form of society – is in a perennial state of unrest. This means that capital's being *is* development, its mode of existence is a ceaseless and insatiable movement of becoming. As Marx and Engels announce in the communist manifesto, 'constant revolutionising of production, uninterrupted disturbances of all social conditions, everlasting uncertainty and agitation distinguish the bourgeois epoch from all earlier ones'.[115] Yet it is never sufficiently developed, with each cycle of accumulation still inadequate compared to the next, so that it 'moves in contradictions which are constantly overcome but just as constantly posited'.[116]

This dialectical slippage between being and becoming is what grounds the capitalist system's openness, as a *historical* rather than *natural* and so 'closed' organic system (although in one sense at least, this distinction ultimately comes down to 'relative speeds' rather than absolute difference) and as a system whose living existence must be grasped in the articulation of reproduction-development (recalling, as I argued in chapter 2, that this hyphenated pairing is the active or processual form of 'natural-history'). The key to this articulation is

---

113  Marx 1976, p. 724.
114  Marx 1993, p. 266. See also Marx 1978a, p. 470: 'the absence of any accumulation or reproduction on an expanded scale is an assumption foreign to the capitalist basis.'
115  Marx and Engels 1976, p. 487.
116  Marx and Engels 1976, p. 487; Marx 1993, p. 410.

the constitutive role of subsumption. Because capitalist reproduction is never fully complete, it is in a continual process of becoming or development, the basic 'logical' form of which may be fixed axiomatically (in the 'general formula' M–C–M') but whose material content is generated in variable and contingent ways by a constantly intensifying subsumption of social and material elements. This intensification or deepening of subsumption, as Echeverría describes it, has 'a progress of totalitarian reach, both extensive and intensive, (as planetarisation and technification respectively)' with no natural or logical state of completion.[117] This means that capital is continually caught in the struggle over integration/transcendence with labour (as well as nature), a struggle which plays itself out primarily in the process of production because it is in production that those elements most directly mediate capital's becoming and thus become moments of its own process, insofar as they determine its capacity to valorise itself and therefore to develop through accumulation. At the same time however, the coordinates of this struggle far exceed production because the social elements that capital strives to subsume in production are themselves shaped by a wide ensemble of factors, relations and practices which traverse the entire social process, including spheres of social activity in which capitalist command has no formal authority (i.e., outside of the workplace). Marx hinted at this when he wrote that capital 'steps as it were from its inner organic life into its *external* relations'.[118] These external relations pertain to an entire compass of forms and practices that determine the compositional totality within which that 'inner organic life' subsists and upon which it depends. In reality then, capital's becoming is nothing but the expression of its successes and failures in the struggle over subsumption *at a social scale*. Deconstructing this struggle and trajectory of development in terms of the real practices and forms of social being through which society reproduces itself is the basis for an open-ended investigation of capitalist subsumption, understood as a contested dynamic of transformation (a 'moving' rather than a static contradiction). As Marx says, 'political economy perceives, discovers the root of the historical struggle and development'.[119] Such a deconstruction is premised on the *non-identity* of capitalist reproduction and the socially reproductive totality despite their historical interpenetration, and the assumption that the interpenetration itself is the object of critical social research (of which capital as a 'mode of production' forms just one aspect or 'layer').

---

117   Echeverría 2005.
118   Marx 1991, p. 135, emphasis added.
119   Marx 1989, p. 392.

Marx himself, however, in reducing his treatment of this broader sense of reproduction (of social relations and their conditions, productive subjects and objective wealth) to the inner dynamics of capital's overall accumulation process, once again raises the threat of a theoretical closure that undermines the deconstructive reading of subsumption. There are various aspects to this 'provisional' or 'tendential' closure in Marx's critique of political economy. Michael Krätke refers to 'at least three heroic abstractions' through which Marx constructed a 'complete and closed system of capitalist relations': 'the abstraction from the diversity or variety of capitalism, the abstraction from the development or history of capitalism, and, last but not least, the abstraction from the capitalist world system'.[120] Shortall, Lebowitz and Bonefeld also take up the problem of closure with reference to *Capital* but focus instead on the neutralisation of the 'variable' dimension of class struggle and the subjectivity of labour, which is suppressed in a functional-economistic model of the social process. As Shortall explains:

> While Marx describes in graphic detail how the rhythms of the accumulation of capital impose themselves, and thereby regulate the conditions of the working class, he is still only concerned with the working class as object; in itself, as the simple aggregation of individual workers, as an objective condition for capital's accumulation. ... The worker, now the working class, remains as mere object regulated by the rhythms of the objective laws of the dialectic of capital.[121]

Or in Bonefeld's account:

> In Marx, there exists a glimpse of economic closure when he argues that the value of labour is solely determined by labour time necessary to reproduce labour power, a value which consists of moral and historical elements which are imposed on capital through the class struggle. This closed formulation is surprising, *since the moral element mentioned by Marx relates to the permanent radical reproduction and production of the separation* [between capital and labour] *and the permanent radical reproduction and revolutionising of the natural conditions on which, in turn, capital depends at the same time.*[122]

---

120  Krätke 2007, p. 122.
121  Shortall 1994, pp. 260–1.
122  Bonefeld 1988, p. 56, emphasis added.

The issue raised in all of these accounts is that, in falling into an 'objectivism' of economic laws, Marx's critique of political economy forecloses a theoretical comprehension of the active potential of labour (as well as other non-economic forces and practices) to disrupt or resist capital's accumulation process (other than as an abstractly registered possibility). But this active element is nonetheless assumed insofar as the inner dynamic of capitalist subsumption on which the accumulation process rests presupposes a constant running up against that which lies beyond the closed organic totality, a totality whose closure is constantly placed into question and undone by this need, contested by the externality upon which its reproduction depends. As Lebowitz argues, 'there cannot be a self-reproducing totality in *Capital* because the necessary presuppositions for capital are not all results of itself but, rather, depend on something outside of capital as such.'[123] These arguments highlight a tension internal to Marx's discourse between what Karatani calls 'a structurally determined *topos* where subjectivity cannot freely intervene' and the necessary openness of the system to that which exceeds it, interrupts it, contests it, but also ultimately acts as the substance through which it lives by subsuming it within its own life process.[124] Shortall cites theoretical exigencies as the reason for Marx's introduction of closure, suggesting that Marx adopted the standpoint of political economy and 'bracketed' extra-systematic factors in order to deconstruct bourgeois society's self-illusion and reveal the cloaked relations of domination that ground it, the objectification of the worker via primitive accumulation, commodification and subsumption to capital in production. For Shortall, however, the closure in Marx's discourse remains 'provisional' (as opposed to the 'capital-logic' and 'systematic dialectics' interpretations where this closure is methodologically absolutised with reference to the object of knowledge).

> [T]he questions of class struggle, rupture and crisis are always implicit in Marx's exposition in *Capital*. While Marx must provisionally close off such questions in order to develop his exposition of the dialectic of capital, he never severs them completely; they are always presupposed.[125]

Marx's writings are thus marked by an ambiguity regarding capital's systematic completeness. As Krätke notes, the closure of the system is interrupted by con-

---

123   Lebowitz 1998, p. 185.
124   Karatani 2003, p. 288.
125   Shortall 1994, p. 122.

stant 'deviations' that are increasingly forceful, particularly with respect to the history of capitalism, so that in fact 'what appear to be digressions from "pure" logical expositions are crucial parts of his argument, pointing to the "openings" and "systematic gaps" of the capitalist mode of production as well as to the logic of its "inner development"'.[126] Schmidt, echoing Adorno, similarly refers to the synthesis of systemic and anti-systemic impulses in Marx's thought:

> Marxian economics is a system and at the same time not a system, for what forms the totality of bourgeois society is equally that which pushes beyond it. As an immanent critic, Marx assumes that the relationships he investigates exist 'in pure form corresponding to their concept.' But as a critic, he knows how little (not only in England in that period) that is the case.[127]

At stake in this issue of 'provisional' closure is the relation between the economic-analytic and the critical-deconstructive aspects of Marx's discourse – that is, between the 'political economy' and the 'critique'. The former points to a functional totality of economic relations that constitute bourgeois society as a structural unity, while the latter, in deconstructing the apparent naturalness of the fetishised economic forms taken by the system, points toward the real processes, practices and subjects that constitute but also exceed and resist the modes of social being generated by capital: 'the totality of social praxis [*begriffene Praxis*] that constitutes, suffuses and contradicts the apparently objective 'logic' of capital'.[128] It is the excessive and actively resistant character of the latter totality that remains problematically ambiguous with respect to the provisionally closed 'organic system' of capital. When Marx wrote to Lasalle that his work was '*at once an exposé and, by the same token, a critique of the system*', was the point to replace the system of bourgeois political economy with a 'truer', more transparent theoretical totality – truer because denaturalised and demystified, shown to depend upon historically specific and therefore alterable conditions – in which exploitation and destruction is revealed to be a generic part of its inner determination? Or was the point, going further, to open up something akin to what Benjamin called a 'constellation saturated with tensions' (between the totalising integrative movement of the system and the de-totalising – and speculatively re-totalising – transcendent movement of

---

126  Krätke 2007, p. 124.
127  Schmidt 1981, p. 54.
128  Bonefeld 2006, p. 85.

the resistant elements brought into its orbit) thus enabling a situated analysis of the ongoing practices and processes of class conflict that constitute social experience?[129]

The ambiguity regarding the relation of the bourgeois system to its historical becoming is brought to the fore through the problem of subsumption because subsumption is the key process that mediates the connection between the formal value-representational surface of the capitalist economic system and the 'totality of social praxis' upon which it is founded and which it takes as its substance.[130] The excess that is bracketed by Marx's closure needs to be re-introduced here if we are to grasp subsumption as more than just a unilateral and automatic *function* of the formal accumulation process, which is the standpoint Marx's critique simultaneously adopted and aimed to deconstruct.[131] This, firstly, requires acknowledging the way in which the factors through which the entire process of accumulation begins – most importantly the value and productivity of labour-power – are politically (as well as socially, culturally, spatially, etc.) determined by conflictual processes *both within and beyond* the domain of 'economic' relations, and that these determinations constitute the terrain upon which the specific struggle over subsumption in production is played out. Secondly, this also means recognising that the dynamic of subsumption is not only driven and shaped in its actualisation by these concrete determinations but at the same time recomposes and transforms them. The entire system of the production, circulation and accumulation of value that moves through the dynamic of subsumption therefore has at its base this politically charged reciprocity, although it is registered within the economic logic of the accumulation process only as the 'variable' aspect of labour-power. One can abstract from the concrete historical dimensions of accumulation and domination for the purposes of theoretical clarification, but ultimately these must be reincorporated in order to critically comprehend the forces of composition, conflict, resistance and rupture animating the social process and subsisting through the sphere of economic relations, because 'between equal rights, force decides'.[132] The reciprocal relation of determination between the

---

129  Benjamin 2003, p. 396.
130  Echeverría 1983.
131  Cohen cited in Lebowitz 2003, p. 24.
132  The theoretical force of *Capital* lies precisely in Marx's use of the 'power of abstraction' to uncover the inner connections and movement as well as outward forms characterising the system of capitalist domination at its 'purest' level. Nonetheless, if this is to be developed into a critical frame through which to engage with real dynamics and practical configurations emerging from the struggle over the subsumption and recomposition of social

individual acts of subsumptive form-determination in production and the consistency of the compositional totality thereby generates an *open* movement of historical development (via the cycle of reproduction) that cannot be grasped at the level of a hermetically closed logical-economic system.

## 5 Subjectivation and Living Labour

Reintroducing the variability of factors animating the dynamic of subsumption and the historical movement of reproduction-development means, in the first place at least, giving theoretical life to the subjectivity and action of labour, which in Marx's discourse continually appears but is just as constantly repressed by the provisional closure of the 'systematic' standpoint. For Marx, labour must be understood to be 'variable' and active in two senses, corresponding to the two poles of its commodity status. The variability of its economic 'value', which is correlated to the basic level of subsistence as determined by 'moral and historical' factors (what the worker receives from capital); and the variability of its 'use-value', which corresponds to the level of its productivity for capital, determined in the struggle over subsumption in production (what capital receives from the worker). Both of these factors are indissolubly bound up with the dynamic of subsumption, particularly in its 'real' form, and constitute sites of resistance and conflict shaping the overall dynamic of accumulation as well as its effects upon the social process as a whole. What is key here is how the resistance of labour (organised or otherwise) exceeds, disturbs and reacts back upon the system's internal logic of accumulation, whilst nonetheless being bound to it as a condition of the worker's existence; or, in other words, how the reproduction of a human society (considered as a practical totality) and the reproduction of capital (considered as an economic totality) dialectically interpenetrate and unfold in their contradictory movements.[133] These two opposed logics of reproduction constitute a further, final moment of the subsumptive relation, played out at the level of the social totality, and completing the series of opposition, contradiction and subsumption between

---

elements, it is necessary to break through the systemic impulse (as Marx himself did in many places) that leads to a flattening out of the concrete contours and antagonistic character of the social process, e.g., 'in order to examine the object of our investigation in its integrity, free from all disturbing subsidiary circumstances, we must treat the whole world of trade as one nation, and assume that capitalist production is established everywhere and has taken possession of every branch of industry'. Marx 1976, p. 727 (fn); p. 344.

133   See Chapter 2 of this thesis; Echeverría 1998a.

capital and labour: (i) use-value/value; (ii) labour process/valorisation process; (iii) social reproduction process/capitalist reproduction process.

In Marx's *Capital*, however, labour's reproduction is presented as a systematic necessity treated in abstractly functionalist terms as a calibrating principle of accumulation, 'the absolutely necessary condition for capitalist production'.[134] In both its 'productive' and 'unproductive' moments labour's activity seems to be fully absorbed within the capitalist totality:

> From the standpoint of society, then, the working class, even when it stands outside the direct labour process, is just as much an appendage of capital as the lifeless instruments of labour are. Even its individual consumption is, within certain limits, a mere aspect of capital's reproduction.[135]

Marx demonstrates this in his reproduction schemas at the end of volume two of *Capital*, in which the working class purchases the means to reproduce itself back from the capitalist class with its wages, whose consumption consequently appears *within* capital's life-process as one of its essential conditions of possibility (the means of realising surplus-value). Marx therefore brackets the independent existence of living labour, reducing its reproduction to the functions it fulfils for the reproduction of capital. In one sense, this is entirely in keeping with the standpoint of the capitalist totality, which reduces the worker to 'nothing more than labour in its being-for-itself'.[136] Moving beyond the partial perspective of those 'certain limits' mentioned above by Marx is however crucial for opening the system to a qualitative dimension beyond capital's unilateral control and direct interest. Such a move is necessary because although the capitalist must cede a wage to the worker in order to ensure his or her reproduction, the capitalists do not directly oversee that reproduction (the worker's eating, sleeping, leisure, caring for others, etc.). Unlike the act of exchange, which effects the formal metamorphosis of money-wages into means of subsistence and commodity-capital into money-capital, the act of 'unproductive' consumption itself, which Marx described in 1857 as the 'destructive antithesis to production', is a moment of practice which occurs outside of the circuit of capitalist accumulation. This is why Marx argues that it 'actually belongs outside economics'.[137]

---

134    Marx 1976, p. 716.
135    Marx 1976 p. 719.
136    Marx 1993, p. 304.
137    Marx 1993, p. 89; Ben Fine notes the theoretical space opened by this caesura in capitalist

This peculiar status of consumption within the system – as both independent of direct capitalist command but simultaneously a *fait social* – is vital for thinking the how the dynamic of subsumption operates at the level of reproduction (i.e., in the contradiction between society conceived as a practical totality and society conceived as an abstract-economic totality). This is because the unproductive consumption through which the labour-power commodity is reproduced *physiologically* (as a bundle of nerves, muscles, organs, etc., capable of abstract social labour) is also a process of production that involves the qualitative formation of the potentially resistant *subjectivity* which capital strives to both utilise and subjugate in its mission to self-valorise. There is thus an invisible thread of continuity linking the struggles over production with the reproductive processes that lie outside of the economic domain, which is to say, linking labour's use-value and value aspects. As an extensive materialist-feminist literature has forcefully argued, it is thus crucial to mitigate Marx's tendency towards value reductionism when it comes to the question of labour's subjectivation through consumption (a reductionism that contrasts starkly with his vivid accounts of subjectivation through subsumption in production) and to situate the conflicts over capitalist subsumption both within *and* beyond the bourgeois economic totality, a 'totality' whose self-sufficient unity is an ideological illusion.[138] The process of consumption cannot, of course, be dissociated from the economic logic determining the production of the objects (and services) through which it is realised or from the circulatory flows determining the distribution and accessibility of those objects, but it must be recognised that the qualitative dimensions of subjectivation play a crucial systemic role that cannot be registered in quantitative value terms alone. A theoretical mediation is required that 'correlates' economic movements with the underlying non-economic processes that shape the subjectivity of those who labour for and against capital. In this respect, considerations of the role of the state are essential, given that capital's mode of existence is founded on an inner drive to negate the conditions of labour-power's reproduction by reducing them to an absolute minimum whilst extracting the absolute maximum surplus-labour.[139]

---

control: '[H]ow do we account for the flexibility in consumption that is a necessary consequence of the value of labour-power being realised in money form (that is, take-home pay and not a bundle of goods)?' (Fine 2008, p. 109).

138  This also opens up the problem of subsumption to the vast literature on consumption, social welfare and the culture industry. For an overview of some of the foundational positions, see Hennessy and Ingraham 1997; for a recent contribution to the debate, see the articles collected in Arruzza et al 2015.

139  Marx 1976, p. 342.

Marx shows that capital would indeed have begun annihilating the working class in Britain, had the latter not resisted and the state not ultimately intervened to secure their reproduction by legislative means. Here too, the state presents a sphere of social action external to the organic system of bourgeois production (if not independent of it) and yet at the same time absolutely presupposed by it.

The principal problematic surrounding the subjectivity of labour is that of the relation of living workers to their own labour activity, a relation at stake in so many of the key moments of Marx's critique: 'original accumulation', fetishism, abstract labour, personification, commodification, subsumption. For Marx, this relation first emerges as a problem by virtue of the dissociation of the worker from their own labour, arising from the historically specific conditions of 'separation' in which capitalism predominates:

> Already the fact that it is *labour* which confronts capital as subject, i.e., the worker *only in his character as labour, and not he himself*, should open the eyes. This alone, disregarding capital, already contains a relation, *a relation of the worker to his own activity*, which is *by no means the 'natural' one*, but which itself already contains a *specific economic character*.[140]

Marx explores this relation at the level of the commodity (where the labour-power commodity is the *bearer* of labour as use-value) and production (where concrete labour is the *bearer* of abstract labour); but what exactly happens to this relation at the level of reproduction (where the living workers are the *'practical bearers'* of capitalist social production process)?[141] At this level, as Lebowitz argues, 'what underlies the struggle against capital and drives beyond capital is the contradiction between the worker's self and her conditions of life',[142] that is, the capacity of living labour, as individual and speculatively as a class, to assert its own being in manner that opposes, exceeds and transcends its status as the mere bearer of a 'substance' that is 'seized upon' by

---

140   Marx 1993, p. 310. This dissociation of intentionality and productive capacity is the most acute expression of the separation of subjective and objective elements of production and their economic synthesis: 'It is not the unity of living and active humanity with the natural, inorganic conditions of their metabolic exchange with nature, and hence their appropriation of nature, which requires explanation or is the result of a historic process, but rather the separation between these inorganic conditions of human existence and this active existence, a separation which is completely posited only in the relation of wage labour and capital' (Marx 1993, p. 489).
141   Marx 1991, p. 957.
142   Lebowitz 2003, p. 154.

capital in production.¹⁴³ Here, where the worker 'no longer belongs to himself but to capital', a specific set of conflicts and mediations are in play. The latter are however dependent upon the obverse moment of the worker reproducing their own capacities, as well as the reproduction of the overall context in which labour exists as *a substance for capital*, both of which introduce distinct but ultimately connected sets of conflicts and mediations that are irreducible to struggles in production. The overall articulation of all these processes within a capitalist framework is defined by the practical dissociation of the capacity to act, to shape reality according to a conscious plan, from the living bearer of that capacity, the subject of that plan, the worker. This why Marx asserts that:

> [A]t the level of material production, of the life-process in the realm of the social – for that is what the process of production is – we find the same situation that we find in religion at the ideological level, namely the inversion of subject into object and vice versa.¹⁴⁴

This movement of inversion is built into the dynamic of subsumption, driving it and at the same time shaping it, thus implying a constant and changing process of subjectivation (or, we might even say, de-subjectivation). On one side, the productive subject enters into the production process, where it struggles to assert itself against the capitalist command that would reduce it to a mere object, as the bare capacity to work and a resource to be exploited, on the other, the subject enters the contiguous sphere of consumption where its intentionality faces no direct capitalist control but is nonetheless constrained by those material facts which have already been decided upon in production.

This movement of de- and re-subjectivation takes on a distinctively new configuration where the dynamic of subsumption asserts itself in production in its 'real' form. With real subsumption, the connection between the reproduction of capital and the reproduction of labour is both intensified and qualitatively transformed by the fact that the two circuits are not simply bound together through mutual economic dependence (as formal subsumption implies) but materially interpenetrate at the point at which the products (i.e., use-values) resulting from a properly capitalist mode of production enter into the consumption of the working class. Marx theorised this in terms of the relation between real subsumption and relative surplus value, which can only be produced once the goods consumed by the working class lower in value,

---

143    Marx 1988, p. 274.
144    Marx 1976, p. 990.

thereby reducing the 'necessary' part of the working day. As the effects of real subsumption are 'socialised' in passing through mediated circuits of reproduction, they assert themselves economically in terms of the 'value' of labour-power. The effects of this movement cannot be fully grasped in economic terms alone, however, as they concern not only a transformation of the material and social mode of production, the means and manner of labour, but also, as a result, entirely transformed *products* which provide the objective social context in which the subjectivity of the working class is formed as well as realised.[145] Here, the development of the producer-subject and the development of the capitalist economy interpenetrate: As the 'density' of capitalist subsumption intensifies, it generates decisive effects in terms of human needs and capacities, just as it does at the level of total social capital.

> The production of relative surplus value, i.e., production of surplus value based on the increase and development of the productive forces, requires the production of new consumption; requires that the consuming circle within circulation expands as did the productive circle previously. Firstly quantitative expansion of existing consumption; secondly: creation of new needs by propagating existing ones in a wide circle; thirdly: production of new needs and discovery and creation of new use values. In other words, so that the surplus labour gained does not remain a merely quantitative surplus, but rather constantly increases the circle of qualitative differences within labour (hence of surplus labour), makes it more diverse, more internally differentiated.[146]

The subjectivity of labour evolves in parallel with the expanded development of capital but is not reducible to it, generating a non-linear dynamic irreducible to the reproduction of capital or labour alone but grounded reciprocally in the interactive movement of the two cycles.

The inner connection posited here between the composition of capital and the composition of the worker is therefore bound up with the question of

---

[145] This also points to the irreducibility of formal and real subsumption to absolute and relative surplus-value, despite their interconnection. There is a different idea of relation at stake (material and political, rather than economic) as Patrick Murray notes: '[T]he categories of formal and real subsumption force the question – where the correlative terminology of absolute and relative surplus value does not – 'subsumption of what under what'. The only answer to the question 'under what?' is under a specific social form, notably, capital' (Murray 2009, p. 174).

[146] Marx 1993, p. 408.

productive forces and capitalist technology. As demonstrated in the previous chapter, Marx clearly identifies a strong correlation between the technical dimension of real subsumption and the formation of the worker's subjectivity. In this sense, the dynamic of capitalist subsumption moves contradictorily with respect to living labour. On the one hand, it constantly strives to increase the productive powers of labour through technical transformation of the labour process and development of productive forces, whilst on the other it represses – as a condition of this technical transformation being at the same time a means to increase the valorisation of capital – the subjective dimension of living labour that asserts itself in the conscious regulation of its metabolism with nature. This conscious regulation is displaced by managerial, scientific and automated forms of workplace control which determine the realisation of labour over and often against the subjective intentions of the workforce. The contradiction, however, appears in a one-sided, mystified form so long as the technical-economic aspects of real subsumption (pertaining to the reproduction of capital) obscure and displace its socio-natural aspects (pertaining to the concrete form of living labour's social reproduction). As Echeverría argues:

> The *effectiveness* of the instrumental field is not reducible to its productivity; this is only its quantitative determination – the degree to which the global instrument enables the subject to dominate or transform nature. Effectiveness is the qualitative content of productivity; it establishes an entire defined horizon of *possibilities of form* for the global object of production and consumption. In this sense, in presenting certain possibilities of form and leaving aside others, in being 'specialised' in a determinate axiological direction, the global effectiveness itself possesses a particular form, which rests upon the technological structure of the instrumental field.[147]

Grasped as a qualitative totality, the process through which society reproduces itself not only endows the objects and in turn the subjects of practical life with a specific form but also shapes the form-giving process itself. Reproduction can thus be seen as a cycle of 'self-activity' through which the subject transforms its own social being via the mediation of its activity upon the object.[148]

---

147  Echeverría 2014, p. 31.
148  'When we consider bourgeois society in the long view and as a whole, then the final result of the process of social production always appears as the society itself, i.e., the human being itself in its social relations. Everything that has a fixed form, such as the product etc.,

The dynamic of capitalist subsumption introduces a unique logic of domination internal to this form of historical activity by dissociating the capacity to determine the form given to the product of labour from the labouring subject that produces it. With real subsumption, this dissociation becomes a material-technical fact, insofar as the objective structure of the instrumental field increasingly presupposes (within 'certain limits') social reproduction on a capitalist basis.[149] This is the sense in which Marcuse argued that 'technology has become the great vehicle of reification – reification in its most mature and effective form', a thought taken up by Krahl as the imperative to transform the critique of political economy into a 'critique of political technology'.[150] Real subsumption therefore operates as a mechanism of *indirect* capitalist regulation of social reproduction (and so by implication, of *subjectivation*) that complements and supports the direct forms of capitalist regulation active in production (although not without a certain degree of practical ambivalence, given that the transformations of the instrumental field effected by capital function necessarily but not *exclusively* reinforce exploitation and accumulation; other uses and abuses of that field may indeed be possible).

## 6    The Generative Dynamic

The key to grasping the openness of the dynamic of subsumption at the level of the social reproduction process lies in the double character of subsumption *per se* as at once a formal metamorphosis and at the same time an 'underlying' process of material synthesis. Marx's analysis of subsumption in production offers an incredibly rich theorisation of the processes and techniques of material synthesis through which the valorisation of capital is effected within a capitalist controlled labour process. Yet Marx only conceptualises the transformative dynamic resulting from that synthesis (which is not only driven by

---

appears as merely a moment, a vanishing moment, in this movement. The direct production process itself here appears only as a moment. The conditions and objectifications of the process are themselves equally moments of it, and its only subjects are the individuals, but individuals in mutual relationships, which they equally reproduce and produce anew. The constant process of their own movement, in which they renew themselves even as they renew the world of wealth they create' (Marx 1993, p. 712).

149   The effects of this on the internal composition of productive subjects are profound, if highly variable, see Echeverría 2009; Negri too emphasises the co-parallel evolution of capitalist and proletarian composition, as an isomorphism tracing linear stages of subsumption, see Negri 1991, p. 123.

150   Marcuse 2007, p. 172; Krahl 2014.

class conflict but also exceeds production and is mediated through the entire social process) from the standpoint of an abstract logic of total social capital's expanded reproduction. This leads Marx to characterise the dynamic of subsumption functionalistically when he claims that a 'specifically capitalist mode of production [i.e., real subsumption] arises and develops *spontaneously* on the basis of the formal subsumption of labour under capital'.[151] As Das rightly notes, however, 'the transition to real subsumption with associated technological change is not automatic, but is a protracted process, mediated by class struggle which occurs in the context of a whole host of factors, including capitalist state interventions.'[152] It is the conflicts between living agents – both capitalists *and* workers – unfolding amongst all of those economic and extra-economic factors that ultimately determines how the dynamic of subsumption acts upon the social and material factors of production, and therefore how it reshapes the reproduction process as a whole.[153] These conflicts are basic to

---

151  Marx 1976, p. 645.
152  Das 2012, p. 179. Das explores this idea with reference to a number of case studies that are of note because of the importance of working class resistance and state interventions in shaping the dynamic of subsumption, e.g., 'in the 1960s and the 1970s, rice fields owned by capitalist farmers were the hotbed of agrarian class tension in Kerala. Supported by multiple unions, including those organised by communist parties, labourers launched political action demanding higher wages and better working conditions including an eight-hour day. Agrarian capitalists responded by retrenching workers, many of whom had worked for them on a long-term basis. They resorted to casualisation of employment. They used tractors to reduce their dependence on labourers. Workers often reacted by forcibly harvesting rice. They were supported by the pro-labour governments in power which refused to intervene on behalf of capital in labour disputes. In Kuttanad area (in Allepey district), the rice bowl of Kerala, labourers even broke up some tractors. This was reminiscent of the Luddite movement Marx talks about in *Capital*. Unions themselves would send in a large number of labourers to farms to complete the harvest in a few hours. Farm owners gradually lost control over the process of recruiting labourers' (Das 2012, p. 189).
153  Considered on a social scale, new determinations and problems pertaining to the dynamic arise that are not evident at the level of the immediate production process, where distinct forms of subsumption (formal, real, hybrid) are analytically separable and empirically identifiable. For example, the socially regulative effects of the practical objects produced under conditions of real subsumption enter into and thus impact upon subjects, processes and spheres of social activity well beyond the productive zones in which they originate. This means that real subsumption in one enterprise, branch of industry or region can – and indeed necessarily does – affect other production processes where formal or hybrid forms operate. This is why the classification of the forms of subsumption loses its explanatory power beyond the immediate production process and must be articulated as components of a dynamic that functions at the level of the reproductive totality. As interconnected moments of the dynamic, hybrid, real and formal subsumption can be deployed as 'flow concepts' that express and explain difference across time and space,

capitalist reproduction and therefore the dynamic is always active, however the latter cannot be translated into a deterministic teleology or schema of material development because that development is only ever a secondary effect of the struggle over valorisation and accumulation, which is the real content of capitalist development.[154] Capital must accumulate in order to be capital, but *how* it does so and the wider material effects of this imperative cannot be specified at such a high level of abstraction. To translate this injunction into a technical teleology is to mystify the real motivations revealed by the theory of capitalist subsumption, as Echeverría argues:

> The theory of subsumption conceives of the apparently natural development of modern technology, together with that which would be, on one side, its essential effect – the 'perfection' of the productivity of labour – and, on the other, it's 'incidental' effect – the destruction of the producer-subject as well as of nature – as a process that, far from proceeding from the *spontaneously progressive need* to apply the advances of science to production, is rather set loose by a *regressive social necessity*, that of perfecting the exploitation of the labour force.[155]

The dynamic of subsumption does not thus primarily denote technological change (although this is its most pronounced and tangible manifestation) but rather expresses the multiple strategies capitalists deploy in their attempts to maximise exploitation and reproduce their capital in expanded form. There is no doubt that capitalist subsumption is characterised by immense advances in the technical complexity and capacities of production (at least at certain

---

therefore forming the basis for a critical investigation into the 'weave of articulations' regulating the composition and relations uniting productive sectors, populations, practices and institutions. Here, the subjectivising effects of capitalist subsumption can be registered, even in the absence of direct capitalist command, at the level of the opposed but interlocking systems of capital and labour's reproduction. (I borrow the idea of 'flow concepts' from Patrick Murray, who uses it in relation to absolute and relative surplus-value. The basic point, namely that the concepts tell us more about changes than about static states, holds equally for the different forms of subsumption employed by capital in the immediate production process. Rather than limiting them to materially or historically descriptive concepts, the different forms should be internalised within a dynamic conception of the process of reproduction-development that constitutes the third and final site of capitalist subsumption, see Murray 2004, p. 248.)

154  'Political Marxists' have also emphasised this point with reference to the transition debate: 'the systematic drive to revolutionise the forces of production was result more than cause.' (Wood 2002, p. 67.)

155  Echeverría 1983, p. 2.

points in global chains of production), yet it can just as well happen that – particularly where the cost of labour is low – the dynamic inhibits or excludes technical advances in production, as 'property owners can respond to class struggle against formal subsumption by way of *reinforcing* formal subsumption and/or introducing hybrid subsumption (which includes mercantile-usury based exploitation)'.[156] Thus arguing against the widespread assumption touched on by Chakrabarty, 'that "real" capitalism means "real" subsumption', Das holds that 'it is the absence of the logic of real subsumption that contributes to the specificity of these [less developed] societies *as capitalist societies*'.[157] The variability with which processes of subsumption affect the social relations and material configuration of production within the frame of global capitalist accumulation thus destabilises any teleological interpretation of the dynamic driving those processes. Rather than guaranteeing progression to a specified technological state, the subsumptive dynamic operates flexibly to inscribe productive units (whether individual enterprises, regions, industries, etc.) within an internally differentiated economic totality characterised by diverse strategies of valorisation.

Thus whilst the dynamic of subsumption presupposes unceasing social transformation and, where real subsumption is in effect, brings about 'a complete (*and constantly repeated*) revolution' in material conditions, the transformative force of the dynamic cannot be adequately comprehended at the level of a closed logical-systemic discourse. This is because it is not a programmatic repetition but an expansive, changing, historical movement. Here, the model of knowledge based on an organic totality – 'the special laws that regulate the origin, existence, development and death of a social organism and its replacement by a higher one' – breaks down and Marx's caution regarding the limits of the dialectical form of presentation become salient.[158] The importance of consumption (considered in the widest possible sense) and processes of subject formation in determining the conflicts over subsumption and therefore the course of historical development points not only to the internal incompleteness of capital as a system but to its extensive dependency on another system, that of the life of labour (not to mention the presence of a political-institutional apparatus at both the national, international and transnational levels which supports and guarantees the reproduction of its basic premises). 'Capitalist society' understood in this way is not a single systematic totality but

---

156  Das 2012, p. 179.
157  Chakrabarty 2000, p. 50; Das 2012, p. 185, emphasis added.
158  I.I. Kaufman cited in Marx 1976, p. 102.

must be comprehended as an (at least) double-sided, contradictory articulation of opposed but interlocking reproductive systems with conflicting 'logics' of existence.

In the course of its own realisation, then, the accumulative logic of the bourgeois system must interact with historically specific conditions, practices and institutions in order to satisfy its own (logically required) conditions of expanded reproduction. The concrete content of this interaction is generated both in its intensive and extensive movement, the deepening of control and productive efficiency in those zones of the social process already entwined within the circuits of capital, along with the colonisation of new spaces, populations, practices and resources. In both of these cases, however, there is no accomplished or 'normal' state of subsumption and the possible paths of development are as vast as they are uneven. The interpenetration between capital's logic and its historical development can therefore be derived no more from a closed logical system than from 'a general historico-philosophical theory', as Marx argued in his famous letter to the editors of *Otecestvenniye Zapisky*.[159] The dynamic of subsumption always points beyond its linear-logical structure and demands a critical engagement with the conjunctural specificity of social forms and struggles. Marx's later writings and correspondence indicate an increasing recognition of the limits of systematic closure and the need for empirical sensitivity, as well as a methodological orientation toward the spheres of externality that disrupt the self-sufficiency of capital as an 'organic system' and place the question of development (which is implied in and in turn implies reproduction) firmly in the field of a complex amalgam of 'realities' whose conjunction is contested. Marx arrived at this standpoint, Tomba argues, 'by making an idea of the development of the forces of production interact with the concrete responses of history; that is to say, the histories of the struggles that, interacting with the atemporal historicity of capital, co-determine its history'.[160]

An open, interactionist approach to the way in which the dynamic of subsumption connects production and reproduction shatters all stageist and teleological assumptions regarding capitalist historical development. Through this perspective, more and less 'developed' regions do not appear as more or less 'complete', they are simply those regions whose reproduction has been subject to a greater duration and/or intensity of formation by capital's logic of accumulation (including the sense in which the very spatial basis of that reproduction is accordingly altered and thus modifies the regional character in question, for

---

159  Marx 1968.
160  Tomba 2009, p. 46.

example from intersocietal to international to transnational modes of differentiation and interaction). The development of so-called 'advanced' regions therefore bears more traces of this formation, where the processes of subsumption (specifically of commodification and capitalist production techniques) are deeper, more entrenched within the reproductive logic of the social body.[161] This is the sense in which Marx talks of capital driving beyond 'all traditional, confined, complacent, encrusted satisfactions of present needs, and reproduction of old ways of life'.[162] That these are emptied of teleological significance should not be taken to imply that pre-existing practices and forms of social existence are simply 'erased' or replaced by fully-developed capitalist forms of life. Capital, as the accumulation of abstract wealth, *posits no use-value content* directly, as Echeverría contends:

> Indispensable as it is to the concrete existence of modern social wealth, capitalist mediation cannot assert itself as an essential condition for its existence, nor can it synthesise a genuinely new figure for it. The totality shaped by it, even when it really does penetrate the process of reproduction and is expanded as one of the technical conditions of this process, is the result of a forced totalisation. It maintains a contradictory polarity: is constituted by the relations of integration or subordination of 'natural wealth' under a form imposed on it.[163]

The dynamic of subsumption introduces a logic of social recomposition into the production process, but it does so only by wrapping itself around, redeploying and reinventing those 'figures' of life which it encounters and runs up against. In doing so, these aspects of the social process are mutated, deformed, suppressed or intensified, inverted or abolished. In whichever way the gradual and progressive re-shaping of this content unfolds, it nonetheless does so in a

---

161  See Kratke 2007, p. 123: 'Marx did not just refer to a difference in terms of more or less here; there is a qualitative change involved, the "higher" form being, in fact, something else and something more complex, more complicated – even more prone to inherent "contradictions".' On other occasions, Kratke frames the same question in somewhat teleological terms: 'The higher the level of capitalist development, the closer one gets to the very end of this specific economic system.' Marx certainly believed that capitalist production 'leads towards a stage at which compulsion and the monopolisation of social development (with its material and intellectual advantages) by one section of society at the expense of another disappears', but whether this 'leading towards' can be compressed into a linear developmentalism is questionable. See Marx Capital Vol. 3, p. 958.

162  Marx 1993, p. 410.

163  Echeverría 2005.

manner that depends upon and works within this social substance and its crystallised historical elements, which form the indispensable medium of capital's realisation. As the mediating role of capital within the reproduction process becomes socially dominant, it progressively recodes the practical significance and social actuality of those elements, functionally form-determining them according to the social logic of abstract accumulation. Capital thus fosters an ever greater dependency upon its accumulative mediation, which superimposes itself upon and subsumes the use-value dimension of social life, giving rise to Castillo Mendoza's 'weave of articulations' as it reshapes the economic and technical basis of reproduction in a process that is both globally integrative and locally generative.[164] This is something Giacomo Marramao has emphasised: Arguing against the idea that capital is a purely homogenising force, he has claimed that even 'the current phase of *mondialisation* ... is characterised by an ambivalent structure, signalled by the paradoxical coexistence of two aspects: *technical-scientific uniformity* and *ethical-cultural differentiation*'.[165]

In this sense, we can analytically separate and critically think together the forms of direct regulation integral to the dynamic of capitalist subsumption (commodification, supervision, technification) and those locally determined ideological and epistemic forms, structures of law, politics, violence and pleasure, etc. with which the dynamic interacts, giving rise to the diverse realisations of capitalist social reproduction and the differential distribution of economic functions at a global level. In so-called 'advanced' regions, then, the subsumptive dynamic can simply be seen to have penetrated the 'elementary civilisationary substratum' of reproduction with a greater 'density', generating a deeper process of conflictual development marked by this 'contradictory polarity'. This indicates, however, no greater proximity to either the perfection or supersession of that mediating dynamic because that which we have come to know as capitalist 'society' and 'culture' is only an *effect* of this contradiction in its unfolding and deepening, the overall development of which lacks a coherent 'holistic' or 'internally' programmatic logic (that is, a developmental logic that could be given 'purely' either at the 'cellular' or 'organic' level). This practical incoherence of accumulation and its subsumptive mechanisms is espe-

---

164  As Marcus Taylor argues: 'While capital may indeed seek to rewrite social life to further the cause of 'endless accumulation', it does not do so – to twist a famous maxim – in conditions of its own choosing ... I prefer to talk of capital as a process that constantly inhabits, remakes, and is fundamentally remade in its interactions with institutional forms, regimes of value and alternative temporalities that have their lineage in other histories and modes of being' (Taylor 2010)

165  Marammao 2012, p. 214.

cially evident in capital's propensity to produce non-development in tandem with its immense technical advances, and, in its most extreme expressions, non-reproduction: surplus population, crisis, environmental destruction, war and death. That tankers dump grain into the oceans to manipulate prices, entire towns lie uninhabited and the cost of life-saving medication is arbitrarily inflated whilst human populations are denied the right to reproduce for lack of property or exploitability are all testaments to the brute fact (summarised in the 'general law of capitalist accumulation') that capital, whilst commanding the greatest productive powers yet known to human civilisation, resolves them in the blind compulsion to incessantly reproduce social reality as a scene of 'absolute artificial scarcity'.[166] At the same time, however, the dynamic of subsumption cannot but give rise to new means, needs and forms of intercourse which point beyond the limited framework of capitalist forms of reproduction. The struggle over and against subsumption is not only a struggle to protect those subjective and objective elements that have not yet been absorbed but also a struggle to redeem those that bear the deepest scars of this society, to provide them with new forms and functions within social reality by giving that reality itself a new form. 'It is as ridiculous to yearn for a return to that original fullness', Marx reminds us, 'as it is to believe that with this complete emptiness history has come to a standstill.'[167]

## 7   Conclusion

At stake in the conceptualisation of capitalist subsumption on 'a social scale' is the conflict of two opposed and contradictory logics of *reproduction* vying to determine the possibilities of social action and thereby the course of historical *development*. As a virulent mediation, capital imposes itself upon and within the social reproduction of living labour and its lifeworld, interrupting the practical correspondence between production and consumption with its abstract productivist agenda. In this way, Marx notes, 'only capital has subjugated historical progress to the service of wealth', by displacing the logics of form-determination proper to the multitude of social elements and reproductive configurations drawn into the orbit of capital's life-process and subjecting them to the exigencies of accumulation.[168] This process of displacement,

---

166   Echeverría 2005.
167   Marx 1993, p. 162.
168   Marx 1993, p. 590.

absorption and formation, however, demarcates a field of tension marked by struggle and contestation, a process that in the course of its own realisation is torn between the two opposed imperatives: production for the sake of living or living for the sake of production. The struggle is not only over the possibility, degree, quality and balance of reproduction but also over the development and transformation of that which is reproduced. But if reproduction and development are both given, the question is: How and to what end do they occur? Here is where the dynamic of subsumption comes into force as a key concept, enabling the boundaries of integration/transcendence to be drawn within which the conflict over the form-determination of the social process itself plays out. This is a contested process of transformation that is far from 'complete', 'total' or 'absolute' in its social reach and effects, but that rather constitutes the base of the ongoing conflicts characterising the reality towards which a theory of capitalist domination must orient itself. A critical engagement with this reality must remain open to the complexity and changeability of the particular forms of command and exploitation in production. Equally, it must remain open to the complexity and changeability of the relation between those discrete sites of subsumption and the compositional totality that conditions and is conditioned by them, the entire 'weave of articulations' regulating the force field within which these struggles play out. Here, the theory of subsumption must mitigate the systemic impulses to totalisation that would enact closure upon the process either diachronically (as the historical completion of labour and society's real subsumption) or synchronically (as the reproductive self-sufficiency and unity of a logically complete capitalist totality). Rejecting such closure opens the way for a far more fruitful engagement with an actively disputed social reality. In contribution to such an engagement, the idea of a dynamic of subsumption can be deployed in order to make sense of the specific forms, regulatory mechanisms and general configurations of domination shaping that reality in disperse and varied ways. Sensitivity to the fluidity and incompleteness of the dynamic also immanently indicates further spheres of critical engagement, not only intensively, at more concrete levels of empirical and historical engagement, but across other social 'sites' and 'logics' that modulate and codetermine the forms and motions taken by the reproductive process, most obviously: politics and state power, racialisation and gender.[169]

---

169  To take one recent allusion to this codetermination: 'Arguably, "race" has never been deployed so variably nor constructed so contingently and quixotically in the subordination of truth to power and life to death as it has since the beginning of the long downturn of the 1970s and its heightening into global recession and industrial restructuring in the 1980s … One cannot, therefore, understand surplus populations without understanding how the

Registered at this level, capitalist subsumption takes on a third form, subsequently to (i) subsumption via commodification and (ii) subsumption in production, and corresponding to (iii) the subsumption of the social reproduction process under the process of capitalist accumulation. In this last form, the opposition between use-value and value contained in the commodity, and the opposition of the labour process and the valorisation process synthesised in production, develop into the opposition between the two principal dimensions of reproduction in modernity: that concerned with the production and consumption of material wealth that sustains the historical existence of human civilisation (what Echeverría terms the 'natural form of social reproduction') and that concerned with the production and accumulation of abstract wealth (expanded capitalist reproduction).[170] Like the other dyads, these two aspects form a 'contradictory unity' in which a relation of subsumption overdetermines the relation between the opposed poles. At each successive level of mediation and concretion, the capitalist pole strives to subsume, control and ultimately refound the material dimension proper to living labour. These two modes of comprehending the social reproduction process as a systematic totality do not, however, form an exhaustive 'ontological' distinction; they do not correspond to two 'realities' but are posed by Marx as the basis for his deconstruction of political economy and the ideology of equilibrium and liberty that arises spontaneously from capitalist-market social relations. Insofar as Marx's critical theory is anti-functionalist, it is because it destroys the apparent coherence, stability and naturalness of capital as an 'organic system' by demonstrating the tension of this system with the other system, that of the production, circulation and consumption of wealth in its 'natural form' (a system which is, as argued in chapter 2, already constituted in a 'bi-planar' tension between its social and natural levels of existence). As capital strives to subsume productive activity under its command and logic, it progressively internalises and transforms the content of this human substratum (its 'substance'). Yet as the crucial mediating point of transition between the two poles, subsumption occurs within a given context – the reproductive framework that unites both aspects in a contradictory totality. It is this framework, in all its concrete historical determinations and possibilities that is revealed by the deconstruction of the apparent capitalist totality.[171]

---

geographical dynamics of accumulation have become increasingly racialised. Nor can one understand the shifting forms of racialisation without taking into account the hierarchical regimes of reproduction that constitute them' (McIntyre and Nast, 2011, p. 2).

170   Echeverría 1994, p. 12.
171   Although there is a contradiction between the expanded reproduction of capitalist wealth

Consequently, what is to be understood is the actuality of the subsumptive dynamic beyond (although not in separation from) the purely 'economic' and in light of the multiple relations of power, collectivity, opposition and action through which the dynamic is constituted within a social process marked by tension and conflict. At this level, the actualisation of the dynamic reveals itself to be dependent upon a specific configuration of economic and political relations, forcing the question of political form and crucially of the *unity of economic power(s) and state power(s)* which act as the basis for the constitution and reproduction of capitalist domination. This is implicit in the realisation of the dynamic on a social scale and points to 'the need to elaborate the links between changes in the capitalist labour process and changes in class composition, in political structures, in the role of the capitalist state (in education as much as the economy) and in interstate relations'.[172] Crucially, the state here emerges as the arbiter of class struggle and ultimately as the unifying power that guarantees the correspondence of the reproductive cycles of capital and of living labour, stabilising and synchronising their contradictory unity as well

---

and the reproduction of practical wealth, as well as an irreducibility of either system or its forms to one another, Marx makes a revealing statement when he claims in vol. 2 of *Capital* that 'money in itself is not an element of real [capitalist] reproduction' but must be transformed into additional productive capital, 'new social wealth', if 'real accumulation, an expansion of production' is to occur (Marx 1978a, pp. 565–7). Here we see that the opposition and subsumption between the two systems is fundamentally registered (although not fully comprehended) at the level of the practical composition of the social totality. In this sense, the most fundamental question posed as a *result* of Marx's critique of political economy seems to be how and in what form practical wealth is (and indeed *might be*) organised, distributed and consumed within the social life process, considered as a process of both *reproduction and development*. Elsewhere Marx also asserts the need for a *material* analysis at the level of the reproductive totality: 'As long as we were dealing with capital's value production and the value of its product individually, the natural form of the commodity product was a matter of complete indifference for the analysis, whether it was machines or corn or mirrors. This was always simply an example, and any branch of production whatever could equally serve as illustration. What we were dealing with then was the actual immediate process of production, which presented itself at each turn as the process of an individual capital. In so far as the reproduction of capital came into consideration, it was sufficient to assume that the opportunity arose within the circulation sphere for the part of the product that represented capital value to be transformed back into its elements of production, and therefore into its shape as productive capital, just as we could assume that worker and capitalist found on the market the commodities on which they spent their wages and surplus-value. *But this purely formal manner of presentation is no longer sufficient once we consider the total social capital and the value of its product.*' Marx, 1978a, p. 470, emphasis added; see also p. 508.

172  Brighton Labour Process Group 1977, p. 23.

as regulating their internal dynamics.[173] But conceived non-instrumentally, the state and its geopolitical foundations constitute a further site of reproduction-development that is equally subject to historical transformation and reinvention. This site is drawn back into the dynamic of capitalist subsumption, just as much as it regulates and enables it: For whereas previous historical forms of political power determined production, in capitalist society production and competition uniquely shape the material and economic basis of political institutions and relations. This is particularly evident in light of the increasing spatial disjunction between the reproduction of capital, labour and political form in the shape of the state. If political form structures the spatial and juridical basis for reproduction, the technical, logistical and communicative transnationality of capital increasingly undermines the capacity of the state to affirm itself as the dominant agent of that form, suggesting a fluidity and ambivalence within the reproductive configuration at the level of its spatial unity and coherence. This points to the need for a less static and far more multiplicitous conception of the powers traversing and regulating the movement of the subsumptive processes that form the 'vertebral column of modernity', recalling Foucault's assertion that 'society is in reality the juxtaposition, the link, the coordination and also the hierarchy of different powers that nevertheless remain in their specificity'.[174] The theory of a dynamic of subsumption offers a perspective from which to think the presence of capitalist domination within this dense constellation of powers, as the central 'moving contradiction' around which all other oppositions and conflicts within the social process turn. This should not be considered as a unilateral hierarchy of influences but as an open framework through which to think the combination of multiple forms of

---

173   'The state's intervention in conflicts is an instrument that aims to monopolise violence and neutralise conflicts, not simply to look after the affairs of one class. Given the fact that, in some historical periods, there may be conflicts between different segments of the ruling classes, and between these and other non-proletarian and not fully synchronised sectors, like smallholders and declassed middleclass strata, what emerges is a conflict between political temporalities that may have different outcomes. The state-mechanism attempts to synchronise these temporalities, even by using asynchronous temporalities against each other' (Tomba 2013, pp. 167–8).

174   Veraza 2008, p. 10; Foucault 2012: 'First, what we may find in the second volume of Capital is that one power does not exist, but many powers. Powers, this means forms of domination, forms of subjugation that function locally, for example in the workshop, in the army, on a slave plantation or where there are subservient relations. These are all local and regional forms of power, which have their own mode of functioning, their own procedure and technique. All these forms of power are heterogeneous. We may not, therefore, speak of power if we wish to construct an analysis of power, but we must speak of powers and attempt to localise them in their historic and geographic specificity.'

exploitation and resistance within a practical reproductive totality. Breaking with the linear exposition of subsumption forms at the analytic level of reproduction and deploying a dynamic conception of capitalist development in its place is, in this way, as essential to a coherent understanding of the emergence of capitalist production as it is to grasping its current composition and the possibilities of action immanent to it.

# Conclusion

The three engagements with the problem of subsumption from which this book departs all share the same critical impulse: to register the mediated structure of an apparently immediate presence or objective reality and to explore the relations and processes by which that mediation occurs as a subsumption of diverse elements under a universal order or set of principles. In every case, this involves rejecting the 'classical' view that subsumption has a merely logical content and validity, that it is an empty or formal category. Instead, a 'critical' approach to subsumption uncovers the synthetic basis of the logical identity it lays claim to in the tautological relation between universal and particular. What is revealed in each case is that productive relations and processes play a decisive form-determining role whose significance is not locally limited to the individual elements that are subsumed but also underpin the global consistency and unity of the systematic totality within which they occur, thus mediating the constitutive relation between discrete forms, mechanisms of formation and the 'compositional totality' within which they are all inscribed. Wherever 'heterogeneous' elements and orders are brought into relation subsumptively, these underlying processes of schematisation, synthesis and ordering are always required to produce the logical identity and systemic coherence implied in that relation. We can thus reconstruct the parallel methodological strategies that allowed Kant to uncover an 'art concealed in the depths of the soul', Hegel to trace the 'labour of the negative' and Marx to descend into the 'hidden abode of production', all in search of the dynamic, active processes and relations that generate the coherence and objectivity of the apparent by subjecting diverse elements to universal principles of adaptation, correlation and transformation. In each case, however, simply identifying the discrete processes of unification and form-determination as the action of some universal upon a set of particulars proves to be insufficient, because the very possibility of this formative relation lies in a structurally overdetermining context within which the subsumed and subsuming elements or orders are both inscribed. Despite their heterogeneity, the multiple orders of being must coexist in a shared medium whose structural unity governs the specific relations of 'production' pertaining to those subsumption acts through which individual elements are formed according to a 'global order'. At the same time, the subsumptive processes themselves are shown to underpin the actuality of that global medium, the totality of composition. There is thus a *reciprocal* determination between the *processes* of subsumption and the *systemic* structure in which they take place, with each grounding the possibility

of the other. At the core of the 'critical' concept of subsumption, then, lie two interlocking processes:
(1) The specific acts of form-determination that give conceptual unity and determinacy to a range of diverse particulars, according to a 'universal' order or system of principles.
(2) The ordination and unification of those subsumptive processes and their results within a structured compositional totality that is the ground of their possibility but at the same time constituted only in and through them.

If this is the shared framework through which Kant, Hegel and Marx all employ subsumption as a 'critical' concept, they nonetheless differ in how the structure and effects of the relation between these two levels or processes are to be conceived. For Kant, subsumption is grounded in a structure of reflexive closure (transcendental subjectivity) which acts as a fixed structure of unity devoid of development within which both concepts and intuitions are 'composed', and it is precisely by virtue of this common ground that they can be related subsumptively (in a 'mechanical' manner). For Hegel, subsumption is posited as both a moment and immanent function of a totality in its dialectical development, which means that the reflexive closure of Kantian apperception has been transformed into the *processual* concept of a subject with distinct stages whose relational structure is transformed as it overcomes its own contradictions. Here, the compositional totality is no longer indifferent to the determinate 'empirical' content produced within it but only exists in and as the unity of this content with its conceptual form, a unity which expresses itself in various structural configurations of reciprocity. This also indicates a transition from a parallel series of universals – a synchronically fixed *set* of 'pure' concepts – to a serial sequence of subjective structures that are immanently connected in their diachronic development (each one giving rise to and dissolving into the next). It is in the course of this developmental process that Hegel decouples the compositional totality grounding form and its systemic function from the finite standpoint of an isolated *consciousness* and generates an intersubjective and ultimately *social-relational* theory of composition and subsumption. This theory, then, opens the possibility of thinking the fluid, changing relation between form and totality, while at the same time enclosing that relation within a speculatively totalised developmental series from whose standpoint subsumptive relations are registered as partial and inadequately developed, mired in the stasis of a posited unity of elements whose opposition has not been sublated.

Marx is the first thinker to break – if inconsistently – with the idealist closure of subsumption and composition, which are, in his writings, no longer modelled on a purely *reproductive* structure of self-same reciprocity (as with

Kantian apperception) nor on the *developmental* structure of a self-perfecting ideal subject (as with Hegel's *Concept*). By dialectically mediating systemic reproduction *and* development through one another in his materialism of the social reproduction process, Marx refuses to ascribe a self-identical unity to the compositional process as a whole that would impose synchronic or diachronic closure upon it. Instead, this process can be seen to be characterised by a radical *openness* at the level of history and *disjunction* at the level of structure that was lacking in either Kant or Hegel's ideally circumscribed totalities. There is still an essential reciprocity here between acts of subsumptive form-determination and the systemic structure that grounds them but for Marx this is a dynamic, changing and unstable reciprocity which cannot be fully captured at the level of a universal or ahistorical theoretical discourse. Such a discourse can merely register the constraints within which this reciprocity takes palce, by stipulating that social reality necessarily occurs as a practical process of production and consumption (i.e. *reproduction*). The concept of subsumption is in this way connected to a logic and immanent dynamic of social forms and the metabolic synthesis underlying their actuality (that is, to 'natural-history') without reducing them to an ideal schema of totality or development. Marx's key modification of the critical concept of subsumption therefore comes with his dislocation of the subject of composition (that which produces or determines form) and the composed/compositional totality (the sphere in which form has its reality and basis, and in which its 'formation' proceeds). This dislocation means that whilst each is always conditioned by and constituted through the other, their correlation can nonetheless only be grasped in a multitude of diverse historical modes, rather than essentially, according to an immutable order of being from which both the particular and the universal would derive their specific characteristics and systemic function.

Marx's theory of the 'subsumption of labour under capital' is the result of concretising this historically open theory of social form-determination and structural reciprocity (as 'subsumption under relations of production') with reference to their specifically capitalist articulation. Despite the partial repression of this theory resulting from the 'provisional' closure of *Capital*, its reconstruction is of central significance to a critical social theory today insofar as it allows us to think through the problem of capitalist power exactly at the points of 'integration' (as well as resistance to it) through which the being, activity and reproduction of living labour is determined as an aspect of capital's life-process. By reflecting critically on these moments and processes of 'integration/transcendence' as well as their specific forms and contradictions, this perspective avoids the theoretical functionalism that would either reduce labour's concrete agency to an already-internal or secondary aspect of capital's 'dialectical totality' or assert labour's absolute ontological independence as a vital reserve of pure potentiality which has simply been 'captured' by an apparatus of capitalist command. Instead, subsumption is the key category of mediation through which the volatile and contested nature of the social process and the struggles to determine its specific and general forms of existence can be grasped. This is something Echeverría noted in the mid-1980s:

> The concept of subsumption has a special importance with respect to the core of Marx's critical discourse – that is to say, the theory of the contradiction between the socio-natural process of production/consumption and the socio-capitalist process of the valorisation of value. *It is the most advanced attempt made by Marx to show in general theoretical terms the way in which those two contradictory processes are articulated.*[1]

If we take the social reproduction process to be the 'compositional totality' through which this contestation is played out and the site where its effects are felt, we find that this subsumptive articulation is operative at three core levels in which the opposition between value and use-value adopts 'distinct moments of presence' or 'different figures'.[2] In each moment, the opposition is suspended or repressed subsumptively, marking a threshold of integration/transcendence, a development of the contradiction into a 'deeper' form (which is to say, a form that affects more fundamentally the social reproduction process as a whole).

(1) Firstly, there is a subsumption of wealth in its 'natural form' (as practical objects or 'use-values') to the generalised commodity exchange and money relations that allows it to enter into economic relation with capital and actualises the value-form of that wealth as a specifically capitalist dimension of social objectivity. Here the contradiction is manifested in the opposition between use-value and exchange-value internal to the commodity, and the subsumption of the former under the latter that occurs within the sphere of circulation. Through commodification, capital and labour are posited as relatable and commensurable – even as mutually presupposing one another – within the compositional totality of bourgeois commercial society. Central to this process is the formal determination of living labour in the value-form of the labour-power commodity, which presupposes historical and ongoing forms of 'so-called primitive accumulation' as well as the generalisation of a legal apparatus

---

1 Echeverría 1983, p. 3, emphasis added.
2 Echeverría 1998a, pp. 26–7.

of property relations and state powers that together constitute a field of economic signification within which the 'spectral objectivity' of value is constituted as actual. It is this extra-economic production and maintenance of economic relations that generates the conditions for labour's subsumption in production: the separation of productive subjects from both one another and the 'practical object' of their labour (means of production), along with their subsequent re-articulation as a result of commodity exchange.

(2) Secondly, there is a subsumption of labour (*qua* activity) under capital (*qua* self-valorising value), which occurs via the management and exploitation of the former in the sphere of production. Here, once the sale and purchase of labour-power has taken place, the contradictions of the sphere of exchange are suspended and a new set of contradictions emerges in the opposition between the labour process and the valorisation process. The conflict over labour's integration and transcendence in production is primarily expressed in the application of capitalist command designed to ensure that labour, in addition to creating use-values, also pumps out surplus-value that capital can appropriate. This occurs (a) in the form of direct interpersonal supervision (what Marx termed 'formal subsumption') and (b) through the technical recomposition of the labour process such that it valorises capital with an ever greater efficacy and certainty (what Marx termed 'real subsumption') as well as (c) the use of 'hybrid forms' in which direct capitalist command is absent but labour nonetheless produces surplus-value for capital via alternative forms of economic exploitation.

(3) Thirdly, there is a subsumption of the 'great total process' of social reproduction under the movement of expanded reproduction proper to total social capital. This occurs as a mediated effect arising from the distinctive capitalist synthesis of (1) and (2), through which society itself, grasped as a practical (compositional) totality, comes to be objectively and subjectively form-determined by capital as the aggregate result of the activity of a multitude of competing private producers. But whilst capitalist subsumption is here operative on a social scale, it is neither final nor complete, nor does it simply represent a quantitative extension of the same basic processes found in (1) and (2). Rather, new contradictions and forms of mediation emerge at this totalised level (e.g., consumption, political institutions, the cultural sphere, etc.) thus generating a *dynamic* of subsumption, connecting and coordinating the specific instances of form-determination in circulation and production. The subsumption of reproduction under accumulation is not direct but mediated through this

dynamic, which expresses the openness and conflict-ridden opposition between the life-process of social individuals and the life-process of capital.

The key to understanding the full subsumption of labour under capital, then, lies in grasping the ways in which it is (1) commodified, rendering it a *formally* exchangeable good subject to economic circulation and purchase by capital; then (2) how it is that capital commands and transforms the labour process in order to make it also function *materially* as a valorisation process, rendering it productive – 'forming' [*Bildung*], Marx says – of surplus-value. The conjunction of these two different acts, finally, effects (3) a subsumption of labour's life-process as such (as a socially reproductive totality) under capital (as a self-expanding economic totality). These three moments of subsumption outline the process of value's autonomisation – from a form of economic mediation and of social objectivity to a medium of exploitation and domination, to the 'automatic subject' of the social process that progressively negates human autonomy and the 'basic politicity' of self-definition proper to the reproduction process. The *reality* of capital's 'real abstractions' is thus not reducible to a discrete moment or act (e.g., exchange, as it is for Adorno and Sohn-Rethel) but is distributed across the entirety of the reproduction process in a series of different forms and through a number of distinct but interconnected processes. Each level of subsumption involves the functional form-determination of an aspect of labour by capital: functional determination within the circulation process, functional determination within the production process, functional determination within the reproduction process. Of these levels, it is (2) that really constitutes the heart of capitalist domination, as the moment in which social individuals are directly subordinated and the constituting, transformative powers of human practice are compelled to serve the end of capital, functionally determined as productive of surplus-value. All three are by necessity coimplicated in the capitalist social relation, but (1) and (3) are simultaneously both conditions and effects of the essential process of exploitation that occurs in (2), around which all other moments of the social process are structured and revolve.

Grasped as a dynamic, this active reciprocity between the conditions, effects and compositional totality must all be thought together such that, for example, direct forms of subordination in production are immanently connected to forms of subjectivation occurring through consumption, culture, law, education, etc. If this expansion complicates our understanding of capitalist subsumption by following the network of relations through which its realisation interpenetrates with the action of states, the working class (in both its reproduction and its 'obstinate but elastic' presence within the production process) and other non-economic forces (surplus populations, non-state actors, 'nature'), it nonetheless does so in a way that brings the theory of subsumption closer to the overarching problem that circumscribes every Marxist theoretical engagement – that of the revolutionary transformation of social conditions. The dynamism of this theory allows a recognition of the central role played by mechanisms of subsumption within the 'logic of the body politic' in capitalist society, without however reducing its presence to an ideal or unilateral schema that would foreclose (or guarantee) the possibility of historical rupture. However, that openness is dependent upon adopting a critical stance that is not purely 'systemic' or capital-centric but instead works *deconstructively* in and against the apparent unity and coherence of the bourgeois system in order to reveal and interrogate the conflictual processes underlying labour's subsumption. If we refuse theoretical closure, then this deconstruction cannot simply aim to grasp an objective totality of relations determining the final truth of social experience (in either the mode of a Kantian apperception or Hegelian *Erinnerung*). As Max Tomba argues:

> It is not a case of giving merely an objective representation of the processes currently underway. We have to understand the subjective insurgencies that disarticulate the process, because the political task is to re-articulate them on new foundations.[3]

It should be noted this does not imply adopting the 'standpoint' of labour or working class as the historical subject (as Postone has criticised) nor does it mean adopting the unmediated standpoint of a politicised field of singularities (as Adorno, Negri and Deleuze do in diverse ways, all of which advocate novel but ultimately hollow theoretical categories of relation – affinity, rhizome, etc. – as if emancipation depended on 'balancing concepts'). It rather means taking the standpoint of the contradiction, synthesis and antagonism subsisting within the logical identity of universal and particular, of departing from the real conflicts that delimit the actuality and possibilities of form in order to both comprehend and practically overcome them.

The point of this critical endeavour, then, is not simply to 'complete' or 'refine' Marx's 'system' with a 'missing' theory of subsumption. Marx's thought is partial in many respects and whichever stance one takes with respect to his 'planned work', the point would not be for us to fill in the blanks but rather to extend, apply and rework his insights in relation to the situation within which

---

3  Tomba 2009, p. 46.

we find ourselves, and in that way sustain the status of Marxism as revolutionary discourse. Because the critical concept of subsumption points beyond the completeness and coherency of a closed totality, identifying instead the points of tension and antagonism between heterogeneous levels or orders of actuality, it opens up systemic discourse to real conditions and their contradictory character. This insight allows us to reconnect the critical-deconstructive moment of Marx's discourse (the 'detour of theory' that pierces through surface appearances of social phenomena and their cohesion) with the materialist impulse to situate knowledge in the 'force field' of real conditions as a practical response to the demands, needs and limits of those conditions, the crystallisation of thought in a 'moment of danger'.[4] The theory of subsumption thus situates itself at the multiple points of tension at which the conflict over integration and transcendence is played out between capital and labour, thus connecting the action of theoretical critique to a revolutionary horizon by focusing on how the inner logic of capitalist accumulation is articulated with the social life process as a permanently unstable and generative process of domination. The combination of systemic and anti-systemic impulses contained in this dynamic approach affirms the following methodological insight of Jairus Banaji:

> In the dialectical method of development, the movement from abstract to concrete is not a straight-line process. One returns to the concrete at expanded levels of the total curve, reconstructing the surface of society by 'stages', as a structure of several dimensions ... And this implies, finally, that in Marx's *Capital* we shall find a continuous 'oscillation between essence and appearance' ... Yet there is a point at which this movement, the very development of the concept of capital, breaks down in *Capital* as we have it today. There is a point at which the 'form of enquiry' is no longer reflected back to us in the dialectically perfected shape of a 'method of

---

4  Benjamin, 2003; Negri makes a consonant point in his commentary on the *Grundrisse*: 'Notebook M elaborates explicitly the method of *determinant abstraction*, the method of the *tendency*, the method of historical materialism; the research embodied in the *Grundrisse* is the first application which grafts the materialist method onto a refined dialectical practice. The synthesis of the two dialectical forces is open in every sense. On the one hand, dialectical reason intervenes in the relation between determination and tendency, it subjectifies the abstraction, the logical-heuristic mediation, and imposes on it a qualification and historical dynamic. On the other hand, the materialist method, in so far as it is completely subjectivised, totally open toward the future, and creative, cannot be enclosed within any dialectical totality or logical unity. The determination is always the basis of all significance, of all tension, of all tendencies. As for the method, it is the violent breath that infuses the totality of the research and constantly determines new foundations on which it can move forward' (Negri 1991, p. 12).

presentation'. To say this is only to say that Marx's *Capital* remains incomplete as a reproduction of the concrete in thought.[5]

Most importantly, the theory insists that the 'presentation' of a revolutionary theory cannot be determined without reference to the global composition of social practices and subjectivities and, in doing so, remains rigorously materialist in orientation. Unlike in closed idealist totalities where actuality and concreteness can be theoretically determined according to systemic place and function, here the concrete has its axial point in the practical context of struggle that synthesises the already constituted amalgam of congealed historical forms with those to-be-constituted (and therefore necessarily multiple and fragmented) or in-constitution (and therefore necessarily ambivalent) within an open process of reproduction-development. The centre of gravity of the dynamic *Darstellung* emanates from this process, measuring the actuality of form by its adequacy to the revolutionary movement it supports. In this sense, the function of critique would be to deconstruct the surface forms of capitalist society in order to bring the essential constituting practice of agents into conscious interconnection with their understanding of, and therefore action within, that society. This is the revolutionary horizon of Marx's critique and the theory of subsumption contained within it. Yet this is not a purely negative or demystifying procedure: In the course of the critique, positive conceptual knowledge is generated in its real connection with social practices. Subsumption is thus, at this further level of concretion, situated at the interstitial point of negative and positive critical knowledge: negative in relation to the economic categories in which oppression appears in distorted form as market fate, and positive in relation to the real processes of practical activity and interconnection through which society reproduces itself. Yet even when conceived dynamically, a 'theory' of subsumption, at the level of generality it has been presented here, cannot replace the more concrete engagements needed to grasp these specific articulations; all it can do is support such engagements by mediating the 'systematic' discourse with a 'historical' one in order to negate closure and thus orient the knowledge of 'general laws' toward real conflicts. The theory of subsumption is not simply a pillar within an expanded 'Marxist system' but a framework for further critical research and engagement. Many more questions and problems remain open and in need of development on the basis of this dynamic, for example: In what way can we rethink the relationship between individuality and subjectivity in light of historical and spatial developments in

---

5  Banaji 2015, p. 40.

the configuration of capitalist subsumption? The paucity of Marx's comments on the state leaves a huge field of enquiry that Marxist theory has only partially broached, one that is key for grasping the conditions under which this dynamic is unfolding, both at a national level and differentially in the relations between and across polities. If the challenge for critical social theory is not to advance toward systematic completeness but to reinforce its historical relevance and operability, then the production of new questions and problems such as these will be a positive rather than negative symptom.

# Bibliography

Abromeit, Josh 2011, *Max Horkheimer and the Foundations of the Frankfurt School*, Cambridge: Cambridge University Press.

Adorno, Theodor W. 1969–70, 'Society', translated by Fredric Jameson, *Salmagundi*, 3 (10–11): 144–153.

Adorno, Theodor W. 1973 [1966], *Negative Dialectics*, translated by E.B. Ashton, London: Routledge.

Adorno, Theodor W. 1976, 'Introduction' [1969] and 'Sociology and Empirical Research' [1957], in Adorno et al. *The Positivist Dispute in German Sociology*, translated by Glyn Adey and David Frisby, London: Heinemann.

Adorno, Theodor W. 1993, *Hegel: Three Studies*, translated by Shierry Webre Nicholsen, Cambridge: MIT Press.

Adorno, Theodor W. 1997, *Aesthetic Theory*, translated by Robert Hullot-Kentor, London: Athlone.

Adorno, Theodor W. 2001 [1957], *Kant's Critique of Pure Reason*, edited by Rolf Tiedemann, translated by Rodney Livingstone, Cambridge: Polity.

Adorno, Theodor W. 2003, *Can One Live after Auschwitz? A Philosophical Reader*, edited by Rolf Tiedemann, Stanford: Stanford University Press.

Adorno, Theodor W. 2005 [1951], *Minima Moralia: Reflections from Damaged Life*, translated by E.F.N. Jephcott, London and New York: Verso.

Adorno, Theodor W. 2006 [1932], 'The Idea of Natural-History', translated by Robert Hullot-Kentor, in Robert Hullot-Kentor, *Things Beyond Resemblance: Collected Essays on Theodor W. Adorno*, New York and Chichester: Columbia University Press.

Adorno, Theodor W. 2008, *Lectures on Negative Dialectics: Fragments of a Lecture Course 1965/6*, translated by Rodney Livingstone, Cambridge: Polity Press.

Adorno, Theodor W. 2018, 'Marx and the Basic Concepts of Sociological Theory', translated by Verena Erlenbusch-Anderson and Chris O'Kane, *Historical Materialism*, 26 (1): 154–164.

Adorno, Theodor W. and Horkheimer, Max 2002 [1944], *Dialectic of Enlightenment*, translated by Edmund Jephcott, Stanford: Stanford University Press.

Albritton, Robert 2003, 'Returning to Marx's "Capital": a Critique of Lebowitz's "Beyond Capital"', History of Economic Ideas, Vol. 11 (3): 95–107.

Althusser, Louis 2003 [1967], 'The humanist controversy', in *The Humanist Controversy and Other Writings (1966–67)*, translated by G.M. Goshgarian, edited by Francois Matheron, London and New York: Verso.

Althusser, Louis and Etienne Balibar 1997 [1968], *Reading Capital*, translated by Ben Brewster, London: Verso.

Anievas, Alexander and Nisancioglu, Kerem 2015, *How the West Came to Rule*, London: Pluto.

Aristotle 1984, *Politics*, translated by B. Jowett, in *The Complete Works of Aristotle: The Revised Oxford Translation* vol. 2, edited by Jonathan Barnes, Princeton: Princeton University Press.

Arruzza, Cinzia et al 2015, 'Gender and Capitalism: Debating Cinzia Arruzza's "Remarks on Gender"', *Viewpoint*, May 4: https://viewpointmag.com/2015/05/04/gender-and-capitalism-debating-cinzia-arruzzas-remarks-on-gender/

Arthur, Christopher J. 2001, 'The Spectral Ontology of Value', *Radical Philosophy*, 107, May/June: 32–42.

Arthur, Christopher J. 2004, *The New Dialectic and Marx's Capital*. Leiden/Boston/Cologne: Brill.

Arthur, Christopher J. 2005, 'Reply to Critics', *Historical Materialism*, 13 (2): 189–222.

Arthur, Christopher J. 2009, 'The Possessive Spirit of Capital: Subsumption/Inversion/Contradiction', In *Re-reading Marx: New Perspectives after the Critical Edition*, edited by Riccardo Bellofiore and Roberto Fineschi, New York: Palgrave Macmillan.

Backhaus, Hans-Georg 1997, *Dialektik der Wertform: Untersuchungen zur Marxschen Ökonomiekritik*, Frieburg, Ça ira-Verlag.

Balakrishnan, Gopal 2014, 'The Abolitionist' (Part 1), *New Left Review*, 90, Nov/Dec: 101–136.

Balibar, Etienne 1995 [1993], *The Philosophy of Marx*, translated by Chris Turner, London and New York: Verso.

Banaji, Jairus 2009, 'Reconstructing Historical Materialism: Some Key Issues': http://eprints.soas.ac.uk/16000/1/Conference%20paper%20%28revised%29.pdf [accessed Dec 2015].

Banaji, Jairus 2011, *Theory as History: Essays on Modes of Production and Exploitation*, Chicago: Haymarket.

Banaji, Jairus 2015 [1979], 'From the Commodity to Capital', in *Value: The Representation of Labour in Capitalism*, edited by Diane Elson, London: Verso.

Bartra, Armando 2006, *El Capital en su Laberinto: De la renta de la tierra a la renta de la vida*, Mexico City: Itaca/UACM.

Basso, Luca 2013 [2008] *Marx and Singularity: from the Early Writings to the Grundrisse* [2008], translated by Arianna Bove, Chicago: Haymarket.

Bellofiore, Riccardo 2009, 'A Ghost Turning into a Vampire', in *Re-reading Marx: New Perspectives after the Critical Edition*, edited by Riccardo Bellofiore and Roberto Fineschi, New York: Palgrave Macmillan.

Bellofiore, Riccardo and Riva, Tommaso Redolfi 2015, 'The *Neue Marx-Lektüre*: Putting the critique of political economy back into the critique of society', *Radical Philosophy*, 189, Jan/Feb: 24–36.

Benjamin, Walter 2003 [1940], 'On the Concept of History', translated by Harry Zohn, in *Walter Benjamin: Selected Writings* Vol. 4: *1938–1940*, edited by Howard Eiland and Michael W. Jennings, Cambridge: Harvard University Press.

Bhandar, Brenna and Toscano, Alberto 2015, 'Race, Real Estate and Real Abstraction', *Radical Philosophy*, 194, November/December: 8–17.
Bonefeld, Werner 1987, 'Marxism and the concept of mediation', In *Common Sense* 2, July: 67–72.
Bonefeld, Werner 1988, 'Class Struggle and the Permanence of Primitive Accumulation', *Common Sense*, 8, November: 54–66.
Bonefeld, Werner 2002, 'History and Social Constitution: Primitive Accumulation is not Primitive', *The Commoner*, Debate 1, March: http://www.commoner.org.uk/debbonefeld01.pdf [accessed Jan 2014].
Bonefeld, Werner 2006, 'Marx's Critique of Economics. On Lebowitz', *Historical Materialism*, 14 (2): 83–94.
Bonefeld, Werner 2014, *Critical Theory and the Critique of Political Economy: On Subversion and Negative Reason*. London and New York: Bloomsbury Academic.
Bowring, Finn 2004, 'From the mass worker to the multitude: A theoretical contextualisation of Hardt and Negri's *Empire*', *Capital & Class*, 28 (2): 101–132.
Brighton Labour Process Group 1977, 'The Labour Process', *Capital & Class*, 1, pp. 3–26.
Burbidge, John W. 2006, 'The Logic of Hegel's 'Logic': An Introduction', Peterborough, ON: Broadview Press.
Butler, Judith 2001, 'What is Critique? An Essay on Foucault's Virtue', *eipcp*, 2001: http://eipcp.net/transversal/0806/butler/en [accessed Feb 2016].
Camatte, Jacques 1988, *Capital and Community* [1976], translated by David Brown, London: Unpopular Books.
Campbell, Martha 2013, 'The Transformation of Money into Capital' in *In Marx's Laboratory: Critical Interpretations of the Grundrisse*, edited by Riccardo Bellofiore, Guido Starosta, and Peter D. Thomas, Leiden/Boston/Cologne: Brill.
Castillo Mendoza, Carlos Alberto 2002, 'Notas introductorias sobre subsunción del trabajo en el capital', *Iralka*, 17: 5–13.
Caygill, Howard 1989, *Art of Judgement*, Oxford: Blackwell.
Caygill, Howard 2000, 'Life and Aesthetic Pleasure', in *The Matter of Critique: Readings in Kant's Philosophy*, edited by Andrea Rehberg and Rachel Jones, Manchester: Clinamen.
Cicovacki, Predrag 2001, 'Paths Traced through Reality: Kant on Commonsense Truths', in *Kant's Legacy: Essays in Honor of Lewis White Beck*, edited by Predrag Cicovacki, Rochester: University of Rochester Press.
Cieszkowski, August 2010 [1838], 'Prolegomena to Historiosophy', in *Selected Writings of August Cieszkowski*, edited and translated by Andre Liebich, Cambridge: Cambridge University Press.
Chakrabarty, Dipesh 2000, *Provincialising Europe: Postcolonial Thought and Historical Difference*, Princeton: Princeton University Press.

Chitty, Andrew 2009, 'Species-Being and Capital', in *Karl Marx and Contemporary philosophy*, edited by Andrew Chitty and Martin McIvor, London: Palgrave Macmillon.

Clarke, Simon 1992, 'The Global Accumulation of Capital and the Periodisation of the Capitalist State Form', in *Open Marxism Vol. 1: Dialectics and history*, edited by W. Bonefeld, R. Gunn and K. Psychopedis, London: Pluto.

Cook, Deborah 1998, 'Adorno on Late Capitalism: Totalitarianism and the welfare state', *Radical Philosophy*, 89, May/June: 16–26.

Dauvé, Gilles and Nesic, Karel 2008, 'Love of Labour? Love of Labour Lost ...' [2002], translated by Endnotes, in *Endnotes*, 1: 104–152.

Das, Raju J. 2012, 'Reconceptualizing Capitalism: Forms of Subsumption of Labor, Class Struggle, and Uneven Development', *Review of Radical Political Economics*, 44 (2), June: 178–200.

Deleuze, Gilles 2008 [1963], *Kant's Critical Philosophy: The Doctrine of the Faculties*, translated by Hugh Tomlinson and Barbara Habberjam, London and New York: Continuum.

Deleuze, Gilles and Guattari, Felix 2004 [1972] *Anti-Oedipus*, translated by Robert Hurley, Mark Seem and Helen R. Lane, London and New York: Continuum.

De Ridder, Widukind 2008, 'Max Stirner, Hegel and the Young Hegelians: A reassessment', *History of European Ideas*, 34: 285–287.

Dussel, Enrique 2001a, 'The Four Drafts of *Capital*: Toward a new interpretation of the dialectical thought of Marx', *Rethinking Marxism*, 13 (1): 10–26.

Dussel, Enrique 2001b [1988] *Towards an Unknown Marx: A commentary on the manuscripts of 1861–63*, edited by Fred Moseley, translated by Yolanda Angulo, London and New York: Routledge.

Echeverría, Bolívar 1983, 'En este número', *Cuadernos Politicos*, 37, July/September: 2–3.

Echeverría, Bolívar 1984, 'La "forma natural" de la reproducción social', *Cuadernos Políticos*, 41, Jul–Dec : 33–46.

Echeverría, Bolívar 1986, *El Discurso Crítico de Marx*, Mexico City: Era.

Echeverría, Bolívar 1994, *Circulación Capitalista y Reproducción de la Riqueza Social, Apunte crítico sobre los esquemas de K. Marx*, Mexico City: UNAM, Facultad de Economía / Quito: Nariz del Diablo.

Echeverría, Bolívar 1995, 'El Dinero y el Objeto de Deseo', in *Ilusiones de Modernidad*, Mexico City: Era.

Echeverría, Bolívar 1998a, *La Contradicción Entre el Valor y el Valor de Uso en El Capital de Karl Marx*, Mexico City: Itaca.

Echeverría, Bolívar 1998b, 'Lo Político en La Política', in *Valor de Uso y Utopía*, Mexico City: Siglo xxi.

Echeverría, Bolívar 2005 [1985], 'Modernity and Capitalism (15 Theses)', translated by Charlotte Broad, *Theomai* 11: http://www.redalyc.org/articulo.oa?id=12420823007 [accessed March 2014].

Echeverría, Bolívar 2009, '*"Blanquitud."* Considerations on Racism as a Specifically Capitalist Phenomenon': http://www.bolivare.unam.mx/ensayos/Considerations%20on%20racism.pdf [Accessed Oct 2015].

Echeverría, Bolívar 2014 [1998], 'Use-value: Ontology and Semiotics', translated by Andrés Sáenz De Sicilia and Sandro Brito Rojas, *Radical Philosophy*, 188, November/December: 24–38.

Elbe, Ingo 2013, 'Between Marx, Marxism, and Marxisms – Ways of Reading Marx's Theory', translated by Alexander Locascio, *Viewpoint*, October: http://viewpointmag.com/2013/10/21/between-marx-marxism-and-marxisms-ways-of-reading-marxs-theory/ [accessed Nov 2014].

Elson, Diane 2015 [1979], 'The Value theory of Labour', in *Value: The Representation of Labour in Capitalism*, edited by Diane Elson, London: Verso.

Fine, Ben 1995, 'Hegel's *Philosophy of Right* and Marx's Critique: A Reassessment', in *Open Marxism vol. III: Emancipating Marx*, edited by W. Bonefeld, R. Gunn, J. Holloway and K. Psychopedis, London: Pluto, 1995, pp. 84–109.

Fine, Ben 2008: 'Debating Lebowitz: Is Class Conflict the Moral and Historical Element in the Value of Labour-Power?', *Historical Materialism*, 16 (3): 105–114.

Foster, John Bellamy 2000, *Marx's Ecology: Materialism and Nature*, New York: NYU press.

Foster, John Bellamy and Burkett, Paul 2006, 'Metabolism, Energy, and Entropy in Marx's Critique of Political Economy: Beyond the Podolinsky Myth', *Theory and Society*, Vol. 35 (1), Feb: 109–156.

Foucault, Michel 2012 [1976], 'The Mesh of Power', translated by Christopher Chitty, *Viewpoint*, September 12: https://viewpointmag.com/2012/09/12/the-mesh-of-power/

Fracchia, Joseph 2004, 'On Transhistorical Abstractions and the Intersection of Historical Theory and Social Critique', *Historical Materialism* 12 (3): 125–146.

Freeman, Alan 2004, 'The case for Simplicity', in *The New Value Controversy and the Foundation of Economics*, edited by Alan Freeman, Andrew Kliman and Julian Wells, Cheltenham and Northampton: Edward Elgar.

Gunn, Richard 1987, 'Marxism and Mediation', In *Common Sense* 2: 57–66.

Hall, Stuart 2003, 'Marx's Notes on Method: A "reading" of the "1857 Introduction"', *Cultural Studies* 17(2): 113–149.

Harootunian, Harry 2015, *Marx After Marx: History and Time in the Expansion of Capitalism*, New York: Columbia University Press.

Haug, Wolfgang Fritz 2006, 'Commodity aesthetic revisited: Exchange relations as the source of antagonistic aesthetization', *Radical Philosophy*, 135, January/February: 18–24.

Heinrich, Michael 2009, 'Reconstruction or Deconstruction? Methodological Controversies about Value and Capital, and New Insights from the Critical Edition', in *Re-

*reading Marx: New Perspectives after the Critical Edition*, edited by R. Bellofiore and R. Fineschi, New York: Palgrave Macmillan: 71–98.

Heinrich, Michael 2012 [2004], *An Introduction to the Three Volumes of Karl Marx's Capital*, translated by Alexander Locascio, New York: Monthly Review.

Hegel, G.W.F. 1953, *General Introduction to the Philosophy of History*, translated by Robert S. Hartman: https://www.marxists.org/reference/archive/hegel/works/hi/introduction.htm [accessed March 2016].

Hegel, G.W.F. 1977a [1802], *Faith & Knowledge*, Translated by Walter Cerf and H.S. Harris, Albany: SUNY Press.

Hegel, G.W.F. 1977b [1807], *The Phenomenology of Spirit*, translated by A.V. Miller. Oxford: Oxford University Press, 1977.

Hegel, G.W.F. 1971 [1817], *The Philosophy of Mind (Part Three of The Encyclopaedia of the Philosophical Sciences)*, translated by W. Wallace and A.V. Miller, Oxford: Oxford University Press.

Hegel, G.W.F. 1991a [1821], *Elements of the Philosophy of Right*, translated by H.B. Nisbett, Cambridge: Cambridge University Press.

Hegel, G.W.F. 1991b [1817, 1830], *The Encyclopaedia Logic (Part I of the Encyclopaedia of Philosophical Sciences with the Zusätze)*, translated by T.F. Geraets, W.A. Suchting and H.S. Harris, Indianapolis: Hackett.

Hegel, G.W.F. 1995, *Lectures on the History of Philosophy vol. 3: Medieval and Modern Philosophy*, Translated by E.S. Haldane and Frances H. Simson, Lincoln: University of Nebraska Press.

Hegel, G.W.F. 1999 [1812], *Science of Logic*, translated by A.V. Miller, New York: Humanity Books.

Hegel, G.W.F. 2004 [1837], *The Philosophy of History*, translated by J. Sibree, New York: Dover.

Hegel, G.W.F. 2007, *Lectures on the Philosophy of Spirit 1827–8*, translated by Robert R. Williams, Oxford: Oxford University Press.

Hegel, G.W.F. 2008 [1831], *Lectures on Logic*, translated by Clark Butler, Bloomington: Indiana University Press.

Held, Carsten 2000, 'Analyticity and the Semantics of Predicates', in *Kant's Legacy: Essays in Honor of Lewis White Beck*, edited by Predrag Cicovacki, Rochester: University of Rochester Press.

Hennessy, Rosemary & Ingraham, Chrys 1997, *Materialist Feminism: A reader in class, difference, and women's lives*, edited by Rosemary Hennessy and Chrys Ingraham, New York: Routledge.

Hess, Moses 2014 [1843], *The Philosophy of the act*: https://www.marxists.org/archive/hess/1843/philosophy-deed/.

Horkheimer, Max 1972 [1937], 'Traditional and Critical Theory', in *Critical Theory: Selected Essays*, translated by Matthew J. O'Connell et al, New York: Continuum.

Horkheimer, Max 2016 [1943], 'On the Sociology of Class Relations', edited by James Schmidt, John Lysaker & David Jenemann, *Nonsite 18: The Subject in Culture*: http://nonsite.org/the-tank/max-horkheimer-and-the-sociology-of-class-relations [Accessed Feb 2016].

Jameson, Frederic 2011, *Representing Capital: A Reading of Volume One*, London and New York: Verso.

Kant, Immanuel 1992a [1762], 'The False Subtlety of the Four Syllogistic Figures', in *Theoretical Philosophy, 1755–1770*, translated by David Walford and Ralf Meerbote, Cambridge: Cambridge University Press.

Kant, Immanuel 1992b [1800], 'The Jasche Logic', in *Lectures on Logic*, translated by J. Michael Young, Cambridge: Cambridge University Press.

Kant, Immanuel 1998 [1781, 1787], *Critique of Pure Reason*, translated by Paul Guyer and Allan W. Wood, Cambridge: Cambridge University Press.

Kant, Immanuel 1999a, *Correspondence*, translated by Arnulf Zweig, Cambridge: Cambridge University Press.

Kant, Immanuel 1999b [1797], *Metaphysics of Morals*, in *Practical Philosophy*, edited and translated by Mary J. Gregor, Cambridge: Cambridge University Press.

Kant, Immanuel 2000 [1790, 1793], *Critique of the Power of Judgement*, translated by Paul Guyer and Eric Matthews, Cambridge: Cambridge University Press.

Kant, Immanuel 2001, 'Metaphisik $L_1$', in *Lectures on Metaphysics*, edited and translated by Karl Ameriks and Steve Naragon, Cambridge: Cambridge University Press.

Kant, Immanuel 2010, *Notes and Fragments*, edited by Paul Guyer, translated by Curtis Bowman, Paul Guyer, and Frederick Rauscher, Cambridge: Cambridge University Press.

Karatani, Kojin 2003, *Transcritique*, translated by Sabu Kohso, Cambridge and London: MIT Press.

Kosík, Karel 1976 [1963], *Dialectics of the Concrete: A Study on Problems of Man and World*, translated by Karel Kovanda and James Schmidt, Boston: D. Reidel Publishing Company.

Krahl, Hans-Jürgen 1974 [1971], 'The Political Contradiction in Adorno's Critical Theory', translated by Pat Murray and Ruth Heydebrand, Telos, 21, Autumn: 164–167.

Krahl, Hans-Jürgen 1978 [1969–70], 'La introducción de 1857 de Marx', in Karl Marx, *Introducción a la crítica de la economía política de 1857*, México: Cuadernos de Pasado y Presente.

Krahl, Hans-Jürgen 2014 [1971], 'The Philosophy of History and the Authoritarian State', translated by Michael Shane Boyle and Daniel Spaulding, *Viewpoint*, September 25: https://viewpointmag.com/2014/09/25/the-philosophy-of-history-and-the-authoritarian-state-1971/

Krätke, Michael R. 2007, 'On the History and Logic of Modern Capitalism: The Legacy of Ernest Mandel', *Historical Materialism*, 15 (1): 109–143.

Lebowitz, Michael A. 1998, *The incomplete Marx* by Felton Shortall (review article), *Historical Materialism*, 3: 173–188.

Lebowitz, Michael A. 2003 [1992], *Beyond Capital: Marx's Political Economy of the Working Class* (2nd ed.), London: Palgrave Macmillan.

Levine, Norman 2012, *Marx's Discourse with Hegel*, New York: Palgrave Macmillan.

van der Linden, Marcel 2008, *Workers of the World: Essays Toward a Global Labour History*, Leiden and Boston: Brill.

Longuenesse, Béatrice 2007, *Hegel's Critique of Metaphysics*, translated by Nicole J. Simek, Cambridge: Cambridge University Press.

Lotz, Christian 2013, 'Capitalist Schematization: Political Economy, Exchange, and Objecthood in Adorno', *Zeitschrift Für Kritische Theorie* 36: 110–123.

Lukács, Georg 1971 [1923] *History and Class Consciousness*, translated by Rodney Livingstone, London: Merlin Press.

Lukács, Georg 2014, 'Moses Hess and the Problem of Idealist Dialectics', in *Tactics and Ethics: 1919–1929*, translated by Michael McColgan, London: Verso.

Macherey, Pierre 2015, 'The Productive Subject', translated by Tijana Okić, Patrick King, and Cory Knudson, *Viewpoint*, October 31: https://viewpointmag.com/2015/10/31/the-productive-subject/

Marammao, Giacomo 2012 [2003], *The Passage West: Philosophy after the age of the nation state*, translated by Matteo Mandarini, London and New York: Verso.

Marcuse, Herbert 2005, *Heideggerian Marxism*, Edited by Richard Wolin and John Abromeit, Lincoln and London: University of Nebraska Press.

Marcuse, Herbert 2007 [1964], *One-Dimensional Man: Studies in the ideology of advanced industrial society*, London and New York: Routledge.

Martin, Stewart 2008, 'Pedagogy of Human Capital', Mute Magazine, Vol. 2 (8): 32–45.

Marx, Karl 1891 [1849], *Wage labour and capital*, edited and translated by Friedrich Engels, https://www.marxists.org/archive/marx/works/1847/wage-labour/ch06.htm [accessed June 2015]

Marx, Karl 1968, Letter to Editor of the *Otecestvenniye Zapisky*, translated by Donna Torr: https://www.marxists.org/archive/marx/works/1877/11/russia.htm [accessed Feb 2016].

Marx, Karl 1969 [1895], 'The Class Struggles in France 1848 to 1850': https://www.marxists.org/archive/marx/works/1850/class-struggles-france/ch03.htm [accessed Aug 2015].

Marx, Karl 1971 [1962], *Theories of Surplus-Value* (addenda): https://www.marxists.org/archive/marx/works/1863/theories-surplus-value/add1.htm [accessed August 2015].

Marx, Karl 1975a, 'A Passage from The Kreuznach Notebooks of 1843', in *Marx and Engels Collected Works*, volume 3, London: Lawrence & Wishart.

Marx, Karl 1975b [1842], 'Leading Article in No. 179 of the Kölnische Zeitung', in *Marx and Engels Collected Works*, Volume 1, London: Lawrence & Wishart.

Marx, Karl 1976 [1867], *Capital: a Critique of Political Economy, Vol. 1: the Process of Production of Capital*, translated by Ben Fowkes, London and New York: Penguin.

Marx, Karl 1978a [1885], *Capital: a Critique of Political Economy, Vol. 2: the Process of Circulation of Capital*, translated by David Fernbach, London and New York: Penguin.

Marx, Karl 1978b, *Thesen über Feuerbach*. In *Marx Engels Werke. Band 3*. Berlin: Dietz Verlag.

Marx, Karl 1985, 'Letter to Engels, 9 December 1861' in *Marx and Engels Collected Works*, volume 41, London: Lawrence & Wishart.

Marx, Karl 1988, 'Economic Manuscript of 1861–63' in *Marx and Engels Collected Works*, volume 30, London: Lawrence & Wishart.

Marx, Karl 1989, 'Economic Manuscript of 1861–63', in *Marx Engels Collected Works* vol. 31, London: Lawrence and Wishart,

Marx, Karl 1991a [1894], *Capital: a Critique of Political Economy, Vol. 3: the Process of Capitalist Production as a Whole* [1894], translated by David Fernbach, London and New York: Penguin.

Marx, Karl 1991b, 'Economic Manuscript of 1861–63' in *Marx and Engels Collected Works*, volume 33, London: Lawrence & Wishart.

Marx, Karl 1992, *Early Writings*, translated by Rodney Livingstone and Gregor Benton, London and New York: Penguin.

Marx, Karl 1993 [1939], *Grundrisse: Foundations of the Critique of Political Economy (Rough Draft)*, translated by Martin Nicolaus, London and New York: Penguin.

Marx, Karl 1994, 'Economic Manuscript of 1861–63' in *Marx and Engels Collected Works*, volume 34, London: Lawrence & Wishart.

Marx, Karl and Engels, Friedrich 1976 [1848] 'Manifesto of the Communist Party', in *Marx and Engels Collected Works*, Volume 6, London: Lawrence & Wishart.

Marx, Karl 1998, *The German Ideology*, translated by S.W. Ryazanskaya, New York: Prometheus Books.

Marx, Karl 2014, 'Feuerbach', in *'Marx and Engels's "German ideology" Manuscripts Presentation and Analysis of the "Feuerbach chapter"'*, edited and translated by Terrell Carver and Daniel Blank, New York: Palgrave Macmillan.

McGlone, Ted and Kliman, Andrew 2004, 'The Duality of Labour', In *The New Value Controversy and the Foundation of Economics*, edited by Alan Freeman, Andrew Kliman and Julian Wells, Cheltenham and Northampton: Edward Elgar.

McIntyre, Michael and Nast, Heidi J. 2011, 'Bio(necro)polis: Marx, Surplus Populations, and the Spatial Dialectics of Reproduction and "Race"', *Antipode* 00 (00): 1–24.

Murray, Patrick 1988, *Marx's Theory of Scientific Knowledge*, New York: Humanity Books.

Murray, Patrick 2004, 'The Social and Material Transformation of Production by Capital: Formal and Real Subsumption in Capital, Volume I', in *The Constitution of Capital Essays on Volume I of Marx's Capital*, Edited by Riccardo Bellofiore and Nicola Taylor, Basingstoke and New York: Palgrave Macmillan.

Murray, Patrick 2009, 'The place of 'The results of the immediate production process' in *Capital*', in *Re-reading Marx: New Perspectives after the Critical Edition*, edited by R. Bellofiore and R. Fineschi, New York: Palgrave Macmillan.

Negri, Antonio 1988 *Revolution Retrieved: Selected Writings on Marx, Keynes, Capitalist Crisis and New Social Subjects 1967–1983*, translated by Ed Emery and John Merrington, London: Red Notes.

Negri, Antonio 1991 [1979] *Marx Beyond Marx: Lessons on the Grundrisse*, translated by Harry Cleaver, Michael Ryan and Maurizio Viano, London: Automedia/Pluto.

Negri, Antonio 2003, 'N for Negri: Antonio Negri in Conversation with Carles Guerra', edited and translated by Jorge Mestre et al., *Grey Room* 11: 86–109.

Negri, Antonio 2005 [1997], 'The Constitution of Time', In *Time for Revolution*, London and New York: Continuum.

Nelson, Anitra 1999, *Marx's concept of money*, New York: Routledge.

Neocleous, Mark 1995, 'From Civil Society to the Social', *The British Journal of Sociology*, 46 (3), September, pp. 395–408.

Noys, Benjamin 2010, *The Persistence of the Negative: A Critique of Contemporary Continental Theory*, Edinburgh: Edinburgh University Press.

Oliva Mendoza, Carlos 2013, 'Los diagramas de Bolívar Echeverría: producción, consumo y circulación semiótica', *Valenciana*, 6 (11): 181–206.

Postone, Moishe 1993, *Time, Labor and Social Domination: a Reinterpretation of Marx's Critical Theory*, Cambridge: Cambridge University Press.

Pippin, Robert B. 1976, 'The Schematism and Empirical Concepts', Kant-Studien, Vol. 67 (1–4): 156–171.

Osborne, Peter 2004, 'The Reproach of Abstraction', *Radical Philosophy*, 127: 21–28.

Osborne, Peter 2007, 'Living with Contradictions: The Resignation of Chris Gilbert', *Afterall* 16: http://www.afterall.org/journal/issue.16/living.contradictions.resignatio n.chris.gilbert.an [accessed Dec 2015]

Read, Jason 2003, *The Micro-Politics of Capital: Marx and the Prehistory of the Present*, Albany: SUNY Press.

Reichelt, Helmut 2005, 'Social Reality as Appearance: Some Notes on Marx's Conception of Reality', translated by Werner Bonefeld, in *Human Dignity: Social Autonomy and the Critique of Capitalism*, edited by Werner Bonefeld & Kosmos Psychopedis, Aldershot: Ashgate.

Renault, Emmanuel 2012, 'The Early Marx and Hegel: the Young-Hegelian Mediation': http://marxandphilosophy.org.uk/assets/files/society/word-docs/renault2012.doc [accessed Feb 2014]

Roberts, William Clare 2009, 'Abstraction and Productivity: Reflections on Formal Causality', In *Marx and Contemporary Philosophy*, edited by Andrew Chitty and Martin McIvor, New York: Palgrave Macmillan.

Robles-Baez, Mario L. 2004, 'On the Abstraction of Labour as a Social Determination', in *The New Value Controversy and the Foundation of Economics*, edited by Alan Freeman, Andrew Kliman and Julian Wells, Cheltenham and Northampton: Edward Elgar.

Rotta, Tomas Nielsen and Teixeira, Rodrigo Alves 2015, 'The Autonomisation of Abstract Wealth: New insights on the labour theory of value', *Cambridge Journal of Economics*: http://cje.oxfordjournals.org/content/early/2015/05/31/cje.bev028.full.pdf?keytype =ref&ijkey=qQFYIkZcO9H4s7y.

Sartre, Jean-Paul 1991 [1985], *Critique of Dialectical Reason, Volume 2 (Unfinished): The Intelligibility of History*, Edited by Arlette Elkaïm-Sartre, translated by Quintin Hoare, London and New York: Verso.

Sartre, Jean-Paul 2004 [1960], *Critique of Dialectical Reason, Volume 1: Theory of Practical Ensembles*, translated by Alan Sheridan-Smith, London and New York: Verso.

Sayer, Andrew 1998, 'Abstraction: A realist interpretation', in *Critical Realism: Essential Readings*, edited by M. Archer et al, London and New York: Routledge.

Schafer, Paul Marshall 1999, *The Praxis of Philosophy: Nature, Reason and Freedom* (PhD dissertation), Chicago: DePaul University.

Schmidt, Alfred 1971 [1962] *The Concept of Nature in Marx*, translated by Ben Fowkes, London: NLB.

Schmidt, Alfred 1981 [1971] *History and Structure: An Essay on Hegelian-Marxist and Structuralist Theories of History*, translated by Jeffrey Herf, Cambridge and London: MIT Press.

Shortall, Felton C. 1994, *The Incomplete Marx*, Aldershot: Avebury.

Simmel, Georg 1997, 'The Concept and Tragedy of Culture', translated by David Frisby and Mark Ritter, in *Simmel on Culture: Selected Writings*, edited by Mike Featherstone and David Frisby, London: Sage.

Skillman, Gilbert L. 2013, 'The Puzzle of Marx's Missing "Results": A Tale of Two Theories', *History of Political Economy*, 45 (3): 475–504.

Skillman, Gilbert L. 2015, 'Production Relations in Agrarian Capitalist Development: A Comment on Das (2012)', *Review of Radical Political Economics* (online), November 27: http://rrp.sagepub.com/content/early/2015/11/25/0486613415616212.full.pdf+ html

Smith, Tony 2003, 'Systematic and Historical Dialectics: Towards a Marxian Theory of Globalization', in *New Dialectics and Political Economy*, edited by Robert Albritton and John Simoulidis. Basingstoke: Palgrave Macmillan.

Sohn-Rethel, Alfred 1978 [1970], *Intellectual and Manual Labor: A Critique of Epistemology*, translated by Martin Sohn-Rethel, London and Basingstoke: Macmillan.

Suchting, Wal 1979, 'Marx's *Theses on Feuerbach*: Notes Towards a Commentary (with a New Translation)', in *Issues in Marxist Philosophy*, Volume 2: *Materialism*, in edited by John Mepham and David Hillel-Ruben, Brighton: Harvester Press.

Taylor, Marcus 2010, 'Histories of World Capitalism, Methodologies of World Labour':

http://www.eisa-net.org/be-bruga/eisa/files/events/stockholm/Taylor%20-%20Histories%20of%20World%20Capitalism.pdf [accessed April 2015].

Tomba, Massimiliano 2009, 'Historical Temporalities of Capital: an Anti-Historicist Perspective', *Historical Materialism*, 17 (4): 44–65.

Tomba, Massimiliano 2013, *Marx's Temporalities*, translated by Peter D. Thomas and Sara R. Farris, Chicago: Haymarket.

Tombazos, Stavros 2014, *Time in Marx: The Categories of Time in Marx's Capital*, Chicago: Haymarket Books.

Toscano, Alberto 2009, 'Chronicles of Insurrection: Tronti, Negri and the Subject of Antagonism', *Cosmos and History*, Vol. 5 (1): 76–91.

Tronti, Mario 2012, 'Our Operaismo', *New Left Review* 73: https://newleftreview.org/II/73/mario-tronti-our-operaismo.

Veraza Urtuzuástegui, Jorge 2008, *Subsunción Real del Consumo Bajo el Capital*, Mexico City: Itaca.

Veraza Urtuzuástegui, Jorge 2012, *Karl Marx y la Tecnica Desde la Perspectiva de la Vida: Para una Teoría Marxista de las Fuerzas Productivas*, Mexico City: Itaca.

Virno, Paolo 2004, *A Grammar of the Multitude: For an Analysis of Contemporary Forms of Life*, translated by Isabella Bertoletti, James Cascaito and Andrea Casson, Los Angeles: Semiotext(e).

Wallerstein, Immanuel M. 2001 [1991] *Unthinking Social Science: The Limits of Nineteenth-century Paradigms*, Philadelphia: Temple University Press.

Watkins, Eric 2009, *Kant's Critique of Pure Reason: Background Source Materials*, Cambridge: Cambridge University Press.

Wiggershaus, Rolf 1995, *The Frankfurt School: Its History, Theories, and Political Significance*, translated by Michael Robertson, Cambridge, MIT Press.

Wood, Ellen Meiksins 2002, *The Origin of Capitalism: a Longer View*, London: Verso.

Wright, Steve 2002, *Storming Heaven: Class Composition and Struggle in Italian Autonomist Marxism*, London: Pluto.

Wright, Steve 2005, 'Reality check: Are We Living In An Immaterial World?', *Mute*, 2 (1): http://www.metamute.org/editorial/articles/reality-check-are-we-living-immaterial-world [accessed Jan 2016].

Zeleny, Jindrich 1980 [1968], The *Logic of Marx*, translated by Terrell Carver, New York: Rowman &. Littlefield.

# Index

absolute idea   89
absolute spirit   78
abstraction   1–2, 8, 21–22, 24, 47, 52, 81, 83–84, 89, 110, 112–69, 172, 178, 184–87, 208, 239
   real   6, 185–86, 192, 237
abstract labour   122–23, 126–27, 130, 137, 140, 215
accumulation   113–14, 117–20, 132–34, 149, 152, 159, 171–73, 181, 192, 196, 202–13, 219, 221–29, 236, 239
actuality   5–6, 63–79, 81–84, 93, 97, 101, 105, 111, 229, 232, 234, 238–40
administration   175, 184–85, 187, 190–91
Adorno   2, 9, 13, 92, 97, 107, 114, 184–87, 189–94, 203, 210, 237–38
agency   183, 185, 234
agriculture   149, 196
Albertus Magnus   3
alienation   2, 67, 87, 127, 129, 131, 135, 163, 168
Althusser, Louis   67, 165
apperception   4, 16, 20, 47, 51, 60
Aquinas, Thomas   3
Aristotle   3, 14, 35, 39, 51, 65, 125
Arthur, Christopher J.   9, 115, 123, 133, 158, 201–4
autonomy   34, 74, 99–100, 102, 110, 182, 190, 194, 237

Backhaus, Hans-Georg   62
Balibar, Etienne   78, 80, 83, 85, 87, 165
Banaji, Jairus   120, 126, 128, 146, 148, 150, 168, 195, 197, 199–201, 239–40
Bartra, Armando   150
Baumgarten, Alexander Gottlieb   3
Bellofiore, Ricardo   109, 142, 186–87, 189
Benjamin, Walter   210–11, 239
Bonefeld, Werner   121–22, 203, 208, 210
Brighton Labour Process Group   171, 197, 229
Burbidge, John   52
Buridan, John   3

Camatte, Jacques   175
capital   9–10, 97–98, 111–23, 126–69, 172–83, 192–96, 198–217, 220–23, 225–26, 228–30, 234–37, 239
   circuits of   134, 223
   commodity   213
   constant   114, 134, 153
   fixed   164, 178
   industrial   114, 120, 149–50
   merchant's   147
   reproduction of   212–13, 216–18, 229–30
   usurer's   147, 150
   variable   132, 140, 167
capitalism   112, 115, 117, 119, 173, 175–76, 183–84, 190, 195, 197, 200, 204, 208, 210
capital-logic   209
Castillo Mendoza, Carlos   62, 164, 173–74, 225
Caygill, Howard   31, 34–35
circulation   94, 102, 108, 117, 125–26, 130, 136, 141, 148, 165–69, 179, 187, 190, 193, 211, 214, 217, 228–29, 235–36
Chakrabarty, Dipesh   222
Chitty, Andrew   46
Cieszkowski, August von   73–74
Clarke, Simon   197
class   114, 118, 121, 131, 145, 158, 164, 174, 176–77, 181, 185, 190, 199, 215, 229–30
   struggle   115–16, 120, 148–49, 165, 172, 208–9, 211, 220, 222, 229
coercion   99, 121, 126, 145–46
colonisation   3, 175, 187, 196, 223
command   9–10, 130–32, 135–37, 139, 142–43, 145–46, 150–51, 155, 167, 170–71, 180–82, 190, 193, 227–28
commodification   113, 116, 126–27, 165–66, 168–69, 179, 196, 209, 215, 225, 228, 235
commodities   118, 120, 122–26, 128–31, 132–35, 137, 143, 146–47, 151, 154, 156, 158–59, 161, 164, 167–68, 186–87, 189, 212, 228–29
commodity exchange   124, 128–29, 135, 143, 145, 168–69, 185, 189, 235–36
commodity-form   116, 126, 131, 135, 142, 154, 170, 189
communism   37, 66, 75, 182, 194
competition   128, 146, 149, 151, 162, 167, 171–73, 180, 230
compositional medium   60, 72
compositional totality   5–7, 46, 57, 62, 79, 111, 207, 212, 227, 232–35, 237

consumption   82, 96, 101–2, 104, 107–8, 123–24, 128–29, 135, 139, 213–14, 216–18, 226, 228, 234, 236–37
contradiction   1–2, 4, 46–47, 61, 70, 72, 122, 125–26, 137, 151, 163, 172, 180–81, 183, 194–95, 207, 212, 214–15, 218, 230, 233–36, 238
cooperation   151–52, 154–58, 160–61, 163, 166s, 195
credit   122, 150
crisis   149, 209, 226
critique   1, 2, 4, 7–8, 21, 26–27, 30, 33, 35–40, 45, 47–49, 62–63, 69, 76, 81, 84, 87–89, 110, 115, 127, 192–93, 210, 239–40
Crusius   3
culture industry   187, 214

Dauvé, Gilles   179
Deleuze, Gilles   26, 133, 238
deindustrialization   196
dialectic   1, 44, 48, 66, 107, 166, 171–73, 178, 185, 187, 189, 194, 204
  of capital   203
  negative   192
  systematic   9, 150, 172, 201, 203, 209
dialectical development   7, 59–60, 95, 206, 222, 233, 239
dialectical totality   235, 239
division of labour   151–52, 155–57, 160–61, 164, 174
Dussel, Enrique   115, 132–33

Echeverría, Bolívar   76–80, 82, 90–91, 96–97, 99, 103–5, 122, 124–25, 207, 211–12, 218–19, 221, 226, 235
economism   108, 111, 172
Elbe, Ingo   189
Elson, Diane   130, 166
empiricism   175
Engels, Friedrich   66, 69, 81, 83, 89, 91–95, 110, 114–15, 170, 206
Enlightenment   94, 185
environment   94–95
epistemology   2, 45, 81
equality   55, 127
equivalence   123, 125, 137, 141, 144, 185–86, 189, 192
exchange   94–95, 116–17, 120–38, 141–44, 152, 165–69, 174, 178, 185–90, 192–93, 196, 213, 215, 236–37

exchange value   116, 123–27, 129–30, 235
exploitation   119–20, 141–50, 163, 165–68, 172, 178–82, 199–200, 219, 220–21, 226, 236–37

factory   161, 164, 177–78
fetishism   90, 125, 133, 187, 189, 197, 215
feudalism   119, 141–42, 144
Feuerbach, Ludwig   61, 66–67, 69, 72, 74–75, 77, 83–86, 89, 92, 97
Fichte, Johann Gottlieb   86
Fordism   177
form-determination   5, 62–64, 73, 112–13, 136, 165, 167–68, 170, 173, 226–27, 232–33, 236–37
  social   112, 234
  subsumptive   170, 212, 234
Foucault, Michel   230
Frankfurt School   186
freedom   6, 26, 33–34, 51, 64–66, 70, 75, 85, 96–97, 99, 101, 106–7, 127, 130, 147

Gattungswesen   70
gender   196, 227
genus   14, 40, 56–57, 86–87, 104
German idealism   6
growth   95, 117
Guattari, Félix   133
Gunn, Richard   113

Hall, Stuart   102, 107
Hardt, Michael   183, 176
Harootunian, Harry   176
Haug, W.F.   120, 184
Heidegger, Martin   99
Heinrich, Michael   115, 124, 172
Hess, Moses   73–74, 86
historicity   106, 175, 223
history   61, 63, 93, 97, 107, 117, 125, 170, 173, 192, 197, 183, 204, 223, 225–26
  natural   92, 107, 117
Horkheimer, Max   184–87, 190–92

ideology   81–82, 84, 112, 189, 214, 225, 228
imagination   13, 20–22, 24, 32–33, 194
immanent critique   67, 69, 210
industrialisation   185, 187

INDEX                                                                                          257

industry   91, 152, 160–65, 174, 195–96, 199, 212, 220, 222
institutions   221, 223
    legal   72
    political   71, 230, 236

Jameson, Frederic   176
judgment   3, 4, 7, 11–14, 16–17, 19, 21–38, 42, 44, 47–48, 51, 53–58, 60, 135, 143, 158, 180, 184
    reflective   22, 25–32, 55

Karatani, Kojin   209
Kliman, Andrew   162
Kosík, Karel   80
Krahl, Hans-Jürgen   112, 114, 123, 192–93, 219
Krätke, Michael   208–10

labour force   143, 221
labour-market   119
labour power   114, 116, 118–20, 126–28, 130, 132, 134, 142–46, 167–68, 177, 194, 196, 199, 208, 211, 214–15, 235
    exchange of   129, 132
    reproduction of   171–72
    sale and purchase of   119, 236
    value of   144, 214
labour process   96–97, 99–100, 102, 136–41, 142–46, 150–56, 158, 160–62, 165–70, 195–96, 198–201, 213, 219, 236–37
labour time   123, 128, 130, 143, 146, 161–63, 208
Lasalle, Ferdinand   210
Lebowitz, Michael   172, 208–9, 211, 215
life   11, 34, 36–37, 62, 67–70, 73–74, 81, 85, 88–89, 92–93, 105, 124, 132, 145, 175, 179–81, 184–87, 194, 196, 212, 225, 227
    ethical   45–46, 59
    natural   91, 93, 99
    organic   95, 105, 207
    rational   36
    time of   177, 179
life-activity   120, 157
living labour   127, 132, 136, 163, 170, 182, 194–96, 212–13, 215, 218, 226, 228–29, 234–35

logic   4, 6–7, 19, 40, 47–52, 60–62, 64–65, 68–69, 71, 81–82, 87–89, 99, 105, 110, 113, 169–71, 173–74, 180, 186, 191–92, 201, 205–6, 210, 212, 219–20, 222–28, 239
    economic   118, 187, 211, 214
    formal   13, 38, 48, 51, 53
    pre-critical   38
    speculative   40, 68, 109
    transcendental   7, 13, 38–40, 48
Longuenesse, Béatrice   66
Lucretius   97
Luddism   220
Lukács, György   86, 90, 189

Macherey, Pierre   131, 250
machinery   151–52, 158–64, 166, 178, 229
management   25, 179, 182, 194, 236
manufacture   152, 155–62, 165
Marammao, Giacomo   225
Marcuse, Herbert   124, 191, 219
Martin, Stewart   176, 180, 194
materialism   5–8, 61–111, 137–38, 133, 234
    historical   64, 189, 214, 239–40
merchants   134, 147
metabolism   8, 94–99, 101, 103–4, 124, 135–40, 164, 170
metaphysics   30, 48, 67, 78, 249–50
modernity   228, 230
Mode of Production   150, 198, 201
Moleschott, Jacob   95
money   118, 122, 127, 129–35, 142, 145, 147, 150, 166–67, 186–87, 189, 213–14, 229, 235
Murray, Patrick   67, 81, 115, 133–34, 147–50, 172, 217, 221
mystification   8, 133, 221

natural forms   28, 30–32, 67, 90, 104, 111, 123–24, 138, 228–29, 235
naturalism   92, 95, 108
nature   28–29, 31, 34, 36, 40, 42, 47, 49, 56–57, 69, 89–99, 105–6, 139–40, 158–64, 173, 185–86, 201–2, 215, 218, 235
negation   52, 68, 74, 85, 112, 124, 160, 181, 185, 193, 195, 205
negativity   109, 129
Negri, Antonio   2, 9, 175–84, 189–90, 194, 203, 219, 238–39
Neue Marx-Lektüre   189

objectification  65, 67, 104, 140, 161, 164, 189, 209, 219
object in general  14
objectivity  4–5, 8, 10, 13–15, 18, 35, 38, 48, 57, 60, 67, 69, 76–81, 83–84, 89–90, 92, 101, 122–23, 129, 132, 134, 168, 186
  social  90, 112, 123–25, 127, 235–37
Ockham, William of  3
Oliva Mendoza, Carlos  95
Operaismo  176–77
Osborne, Peter  2, 114, 185

particularity  2–4, 13, 22, 29, 31, 35, 40, 52–54, 58–59, 60, 63, 65, 66, 70–71, 109–11, 113, 126, 232–33
peasants  118–19, 145
periodisation  9, 165, 175, 194, 197
personification  157, 215
political economy  1, 109, 117, 128, 133–34, 189, 207–10, 228–29
  critique of  6, 8, 62, 110, 112, 115, 172, 219
Pollock, Friedrich  190
postmodernity  176
Postone, Moishe  9, 114, 116, 238
primitive accumulation (so-called)  116–18, 120–22, 134, 136, 156, 186, 196, 209, 215, 235
production  9–10, 36, 83, 91, 93–94, 101–4, 108–14, 116–22, 126–27, 132–37, 139–52, 154–73, 175, 177–82, 189–92, 195–202, 204–17, 218–23, 227–29, 236–37
productivism  179–80, 226
pseudo-Aquinas  3
purposiveness  28–33, 36

race  186, 227–28
Read, Jason  9, 176
reason  11–12, 19, 25–27, 31, 33–34, 37–38, 42–43, 51, 55, 69, 71, 74, 114, 185, 191, 193
  instrumental  185, 192
recognition  13, 16, 24, 44–46, 89, 92, 119, 134, 223, 238
Reichelt, Helmut  123, 189
reification  127, 189, 203, 219
relations of production  133, 200–1
religion  69, 216
Renault, Emmanuel  64, 66, 74
representation  4, 11–20, 23–27, 29–37, 40, 46, 48, 73, 77, 80, 165–66, 186, 238

repression  119, 125, 140, 182, 202, 218, 234
repressive desublimation  191
reproduction  61–112, 114, 119–20, 122–23, 129, 131–32, 139, 150–51, 165, 167, 169–83, 195–98, 201, 203–9, 212–40
resistance  10, 115, 163, 182, 184, 198, 203, 211–12, 231, 234
revolution  5, 64, 67, 72, 75, 80–82, 84, 87–88, 106, 135, 169, 170, 183–84, 193, 199, 222, 239–40
  industrial  145
Riva, Tommaso Redolfi  109, 187, 189
rhizome  2, 238
romanticism  38
Roberts, William Clare  115, 126, 142, 155
Ruge, Arnold  66
rules  4, 11–17, 18–19, 21–24, 26, 28, 33–34, 37, 43, 49, 114

Sartre, Jean-Paul  78, 90–91, 99, 106, 122
Sayer, Andrew  106, 197
Schelling  93
schematisation  9, 13, 16–25, 33, 119, 123, 128–29, 185, 187, 232
Schmidt, Alfred  81, 94–95, 98, 105, 109, 112, 133, 204, 210, 249, 253
science  48–49, 64, 72, 75, 78, 81–83, 91, 94, 112, 153, 164, 173, 185, 192
self-consciousness  39, 43–47, 59, 83–4, 85
sensation  14, 21, 30, 32, 34, 43
sensibility  13–18, 45
sensible intuitions  14, 19, 38, 41, 58, 77
sensus communis  35–36
Shortall, Felton  208–9
Simmel, Georg  97, 253
singularity  2, 17, 20–21, 52–54, 58, 85, 109, 162, 238, 244
Skillman, Gilbert  115–16, 156–47, 150, 174, 253
slavery  114, 120, 200, 230
Smith, Adam  117, 118, 129, 253
socialism  73
social relations  46, 60, 62, 73, 75, 85–86, 106–8, 113, 121–22, 125–26, 133–34, 142, 159–60, 165, 167–69
social reproduction  6, 8, 10, 104, 107–18, 121, 123, 139, 141, 165, 170, 172–75, 187–9, 203, 218–19, 225–26, 228, 234–35

society   6, 9, 70, 86, 88, 91, 110–12, 121–28, 141, 153, 169–70, 172–73, 176–79, 190–96, 205–7, 212–14, 218, 225–27, 235, 239–40, 243–44
   civil   70–71, 86
socio-natural   6, 8, 92, 97, 103–7, 116, 124–25, 138, 218, 235
Sohn-Rethel, Alfred   185–86, 189, 237, 253
space   17, 25, 35, 105, 127, 153, 172, 177, 213, 220, 223, 230
speculative philosophy   51, 66–67, 73, 79, 82, 88
Spinoza, Benedict de   184
structuralism   87, 197
Structure-in-process   112, 108, 169
subjectivation   100, 104, 106, 119, 212, 214, 216, 219, 221, 237–39
subjectivity   38–39, 42–48, 56, 58–59, 72, 76, 78–80, 85, 92–93, 98–100, 102–3, 119, 167, 177, 182, 212, 214, 218, 240
   transcendental   19–20, 40, 42, 44, 233
subordination   12, 13, 99, 113, 115, 131, 140, 146, 162, 165–66, 205, 227, 237
subsistence   65, 118–19, 126, 128, 133, 137, 148, 159, 167, 213
subsumption
   formal   140–42, 144–46, 149–52, 154, 160, 163, 165, 196, 202, 216, 220, 222
   hybrid   146–50, 166, 195–96, 220, 222, 236
   ideal   147
   of intuitions   16, 19, 45, 59
   real   146, 149–55, 158, 160, 163, 165, 168–70, 176–81, 183–84, 192, 195–96, 198–200, 216–20, 222
   total   9, 175, 177, 187, 194
   transcendental   13, 19, 21, 23, 49
Suchting, Wal   8, 75, 78, 82, 86
surplus labour   136–37, 142, 144–45, 147, 151, 154, 199, 214, 217
surplus populations   120, 149, 226–27, 238, 251
surplus-value   128, 136–37, 142–48, 150–52, 161, 167–68, 174, 180, 182, 190, 206, 213, 217, 229, 236–37
   absolute   145, 196
   relative   152, 196, 216–17, 221
syllogism   12, 15, 26, 34, 51, 57–58, 60, 107, 180

synthesis   4–5, 8, 9, 11, 16–17, 19–21, 23–25, 31, 33, 36, 41, 50–51, 62–63, 97, 112, 166–69, 170, 186–87, 215, 236, 238–40
   metabolic   5, 8–9, 166, 232, 234
synthetic unity   4, 25, 41, 46–47
systematic dialectic   150, 172, 201, 209
system-in-process   1, 112

Taylorism   177
technology   134, 141, 151, 164–65, 173, 196, 199, 218–19, 222, 226
teleology   9, 27, 98, 101, 134, 220, 221–23
temporality   28, 98, 104, 107, 121, 127, 143, 156, 225, 230
thermodynamics   94
time   6, 16, 105, 182, 206, 211, 233
Tomba, Massimiliano   121, 178, 223, 230, 238
Tombazos, Stavros   81
tools   24, 147, 153, 156–60
Toscano, Alberto   176, 183, 186, 245, 254
totalisation   12, 60, 65, 93, 104, 108, 122, 175–76, 181, 184, 187, 189–91, 195, 197, 204, 210, 227, 233
   diachronic   194
   historical   173, 184
   systematic   173
totality   7–8, 40, 50–54, 58, 60, 65, 68, 85–88, 91, 95, 106, 108–12, 125–26, 133, 173–76, 181, 187, 191–92, 198–202, 205, 209–10, 214, 218, 228, 233–34, 238–40
   economic   212, 214, 222, 237
   organic   88, 105, 209, 222
   social   85, 90, 139, 168, 179, 187, 193, 195, 201, 212, 229
   transcendental   1, 4, 7, 14, 16, 19, 20, 22, 24–29, 32–34, 39–43, 47–48, 76, 80, 86, 108, 112
transcendental object   187
transhistorical   8, 109, 123
Transindividuality   85
transnaturalisation   82, 98, 105
Tronti, Mario   176–77, 254

unemployment   162
universals   3–4, 13, 58–59, 62–63, 83, 113, 233
use-value   103, 111, 114, 120, 122–30, 137, 140, 143, 178, 214–16, 225, 228, 235–36
usury   134, 147–50

valorisation   116, 118–19, 129, 132, 136–39, 140, 142–45, 148, 152, 156, 165–68, 170, 174, 189, 198, 207, 221–22, 228, 235–37
value   90, 112–14, 117–18, 120–30, 133–37, 143–45, 151–52, 165–66, 168, 178, 180–81, 186, 189–90, 208, 211, 216–17, 228–29, 235–36
   law of   146, 178–80, 194
value-form   113–14, 123–25, 179, 185–86, 201, 235
value theory   129, 166
Veraza, Jorge   230
Verri, Pietro   96
violence   113, 118–19, 121, 128, 142, 145, 225, 230
Virno, Paolo   182

wage-labour   114, 116–17, 120, 131, 134, 136, 144–48, 167–68, 195, 206, 215
wages   122, 129, 132, 134, 136, 139, 143, 146–48, 151, 171, 196, 213, 220
Wallerstein, Immanuel   148
Weber, Max   189
workers   99–100, 118–20, 126–28, 130, 132, 135–39, 142–47, 149, 151–64, 177–78, 181–82, 199, 208–9, 212–13, 215–18, 220
working class   120, 145, 164, 177, 208, 213, 215–17, 220, 237–38
working day   144–45, 151, 161, 163, 178–79, 217
workshop   155–59, 161, 163, 230

Young Hegelians   66–67

Zeleny, Jindrich   67, 81–82, 91, 112, 254

www.ingramcontent.com/pod-product-compliance
Lightning Source LLC
Chambersburg PA
CBHW070616030426
**42337CB00020B/3815**